Cybercrime
Investigators
Handbook

Cybercrime Investigators Handbook

GRAEME EDWARDS,PhD.

WILEY

For general information on our other products and services or for technical support, please contact our Customer Care Department within the United States at (800) 762-2974, outside the United States at (317) 572-3993, or fax (317) 572-4002.

Wiley publishes in a variety of print and electronic formats and by print-on-demand. Some material included with standard print versions of this book may not be included in e-books or in print-on-demand. If this book refers to media such as a CD or DVD that is not included in the version you purchased, you may download this material at http://booksupport.wiley.com. For more information about Wiley products, visit www.wiley.com.

Library of Congress Cataloging-in-Publication Data
Names: Edwards, Graeme (Financial and cybercrime investigator), author.
Title: Cybercrime investigators handbook / Graeme Edwards.
Description: Hoboken, New Jersey : John Wiley & Sons, Inc., [2020] |
    Includes index.
Identifiers: LCCN 2019023231 (print) | LCCN 2019023232 (ebook) | ISBN
    9781119596288 (cloth) | ISBN 9781119596325 (adobe pdf) | ISBN
    9781119596301 (epub)
Subjects: LCSH: Computer crimes—Investigation.
Classification: LCC HV8079.C65 E39 2020 (print) | LCC HV8079.C65 (ebook)
    | DDC 363.25/968—dc23
LC record available at https://lccn.loc.gov/2019023231
LC ebook record available at https://lccn.loc.gov/201902323

Cover Design: Wiley
Cover Image: © South_agency/iStock.com

Printed in the United States of America
V10012796_081219

To Marie and Bob. Long gone but not forgotten.
To Liz and the girls. Thank you for putting up with the numerous hours
I have spent on work, study, and research for this book and all the support
you have given.

Contents

List of Figures

About the Author

Dr. Graeme Edwards is a financial and cybercrime investigator located in Brisbane, Australia. He has 26 years' experience in policing, with 17 years as a detective specializing in the investigation of financial crimes and cybercrimes.

He has successfully completed a doctorate in information technology with his thesis, "Investigating Cybercrime in a Cloud-Computing Environment." He has also successfully completed a master of information technology (security).

Dr. Edwards is a regular conference presenter, speaking on a wide range of topics related to financial crimes and cybercrimes; he also conducts training events for organizations and senior management as well as undertaking post investigation analysis of cyber events. He was the president of the Brisbane chapter of the Association of Certified Fraud Examiners from 2016 to 2018.

Foreword

CYBERCRIME INVESTIGATION is a discipline relevant to an increasingly diverse audience. It's a profession that has evolved with technology and that is constantly being presented with challenges in determining the truth behind alleged events. As part of the broader cyber security profession, investigators in large part are valued for their practical experience, vendor certifications, and trustworthiness in delivering investigative outcomes—whether that be to prove or disprove alleged offending.

Graeme Edwards embodies these qualities. He forged a career as one of Australia's first true cybercrime detectives with the Queensland Police Service. Like many in our profession he took it upon himself to continue to self-develop, through learning about and adapting to new technology environments, and through advancing his own education. His doctorate furthered his expertise in cloud investigations and forensics, anticipating the growing need for this subspecialization.

Cybercrime Investigators Handbook is a life work for Graeme. It provides an opportunity for readers to directly benefit from his unique expertise and lifelong learning experiences. Its content steps readers through the investigative process from a cybercrime perspective, capturing key practical and observational gems readers can readily apply to their own challenges.

Thanks to authors like Graeme, our profession can continue to evolve and benefit from the passing on of key lessons and knowledge for the betterment of practitioners and those looking to move into the exciting field of cybercrime investigations. It's a very timely contribution. I trust you'll benefit from its content as much as I have. Thank you, Graeme, for advancing our profession in this very meaningful way.

Professor David Lacey
Managing Director, IDCARE
Director, Institute for Cyber Investigations and Forensics, USC

Foreword

Acknowledgments

I T IS APPROPRIATE to thank those who have supported the writing of this book.

First, thank you to my family for putting up with the numerous hours I have spent studying, researching, and working the very antisocial hours a police officer on shift work dedicates to their profession. Without your support, this book and years of study and research would not have been achieved.

I also wish to thank Dennis Desmond, a former agent for the FBI National Computer Crime Squad in Washington, DC, and Professor Lacey, both now members of the Institute for Cyber Investigations and Forensics in Queensland, for their peer review of the contents of this book. I would also like to thank Professor Lacey for his foreword.

Cybercrime Investigators Handbook

CHAPTER ONE

Introduction

C YBER-ATTACKS AGAINST businesses and individuals have been occurring for decades. Many have been so successful they were never discovered by the victims and only identified while the data was being exploited or being sold on criminal markets. Cyber-attacks damage the finances and reputation of a business and cause significant damage to those whose data has been stolen and exploited.

From the criminal's perspective, the current cyber environment effectively gives them a free pass when it comes to attacking their target. They can do whatever they like to an individual or business online, cause immense damage of a professional or personal nature, and make large sums of money safe in the knowledge the complainant will rarely report the matter to police. In fact, this is a strange anomaly about cybercrime: a company has millions of dollars of intellectual property (IP) stolen from them, has all the personally identifying information (PII) of the staff and clients stolen, and the action of reporting it to police or investigating who is behind the attack is rarely considered or undertaken unless forced by local legislation. Consequently, from the criminal's perspective, there is little to no downside to being a cybercriminal. They operate on a high-financial-return, low-risk model.

Due to the high volume and complexity of cyber-attacks, should a victim decide to refer a complaint to police they cannot always rely upon them to be available to undertake an investigation and locate the offender. Police resources are stretched and skilled cyber investigators in law enforcement are few and overworked. This means organizations subject to a cyber-attack that wish to find information about who is behind the attack will need to hire an experienced cyber investigator (scarce and very expensive) or investigate the matter themselves. Alternatively, they will not conduct an investigation and instead focus on increasing security.

The decision by victims to not investigate a cybercrime is made for many reasons, including the time and money to be expended on an investigation, the focus of the business being directed on the investigation, the internal disruption it causes, and the reputational harm caused when the community finds the company security has been breached and all the data entrusted to them stolen. Also, directors would not look forward to the day that they stand before a public annual general meeting and explain to the shareholders that all the company data was stolen on their watch and that they have made no effort to recover it or identify who took it.

To the members of an incident response (IR) team or the cyber investigator, responding to an attack is often an inexact science as the attackers' motives and skill levels vary. Whereas an attack against a single desktop computer may be easily contained and investigated, an attack against a complete distributed corporate network will require significant resources and an experienced response team to protect the company, their data, and clients. As the attack methodologies vary, the investigation strategy will not necessarily follow the exact same path each time.

Investigating a cyber-attack may be a critical part of the continuation of the business. When the attack is discovered, a mixture of panic, stress, anxiety, and fear is seen among staff, and those tasked to mitigate and eradicate the attack may feel the future of the company rests upon their shoulders. Many employees will be concerned as to their personal future, as they will be familiar with the many stories of businesses hit by a cyber-attack that no longer exist six months later. Staff members of the organization being interviewed as a part of the incident response may also feel that they are being held responsible and that the interview is a method of laying blame at their feet.

So why conduct an investigation and gather evidence? Why should a company start investigating the cybercrime and try to track down the offender? With the proliferation in the instances of cybercrime, there is an expectation among the community that those who are entrusted with their PII take their responsibilities seriously and ensure their data is secure.

Shareholders of companies who find that the value of their shares and/or dividends is affected by a breach may demand efforts by the company to identify and prosecute the attacker. In the initial aftermath of the attack, there may be the possibility of locating the suspect and the digital property taken and recovering it before it is exploited. It may be argued that the duties and responsibilities of a director include trying to recover the stolen corporate data before it is exploited.

Outside of law enforcement and several large businesses, such as the major accounting companies, there are few options for those who want to have an investigation into a cyber-attack conducted. The IR team may find evidence pointing to a suspect, but it is generally not their job to prepare a case for referral to police or lawyers. A cyber investigator is a very specialized position and is roughly the equivalent of a police detective conducting a criminal investigation, as the rules of evidence the court demands are the same whether you are an experienced detective or a civilian investigator.

The cyber investigator is viewed as the person who is tasked with finding evidence of the person behind the attack, and in some cases preparing a referral to police or commencing a civil prosecution. While many attacks originate from overseas and are hidden behind multiple legal jurisdictions, anonymizers, bots, or other technology, people have their own motivations to commit crimes—and these people may include current or former employees residing within your local jurisdiction.

The role of the cyber investigator is an extension of the digital investigator. For the benefit of this book, the digital investigator is the person who conducts a forensic examination of a device or network and produces a report on the evidence seized and identified.

This book is intended for the person assigned the task of investigating the cyber event with a view to gaining a full understanding of the event and where possible recovering the IP/PII before it is exploited. They may also be tasked with finding evidence to support an action in a tribunal (e.g., employment court) or a potential prosecution in a civil or criminal court should the attacker be identified. It will also be of benefit to the manager/executive/lawyer who is tasked to review an investigation to understand the actions of the investigation team and why certain decisions were made and to gain an understanding of the evidence available from a cybercrime scene and the follow-up investigation. This is not a book that describes how to technically respond to and mitigate a cyber-attack, as there are many books covering this topic in great detail. There are also many courses offered by organizations that teach the many aspects of responding to a cyber-attack from the technical perspective.

Although this book makes some references to material from third parties, it is not intended to be an academic book. This is because much of the material is not from academic literature or web sources, but from the experience of the author as a cybercrime investigator. The major exception to this is Chapter 12, which relies on evidence from the author's doctoral thesis on cybercrime investigation in a cloud-computing environment and where academic references from a literature review are noted. Where explanations are provided, as in the glossary, they are largely kept at a low-level technical definition to allow those new to this field of work to understand the material and its relevance without having to learn a whole new language called technology.

Due to the dynamic nature of evidence, advances in technology, and the evolution of legislation/court decisions, this book is not intended to be an exclusive guide in every legal jurisdiction or to cover every potential cyber event. Where material in this book conflicts in any way with the laws of your jurisdiction, the legal environment(s) you operate in will always take precedence. The book intends, however, to provoke critical thinking among management, IR team managers, and investigators facing a complex legal and technical environment should a suspect be identified and subsequent evidence need to be presented to a tribunal or court.

This book contains many of the steps a cybercrime investigator will undertake, from the initial identification of a cyber event through to considering a prosecution in court. There are many lists of things the investigator may consider. These are not exhaustive lists and are provided to expand the thinking as to what to do, where evidence may reside, and how to legally obtain and manage it. Use this book as a prompt and not as a definitive step-by-step template, as each cyber investigation is different and each jurisdiction has its own legal requirements.

The lists in this book provide a handy point of direction in each stage of the investigation. As you will discover, at each stage there are many things to be done and no one can remember them all every time. So, the lists are provided as a memory prompt of things to consider and apply as the circumstances, legislation in your jurisdiction, and your experience dictate. Not all items in the lists will be relevant in all instances. The explanations are in plain language and technical terms are kept to a minimum to assist your understanding of new concepts.

In Chapter 2 we provide an introduction to the cybercriminal and a series of offenses an investigator may be called upon to investigate. These will vary according to the laws of the jurisdiction(s) you are operating in and terms for the offenses will vary. By gaining an understanding of the cybercriminal and their chosen cybercrimes, we gain an understanding of how the crime was committed and why it was committed in the manner it was, as well as gaining some understanding of the type of identity we are seeking.

Once we understand typical offenses, in Chapter 3 we look at the motivations of the attacker. In some instances, understanding the attacker's motives will provide a strong pointer as to who the offender is, especially in cases of internal offenses. Motivations will vary across the many forms of cyber-attack you will investigate. It is worth understanding the reasons why a criminal attacks a specific target, as this will make great sense to them, even if the motivation seems unusual to the investigator.

In Chapter 4 we will look at examples of the alerts that may be the first indicators of the cyber event, as well as the offender's methodologies. These alerts and methodologies may be evidence in their own right and provide indicators as to the identity of the offender. While an alert will be generated before the investigator is brought in, the evidence from the alert will provide direction for the investigator to use as a platform for their investigation.

In Chapter 5 we will learn the process of commencing a cybercrime investigation. We will discuss the many reasons why an investigation is commenced and introduce who a cyber investigator is. While the common response to a cyber event is to fix the system and prevent an attack from happening again, we also will ask whether there is a responsibility on the part of the data owner to identify the attacker and attempt to get the stolen data back before it is exploited.

Once we have an understanding of offenses, offenders' motivations, initial alerts, and attack methodology, in Chapter 6 we will learn about the role of the law in your investigation. Should an attacker be identified and presented before the court, every aspect of your investigation is subject to critical examination in court by the defendant's lawyers, and your actions and their legality may be as much on trial as the activity of the defendant.

Whether you are conducting a civil or criminal investigation, the complainant will provide direction to the investigation they want from you. They will have information on which to base your investigation as well as the authority to provide the resources you require. In Chapter 7 we will cover the many aspects of your initial meeting with the complainant, including numerous questions you may find relevant to ask them at this meeting.

Chapter 8 provides a general introduction to the role of the digital investigator for the cyber investigator. Although the cyber investigator will not necessarily be involved in the technical aspect of the incident response while the attack is underway, it will be of benefit to them to understand what the IR examiners are doing and the consequences of their actions involving the digital evidence.

The cyber investigator will be involved in preserving evidence and in discussion with the digital investigator and IR teams as to the seizure of evidence, including placing a priority on preserving digital evidence, especially that which is most volatile.

The cyber environment provides many unique challenges to the investigator, and a variety of these challenges are introduced in Chapter 9. As you are operating in a dynamic environment, the challenges you face will vary according to the circumstances of your case and the evidence you are seeking.

In Chapter 10 we move into the cybercrime scene investigation and cover many of the areas of a search you need to be aware of and understand. Cybercrime investigations involve unique challenges to the investigator and these are identified and discussed. As you are operating in a physical and digital environment the challenges faced will differ among investigations, and the investigator will need to expand their thinking to understand their changing environment.

Log files are critical to cybercrime investigations: when activated and secured, they will tell you a lot about the attacker, their methodologies, and the data they accessed. In Chapter 11 we will introduce many log types, where they can be found, and what they mean to you as an investigator.

Log files are like video cameras at a crime scene. They can be effective—or, like a camera, if they are turned off or output not preserved, can be totally unusable. Log record activity on a device and network may provide very valuable evidence as to what happened, how it happened, when the breach occurred, and in some instances, who was behind it. The investigator may need to work with the digital investigator to understand what the logs are saying; however, this form of technical evidence may be crucial to your investigation—to the point where you may be criticized in court if you did not follow this potential evidence trail.

Chapter 12 addresses legal and technical issues involved in locating and lawfully seizing evidence from a cloud-computing platform. As data is now stored on multiple computer servers in multiple legal jurisdictions, evidence identification and preservation has become a far more complex procedure than when the examiner could physically seize a device that was suspected of being breached. Chapter 12 covers many of the legal and technical issues to be considered by the investigator, with suggested pathways to advancing your investigation in the cloud.

Chapter 13 provides a very brief introduction to the Internet of Things (IoT), which includes the multitude of devices now connected online. Evidence may now be gathered from anywhere there is a device connected to the Internet, and the digital investigator may use this technology to support their investigation.

Open source material is material that can be captured from online sources. There are numerous forms of open source information available online and many cyber investigators are finding valuable information to support their investigations by conducting online searches. Chapter 14 introduces a sample of the many forms of open source information available and how this information can assist your inquiries.

As cybercrime has become more professional over the past decade, the criminal community has created specialized markets where they can trade goods and services with customers. Criminal markets such as Silk Road and AlphaBay obtained a great deal of publicity through identifying the manner in which members of the criminal community operate and the level of support provided to each other in training and other support mechanisms. In Chapter 15 we will introduce the dark web and discuss its relevance to the investigator, with a warning not to venture into the criminal markets unless you as an investigator are well trained and understand the environment in which you will be operating. In some jurisdictions, it is an offense to access the dark web.

Interviewing witnesses and suspects is an art that many police officers and investigators take years to master. It is not a simple process, as each interview is unique and may be evidence in its own right. Chapter 16 will discuss many of the considerations to be undertaken when conducting an interview and safeguards that may be applied depending on the jurisdiction you are operating within.

Chapter 17 discusses how to review evidence collected and provide direction as to how to proceed. Sometimes you will have strong leads to the suspect, sometimes you may have enough evidence to commence or refer an investigation, and sometimes you will be facing a dead end with a recommendation to complete your investigation.

Should you have enough evidence to refer to a tribunal, civil court, or police, Chapter 18 discusses ideas for how to prepare your evidence for court. Each jurisdiction has its own rules, and your priority will be to obtain experienced legal advice to ensure the requirements of the law and court are met. How you present your evidence is sometimes as valuable as the strength of your prosecution.

Finally, in Chapter 19 we provide a summary of the contents of the book.

A glossary is also provided. It is prepared using nontechnical language, as readers will come from many backgrounds, many of which are not technical. Its aim is to provide a very general understanding of the new terminology mentioned, so you may continue reading with an understanding of the concept and the circumstances in which it is referenced. Should you require a more technical understanding of these concepts, there are many online resources available to you.

As a prime reason cyber security exists is the cybercriminal, we commence this book with an examination of the potential criminal offenses that may be committed in a digital and cyber environment.

2

Cybercrime Offenses

THE POTENTIAL offenses a criminal may commit against an entity or individual is limited only by the imagination of the attacker. The cybercriminal may be a long-term trusted employee within the organization or a person located on the other side of the world. They could also be a contractor who takes advantage of operating within the corporate network to install malicious software or access information by installing a server on the network to intercept and record all traffic without the authority of the system's administrator.

This chapter seeks to present to the investigator an understanding of the many forms of cybercrime they may be required to investigate. While the investigation techniques presented in this book may be similar across each crime type, an understanding of the crime goes a long way toward understanding the criminal. This then provides direction as to where to locate digital evidence within the physical and digital crime scene as well as to understanding the criminal's motivation.

As technology evolves, so do the opportunities for the criminal community to evolve with it. As new technological products are released into the marketplace, criminals view the product or service with a view as to how it may be exploited to progress their criminal ventures. For example, when gaming consoles provided an internal hard drive to store the games as well as to provide

Internet connectivity, criminals started storing evidence of their crimes—such as Child Exploitation Material (CEM)—within the hard drive of the console, so should police conduct a search warrant at their address, they were less likely to seize a gaming console than a laptop or desktop computer. As criminals develop these skills, law enforcement reacts to them and develops their evolving field of investigative knowledge.

Cybercriminals share their knowledge on open source and closed criminal forums, resulting in a higher standard of criminal who can seek experienced assistance when their attempted crime meets a hurdle. Cybercriminals also provide tutorials for those new to the industry, including step-by-step methodologies on how to commit cybercrime without leaving behind digital evidence leading to their identity. Should it be required, some sites provide one-on-one tutorials and peer review. In essence cybercrime is a profession, with many resources available to the criminals. These same resources can also be useful to the investigator in understanding developing methodologies and the ways criminals conduct their activities.

An advantage of cybercrime to a criminal, when compared to other forms of crime, is the lack of structural complexity. When compared to a crime such as illegal drug trafficking, cybercrime lacks the structural managerial complexities that are prevalent in crimes involving physical property. A drug trafficker may be required to structure the business, distribution, processing, transporting, competition, physical threats, sales network, and money laundering. In cybercrime, there are fewer of these considerations involved. As opposed to the illegal drug trade, where parties involved maybe personally known to each other and build relationships, those involved in partnerships in cybercrime may not ever physically meet each other, assisting each other based on their areas of expertise. Also, a valuable consideration is there are no turf wars involved in cybercrime, as there are in the illegal drugs trade.[1]

There are many other reasons why cybercrime is attractive to the criminal. One of these is the financial reward available compared to other forms of crime. Joseph Schafer and his colleagues found that on average the bank robber may obtain $2,500, the bank fraudster $25,000, and the cybercriminal $250,000. They also found that the cost of the theft of technology to an organization is approximately $1.9 million.[2]

Alongside the financial rewards, a further attraction of cybercrime to the criminal is that the actions required are easy to carry out and hard to detect. The Internet provides anonymity for skilled cybercriminals, who use available technological resources (such as free web-based email accounts). Schafer and his colleagues found that the anonymity cybercriminals are operating under online reduces their personal inhibitions, especially since the potential for being identified and held accountable for their actions is low.[2]

Of further benefit to the cybercriminal is that the proceeds of their crime (data) can be virtualized and geographically distributed, creating technical and jurisdictional challenges for law enforcement and other investigating agencies. Digital forensic investigations to obtain evidence may not be able to be obtained in a timely manner, meaning valuable evidence may be not available to investigators.[3]

An additional benefit to the cybercriminal is that their crimes can be committed anywhere. Data can be disseminated very quickly, and the cross-jurisdictional manner of the crime results in the need for collaboration between police services at the national and international level.[2] To add a further layer of complexity for an investigating agency, cybercriminals may operate in failed or failing states that provide a safe haven.[4]

The specific civil or criminal offense in each instance depends upon the legal jurisdiction and the wording of the specifics of the offense as defined in legislation. While there are many forms of civil and criminal offenses involving technology, this chapter lists examples of offenses where technology is a major factor in the crime the cyber investigator is required to respond to. Also understand that when you are dealing with a cyber event and the suspect lives in a foreign legal jurisdiction, even though their action may be a very serious criminal or civil offense in your jurisdiction, the act may not be an offense in their country. In effect, in their jurisdiction they are doing nothing wrong.

As an investigator, be aware there may be more than one offense occurring at the same time. While you are responding to a certain form of cybercrime, this may be merely a distraction to divert the attention of the Incident Response (IR) security team, as the attacker's main goal may be elsewhere on the network. For example, there may be an attack against the company web server, and while the IR team is focused on mitigating this attack, the criminal can be stealing data from the email server or corporate database.

The remainder of this chapter provides examples of different forms of cybercriminal offending followed by a brief explanation. These are not listed as specific offenses, as each jurisdiction will have different wording for these activities and there may be multiple offenses you can identify from a single description.

▦ POTENTIAL CYBERCRIME OFFENSES

Each of the following sections will provide some consideration the investigator may think about to support their investigation. There will be replication across the offenses; however, the comments are presented to provide a few thoughts to advance your investigation.

Industrial Espionage

This offense is also sometimes called corporate espionage. This is a standard form of cybercrime, with the criminal breaking through the defenses of a company to locate the Intellectual Property (IP) for sale or their own use. A competitor may itself conduct the attack, or the attack may be random, with the criminal breaking in to see what they can find and exploit. This offense has well predated the Internet, with insiders being used to steal IP or documents being stolen from trash bins after being discarded.

As companies develop new products, competitors may find a strategic advantage in knowing where their competition is planning on being in 12 months. The theft of strategy and development plans allows the attacker to develop their countermeasures, saving years of development and expense in new product design.

Specific IP may be submitted for patent by the developer, ensuring a level of industry protection against it being copied by competitors. However, should the IP be stolen prior to the patent being issued and then submitted for patent by the thief, complicated and expensive court cases or even overall loss of the developed IP may result.

Along with corporate IP, tender documents, which are due to be submitted in the following days, are a valuable target. With this information the business competitor who initiated or contracted a hacker to undertake the attack on their behalf may update their documents to increase their chances of winning the tender against the victim company.

Investigator Considerations

Industrial or economic espionage is a very serious criminal offense, as the future of the victim company may be at stake. Companies put very serious money into the development of IP, and having it stolen by competitors or put up for sale to the highest bidder will cause very serious stress to the complainants. In the instance of public companies, disclosure of IP being stolen may have a negative effect on their share value.

As the investigator at the scene, always respect and understand the stress of the company executives and owners. Identify who may benefit from the theft of the IP, such as competitors or new companies seeking to establish themselves.

It may be of benefit to contract with a company that specializes in operating in the criminal markets to identify whether it comes up for sale.

Do not discount the potential for an internal employee to be the party taking the IP and seeking to establish them in a rival business in the near future. If the IP is of significant financial value and not patented, recommend to the complainant that they still go through this process, as they will have the product development history to support their claim as to ownership of the IP.

An investigation such as this may need to be conducted into the future in a monitoring phase, as the complainant monitors who in the industry develops a product very similar to their IP or seeks to patent it. This now provides you with a reverse starting point with a suspect. By this time you will have conducted your initial investigations; when a suspect has been identified, you may resurrect your investigation with a suspect in mind. This is equally applicable if the suspect was involved in the initial theft of the IP or purchased it through the criminal markets.

Theft of Information Such as Identities, Staff Files, and Accounts

Similar to industrial espionage, this may be a specifically targeted or random attack. The identities may be sold online, held for later exploitation, or sold back to the company as a ransom. These attacks may be internal or external to the network.

Examples of Personally Identifiable Information (PII) stolen include names, addresses, Social Security numbers, passwords, phone numbers, email accounts, credit card numbers, next-of-kin details, mother's maiden name, and so on. The value of this information to the attacker is that it may be useful in creating databases on persons of specific interest within the organization; other data can then be located through open source investigation (such as social media) to develop a more detailed profile of the individual. The profile may be used to commit identify theft against the organization or a financial institution, or sold on the criminal markets as a product.

Investigator Considerations

Although this is a very common crime, with hundreds of millions of identities and credit card details stolen every year, the consequences to victims are not lessened. There is a saying in the law that you take your victims as you find them, and while one victim of identity or credit card fraud may take the news and move on without concern, another may suffer severe financial and emotional stress.

As a very general although not exclusive rule, stolen identities are sold on the criminal markets. Investigating in this environment is the task of a very skilled and experienced investigator, and if you do not have these skills, seek them elsewhere, as these cybercriminals employ countersurveillance, which you need to avoid.

The evidence you will locate may come from the initial investigation of the digital evidence. Did the cybercriminal proceed straight to this evidence or did they navigate their pathway through the network before locating this evidence? Look at the business of the victim company and whether it is a company whose collection of such information is a byproduct of its core business or actually the core business itself, such as being a payment gateway. This information will assist in understanding the attacker's motivations and the type of cybercriminal you are seeking.

Chapter 15 will provide more information as to conducting investigations in this environment and evidence you may locate through criminal vendors.

Computer Hacking to Gain Access to System Resources

Corporations and educational and governmental organizations have access to large and powerful computer systems with processors and bandwidth. An attacker may break into a system to host a criminal site (such as a fraudulent online pharmacy) or to use the bandwidth to launch a Denial of Service (DoS) attack against another target. Alternatively, they may seek to use these resources to mine Bitcoin.

This form of attack may be lost in the traffic of normal day-to-day activity where there is a high volume of activity on internal and external networks; however, use of the bandwidth resources confers a cost to the victim company.

Investigator Considerations

This is a unique form of investigation, as many victims of this form of cybercrime do not make complaints due to the potential for reputational damage. If you are entrusted to investigate these crimes, look toward who is the beneficiary of the offense, such as the online pharmacy or the Bitcoin miner. Details about the compromise may also be of interest, as the obvious offense may be the byproduct of an initial hack seeking IP and student/staff details.

Academic institutes are a haven for valuable IP being developed by postgraduate and doctoral students, which is highly prized by nation states, especially in fields such as robotics, artificial intelligence, and nanotechnology. Look very closely at what else the cybercriminal was doing, especially before the takeover of the infrastructure, and do not focus exclusively on the most obvious offending you have been tasked to investigate.

Gaining or Exceeding Authorized Access Levels to Obtain Highly Restricted Data

Users of a network may seek to increase their level of access to highly confidential data. Alternatively, a hacker may gain a user's credentials within the organization and work on escalating their access to the confidential data through compromising accounts associated to the user. For example, a hacker may gain access to the personnel clerk's internal account, then use this to gain access to their supervisor's account, then use this to gain access to the personnel manager's account, and so on.

This is a major concern for all organizations and government agencies and their contractors who have been compromised in this manner.

Investigator Considerations

Escalating privileges involves navigating a pathway through a series of users' accounts from low to higher levels to find where users gain access to confidential data. You may have to work backwards from the point of identification of the breach to find whose account was compromised in the first instance and how this was achieved. This will provide evidence of the attacker entering the organization and gaining the lowest levels of privilege. You may, for example, find a link between the attacker's Internet Protocol address found at the initial compromise of the junior personnel clerk's account and the Internet Protocol address the stolen data was forwarded to.

Understanding pre-offense behaviors, including reconnaissance, testing of vulnerabilities, and phishing attacks, may provide details about offender behavior and attribution.

Exploiting Information Security Weaknesses through the Supply Chain, Including Third-Party Contractors

Third-party contractors often fail to provide the level of security their client is capable of providing. For example, independent contractors in Hollywood may have been the ones hacked when movies are taken and held for extortion prior to release to the public. The criminals have determined it is easier to hack into the computer of a contractor rather than a major Hollywood studio, which has more resources to defend itself.

Investigator Considerations

Look closely at what was taken and who may benefit from the attack. In the example given of a Hollywood contractor, look to see whether the offender went directly to the IP or whether the IP was only located as a byproduct of examining the system.

While we may think cybercriminals are very structured, motivated, and skilled types of people, sometimes they are lucky and stumble across very valuable IP without initially understanding the target they are hacking. In effect, they got lucky.

Stealing Credit Card Data for Selling Online, or Card-Not-Present Fraud

These attacks deliberately target credit card information for exploitation or for selling online through the criminal trading markets. This information includes names, addresses, credit card numbers, dates of birth, next of kin, phone numbers, and so on.

The card numbers are used to purchase goods from online retailers using Internet services, with the cybercriminal having the goods delivered to a predetermined address. This may be an unknowing colleague's address, work address, rental property, or a pickup point that specializes in receiving parcels for clients, as some postal services operate. This is known to retailers as "card-not-present" fraud and carries a significant financial cost for the retailer, as the credit card company reverses the charge to the retailer.

As an alternative, a cybercriminal may sell information from the cards to clients as a bulk item, charging per unit or at a volume discount. Should the information be from cards of particular value, such as an American Express Platinum card, it may be sold individually at a negotiated price.

Investigator Considerations

These tend to be large-volume crimes, with hundreds of millions of credit cards available for sale online in the criminal markets. As mentioned previously, do not even consider going onto the criminal markets unless you are very skilled in online tradecraft, or even better, have brought in cyber investigator who is experienced in this field.

Identifying who is the beneficiary of the transaction is a more productive pathway for the investigator investigating individual card-not-present frauds.

Gaining Access to a System or Device through Malicious Software

These attacks seek to gain access to a computer system through the delivery of malicious software. This may be either an internal or external attack. An example is an Advanced Persistent Threat (APT), where a person gains unlawful access to a computer device and maintains their hidden presence, gathering new data each day. An APT may be present from a week up to several years before being found.

Investigator Techniques

Identifying the malicious software used in the crime is one of the first steps for the investigator. Contact the organization's security vendor, which may have resources available to immediately identify the malicious software and its characteristics. Many of these companies have very knowledgeable investigators who can provide you with information about the persons and/or syndicates behind the attack. You may use this valuable information to leverage off their technical inquiries.

This will be a portion of your investigation and supplement the investigation into the crime committed via usage of the malicious software.

Damaging the Reputation of a Competitor to Gain a Market Advantage

As competition is tough in the marketplace, damaging the reputation of a competitor may provide the attacker an advantage. An example would be a tender submitter launching an online attack on a competitor just before a tender committee sits to decide who will win the latest tender, raising serious questions about the victim's cyber security.

Investigator Considerations

In the early days of the investigation, look to see who is the beneficiary of the reputational damage of your client. While this may be a random attacker with an extortion motive, if the company is in the process of delicate negotiations with a potential client or tendering for a new contract, there may be clear signals as to who the potential suspect may be. Your client may be able to point you in this direction.

Changes to Computer Systems or Devices

This is a particularly difficult crime for a company to manage, as the attack will be targeted at modifying the data of the company. As the victim company makes subsequent strategic decisions, they will be made with incorrect data, meaning tender documents may be uncompetitive or overly cheap.

Investigation Considerations

This is a very personal attack where there is no obvious suspect. Damaging data to induce the company into making poor business decisions is not of any great benefit to the average cybercriminal who is seeking a personal financial return.

Speaking to the complainant will provide direction as to potential beneficiaries of the crime. Also understanding how the action was identified will provide further direction of assistance.

A person motivated to commit such an attack would include a disgruntled former employee who modifies the data before they leave as retribution for a perceived grievance. Never underestimate the motivation of an angry ex-employee.

Vandalism to Prove the Skills of the Attacker

Hackers like to prove their skills and build their portfolio of companies that they have successfully attacked. A company may be the random victim of a hacker who is seeking to build their credibility in the hacking community.

Investigator Considerations

As the victimology of this crime may be put down to pure bad luck, there may be few leads for the investigators to consider from the perspective of motivation.

Investigators who know their way around the bulletin boards and websites cybercriminals communicate on may pick up some details on who was behind the attack. New cybercriminals testing their skills like to let everyone know about their successful attacks for the purpose of building their reputation. Use these criminals' vulnerability related to the need to promote themselves to see what you can find out about them and to build profiles on them.

Drive-by Downloads of Malicious Software

An effective form of cyber-attack is the taking control of the website of a legitimate company, installing malicious software, and waiting for visitors to the site to unknowingly download the malicious software. As it is a reputable site, the visitors will not view the site as high risk, raising the prospects of more success for the attacker.

Investigator Considerations

Investigating this form of cybercrime involves gaining an understanding of the technical vulnerabilities of the site exploited. Look to see where the repository of the data has been sent, which is usually a website controlled by the attacker. As noted previously, discussions with cyber security companies (such as Sophos and Symantec) may provide you with information as to the technical components of the attack and the leads you may generate from them.

Interfering with Access to a Network

Denial of Service (DoS) and Distributed Denial of Service (DDoS) attacks are technical attacks to overload the website and server, restricting customers and staff from accessing the Internet.

Ex-employees have been known to cause damage to networks before ceasing their employment by loading malicious software onto the system, installing backdoor pathways into the system to allow access once their legitimate access has been removed, or deleting valuable files.

Investigator Considerations

Reasons for a DoS or DDoS attack may be as simple as an extortion attempt, political motivation (as a party holds a personal grudge against the target), or business reputational damage, as previously discussed.

Speaking to the complainant may provide some valuable information, especially if there has been communication with the attacker. In these cases, there may have been a demand for a ransom to be paid to a virtual currency account or a demand to modify a stated company philosophy.

Ransomware

Here, the attacker encrypts the hard drives of the devices they can access and also encrypts the backups, if accessible. If the victim has no offline backups, they are required to pay a ransom to the attacker to regain access to their data. This attack may also include the theft of data from the device or network before the encryption process commences.

Investigator Considerations

As previously discussed, there will be a form of communication from the suspect. Usually this is in the form of an email or note left on the victim's computer. Identify the virtual currency account that payment is to be made to and identify the volume of payments being made to it. In the case of Bitcoin, you can use Block Explorer on the Blockchain site (https://www.blockchain.com/explorer) to input the address where the Bitcoin payment is to be made to gain an understanding of the magnitude of the crime and whether it is a random attack or specifically targeted.

Phishing Attacks and Money Laundering

Fraudulent emails are sent to induce persons to log on to a site they are a member of (such as a bank, credit card, or finance company) by using their user names and passwords. The link included in the email is to a site the criminal has created, which is an exact image of the legitimate site the potential victim is familiar with.

Once the account owner enters their user name and password, the cybercriminal has access to the client's account. The difficulty for the cybercriminal is if the victim has two-factor authentication on their account; then they will have to develop a further strategy to defeat this level of security.

The next stage for the cybercriminal once they have direct access to the account is to remove the funds. This may present a further logistical hurdle if they are in a different country from their victim and they cannot directly transfer the proceeds of their crime overseas.

The experienced cybercriminal may monitor the account for several weeks to get a full understanding of how money flows through the account. Examples of activities of interest include when the victim's pay goes into their account and when mortgages and utilities are paid, effectively mapping the flow of money to identify when in a pay cycle there is the most money in the account.

Some financial institutions have daily limits on transfers of money from an account. To maximize the financial return cybercriminals will transfer the balance of the daily available funds at 23:59 hours and then the new daily balance at 00:01 hours the following day.

When the funds have been accessed and the money is to be moved across international borders, the cybercriminal will need another victim or unknowing associate to assist in moving the funds to a jurisdiction they can access. The unknowing associate becomes in effect a money mule.

The money mule is an unknowing person who believes they are involved in a legitimate business venture or who has been socially engineered to believe they are in a relationship with a legitimate person. These shall be viewed separately. As these are common methods of removing money across international jurisdictions, the investigator may be required to interview them to identify their level of culpability.

Business Money Mule

The business money mule is a person who has responded to an online advertisement for what they believe is a legitimate job. The most common job they are recruited for is to receive money into their bank account on behalf of the company employing them while it sets itself up in the host country.

As money is placed into their account, they are required to immediately send it to a specific account or to a person using money transfer services, exchange it into virtual currency, or use their personal bank account to transfer the money overseas. They are permitted to keep a specified amount as a commission, which reinforces their belief they are involved in a legitimate business venture.

This is a risky time for the cybercriminal, as they are trusting a third party to be an integral party of their cybercrime. To mitigate the risk, they may immediately contact their money mule by phone and keep them on the phone while the money is obtained and transferred. This may require an investment of several hours of their time but helps to mitigate the risk of the money mule deciding to keep an apparent financial windfall for themselves.

Socially Engineered Money Mule

This is a very different type of person from the business money mule, as they believe they are in an established relationship with another person. This relationship may be several years long. The most common form of person to fit this category is a person who has been victimized through online relationship fraud, where they have sent money to their new friend to support them and bring them to their home country.

As the relationship develops, the victim is asked to receive money into their bank account to help facilitate a business venture their online friend needs to complete to finalize their travel to meet the victim. At this time, there is a very strong emotional tie between the victim and the cybercriminal, and the victim believes what they are being told.

Investigator Considerations

To an investigator who has not encountered examples of individuals meeting people on the Internet, falling in love or believing what may appear to be obvious frauds, the inclination is to suspect that these victims are involved in the fraud and need to be charged. While this may be applicable according to the laws in your jurisdiction, it is unfortunately a very common occurrence. On most occasions, these people have been socially engineered and have no understanding that they have been dealing with professional criminals.

To advance your investigation, seek the cooperation of the money mule to obtain as much information as you can to identify information about the cybercriminal. Email communication, Skype addresses, recorded communication, phone numbers, contact names of those receiving money sent via money transfer services, and the history of the employment/relationship may be used to advance your investigation.

Business Email Compromise Fraud

Business email compromise fraud is where an email, that represents itself to be from a senior executive of the company is received by a staff member. They are seeking money to be paid urgently to a new bank account. Alternatively, a customer asks for an established payment to be made to a new bank account; however, the email is not from the customer, but a fraudster impersonating the customer.

A further alternative to this fraud is the criminal gaining access to the email account of a creditor to a company and sending a legitimate email requesting that an upcoming payment be paid to a new bank account. The victim confirms this as a request from a regular creditor and has no reason to believe the email is fraudulent.

Investigator Considerations

Evidence may be located from confirming the attack strategy through an examination of the email containing the request to change the bank account details. If the email is a close copy of the creditor's regular email address, it is most likely an indicator the creditor has not been compromised and that the attacker has created a domain name very similar to the creditor's. An examination of the domain records of the suspect domain will tell you when the domain was registered and possibly by whom, allowing for the reality that many of the domain registry details are false. Even this information will lead you to further inquiries, as you will be interested in identifying how the attacker knew a payment was due to the creditor and who within the victim company the email was to be sent to.

If the email containing the false request to change bank account details is a true email from a known creditor, there has most likely been a security breach of the creditor business where an attacker has accessed the corporate email account, monitored the accounts receivable system, and identified when an account payable by the target company is to be paid.

Examination of where the funds were paid will lead to further information. Often the recipients are money mules and inquiries can be continued as previously discussed.

Social Engineering Fraud

Social engineering is the art of inducing a person to commit an act or series of acts against their interests that they would not do if they fully understood the reality of what they are being told to do. In effect, online social engineering is a series of lies told by a cybercriminal to induce a person to send them money or data, or to provide access to personal devices or corporate networks.

These crimes have been in existence since before the Internet; however, the reach of the online environment has allowed the cybercriminal to reach potential targets in any corner of the world. In fact, it is easier and safer to defraud a person on the other side of the world than it is your neighbor.

There are many strategies available to the cybercriminal; however, undertaking research on their target is used across all strategies. Social media sites are researched as well as search engine inquiries. When required, they will research genealogy sites to provide background on their target, so when an initial approach is made to the target, the criminal has personal information which can be corroborated.

The business email compromise discussed previously is a form of social engineering, and we will briefly introduce a series of other examples.

Relationship Fraud

This crime targets the human vulnerability of loneliness and exploits the hope that a person may find a partner online. This is a particularly cruel form of crime, as victims state they find it hard to understand which was worse: losing their money in the fraud or being defrauded emotionally.

A victim may be located on a relationship site or through social media. The relationship sites are particularly valuable to the attacker as they can identify a lot about the victim from their profile, including their background, their current status, their likes and dislikes, their hopes for the future, and the attributes they are looking for in a future partner. The fraudster will use a technique called "mirroring" to reflect the values and desires of their target back to them by creating a profile for that purpose or modifying an existing fraudulent profile. For example, if the target likes taking long walks on the beach with their Labrador dog and having an evening glass of red wine before the fire, then the fraudster's profile will say exactly the same things. If a victim's profile says that they have lost a partner due to a specific disease, the fraudster will disclose a very similar life event, providing a strong emotional connection. As stated, these are particularly cruel crimes.

In the initial communication, the criminal will seek as much information about the victim as possible, asking numerous questions and filling in their database of knowledge with which to exploit their target. The victim will not be used to the level of interest in them being shown and the criminal will commence using emotional language. To the victim, the purpose of going on the relationship site—meeting a compatible match—will appear to be fulfilled.

Over the coming days and weeks they will receive numerous positive messages, including "I think I love you." While it may seem very unusual to fall in love with a person you have never physically met, there are literally hundreds of thousands of normal people throughout the world who have been socially engineered by this form of crime with the psychological trigger of loneliness abused.

Victims will send money to the fraudster to assist them in traveling to the victim's country, including the cost of completing business ventures, required government charges, and so on. Each payment is met with a new request for more money. The cybercriminal is very skilled at this, as they will have learned when the victim receives their pay, when accounts are due, and the like.

The cruelty of this crime type is shown by the manner in which the victim is socially engineered. In a relationship where people live together, the last person you usually speak to in the evening is your partner. The first person you speak to in the morning is your partner. In relationship fraud, the cybercriminal will call last thing in the evening to tell their victim, "I love you … Goodnight," and again first thing in the morning to make a comment along the lines of, "I have been thinking about you all night. I love you … Have a great day." These are very powerful messages.

Investigator Considerations

The cybercriminal is usually in a foreign jurisdiction using disposable web accounts, disposable phones, and fake identities. This is a very difficult crime to investigate, and it is very difficult to identify a real-world suspect.

You will require cooperation from law enforcement or civilian investigators in foreign jurisdictions. Your local evidence will include phone records, Internet Protocol addresses, and money transfer receipts, as well as copies of text communication on applications such as Skype.

Inheritance Fraud

With the abundance of material available about people online, learning the background of people is easy, with social media and genealogy sites providing valuable resources to the cybercriminal.

An inheritance fraudster will prepare a letter of introduction to their target using the name of a legitimate foreign law firm and identify a relative of their target who research shows lived and died overseas. The fraudster will represent that the relative left a large sum of money to the target. The letter of introduction will include many family references, which can be independently verified by the target.

The victim will be instructed to make payment of fees, charges, taxes, and the like before the funds can be released. Depending on the skill of the cybercriminal, these costs can reach into the hundreds of thousands of dollars.

Investigator Considerations

As with the relationship fraud, the offender will usually be overseas and hidden behind layers of technology. The large sums of money sent may provide avenues of inquiry in the foreign jurisdiction, as will phone records, message records, and IP addresses.

These are several examples of the many cyber-related attacks you may be involved in investigating in your career. There are many more and each requires a level of lateral thinking by the investigator to understand attack methodologies, motivations, and consequences.

Chapter 3 will identify a series of factors motivating people to commit a cybercrime, including why specific companies or individuals are targeted.

CYBERCRIME CASE STUDY

A male was on an online relationship site when he met a person he felt he had a future with. He invested a lot of time with her and built a strong emotional relationship despite their being in separate countries. She encouraged the building of the relationship saying all the phrases he needed to hear, such as "I love you," which was a very powerful phrase he felt he would never hear again.

At some stage in the early grooming phase, he disclosed that his brother had died of a congenital heart defect and that this placed an emotional burden on his life. The fraudster identified this as a form of vulnerability and later introduced him to her son. Over time the fraudster convinced him that they had a future together, and her four-year-old son started asking, "Are you going to be my new daddy?" This sealed the relationship as far as the victim was concerned, as he was desperate to be a parent.

Once the relationship was secured, the child mysteriously developed a congenital heart defect requiring regular sums of money for medication and later surgery. The victim was determined that the child was to receive the best of health care and sent large sums of money for the child's health care, medication, and the like. He cashed in his pension, paid all costs as they were incurred, and was provided medical receipts, which were later proven to be fake. As the child's health failed, he paid for an urgent heart transplant at the request of the mother, her pastor, physician, and other "friends of the family."

Upon identification of the fraud, a search warrant was conducted at the suspect's address that identified communication logs, phone records, financial receipts, and partial admissions, proving the guilt of the female. She was sentenced to five years' imprisonment.

NOTES

1. G. Stevenson Smith, "Management Models for International Cybercrime," *Journal of Financial Crime* 22, no. 1 (2015): 104–125, https://www.emeraldinsight.com/doi/full/10.1108/JFC-09-2013-0051.
2. Joseph Schafer, Michael E. Buerger, Richard W. Myers, Carl J. Jensen III, and Bernard H. Levin, *The Future of Policing: A Practical Guide for Police Managers and Leaders*, 1st ed. (Boca Raton, FL: CRC Press, 2011).
3. Christopher Hooper, Ben Martini, and Kim-Kwang Raymond Choo, "Cloud Computing and Its Implications for Cybercrime Investigations in Australia,"

Computer Law and Security Review 29, no. 2 (2013): 152–163, https://www
.sciencedirect.com/science/article/pii/S0267364913000241.

4. Roderic Broadhurst, "Developments in the Global Law Enforcement of
Cyber-Crime," *Policing: An International Journal of Police Strategies and Management* 29, no. 3 (2006): 408–433, https://papers.ssrn.com/sol3/papers
.cfm?abstract_id=2089650.

Motivations of the Attacker

A S WE HAVE seen in Chapter 2, cybercrime offenses cover a wide range of territory. The boundaries of offending are limited only by the imagination of the attackers. Cybercriminals come in many shapes and sizes and are motivated by reasons that make sense to them at the time of their attack. Once identified, the attack, motivation, or methodology does not necessarily have to make sense to the victim or investigator, as they are not the ones who decided their reasons were sufficient to commence the attack in the first instance.

While the investigator may commence an investigation with a perceived understanding of what they are going to locate over the coming days, the reality of what they discover may be very different. If they commence their investigation with a tunnel view of what happened, they will misread the evidence and ignore that which does not suit their unconscious bias. In short, follow the evidence and make your mind up as to what happened and the reasons why at the end of the investigation. If you have an open mind, the evidence will lead you on the correct path.

Without knowing the identity of the attacker, the motivation for an attack may be identified from the methodology used or the damage that was caused. Alternatively, an attacker may contact their victim after the attack has been discovered and make their motivation clear by making an extortion demand.

Examination of the pathway through a network that an external hacker has traveled may show their level of familiarity with the internal network, especially if they travel directly to the target and take the data sought. Alternatively, the attacker who stumbles around the network missing key data may be evidence of a cybercriminal with limited skill looking to see what they can find. An examination of system logs prior to the attack may find evidence of the attacker conducting extensive reconnaissance of the network and its security.

The cybercriminal may be internal or external to the network, or a contractor. While the usual understanding of a cybercriminal is a person physically remote from the network they are attacking, an internal employee may be taking copies of valuable IP with them to their next employer or selling it to competitors. A malicious internal employee may also be prepared to execute a program on a USB device, allowing an attacker they know remote access to their employer's corporate network.

COMMON MOTIVATORS

The following are examples of cybercriminals' common motivators for their crimes. The list is not exhaustive, as the important point to understand is that the motivation for the attack will make sense to the criminal during the time of preparing for and committing the offense. Therefore the list of potential motivations may be far more extensive than this list.

Revenge

An attacker may commit a criminal offense against a company after a perceived injustice against themselves. The attacker may be a current or former employee, a competitor, or an issue-motivated group. A current or former employee may be motivated by having been passed over for a promotion, by having not received a pay raise that met their expectations, or by having been disciplined for their behavior and having not met job performance standards.

The form of attack will vary based on the skills and resources available to the attacker.

Opportunity

In the instance of an internal employee, there may be no initial motivation by the employee to commit any form of crime against their employer. However, while undertaking their duties they may identify a vulnerability in the internal systems where money or data could be removed without anyone else being able to identify their actions. From there, they may decide to exploit the vulnerability to their benefit and commence taking money or data to be sold to other parties.

The decision to commit the offense may develop a significant period after identifying the potential vulnerability, when the opportunity proves too much of a temptation to them. Examples include accounting staff adding fake employees to the accounting system and sending the pay to their bank account, the accounting manager operating a second set of books to hide their dishonest behavior, and the creation of false invoicing, with the creditor's payment going to their personal bank account.

Greed

No surprises here. Greed is a common motivator for the criminal, whether internal or external to the company. The potential to enrich their lives at the expense of others is an enticing option to them, with little to no concern as to the damage they do to others. Greed is not listed as one of the seven deadly sins by accident.

The investigator may uncover this motivator very quickly, in which case the emphasis will be on locating the proceeds of the crime with a view to mitigating the potential damage.

Test of Skill

Some cyber criminals may commit technical attacks against others as a training exercise to develop their skills for a more financially lucrative attack. They may also use these attacks to advertise their skill set and their successful system compromises to build their credibility on cybercriminal websites.

Script kiddies are new entrants to the cybercrime community who rely heavily upon the technology and education provided by more experienced cybercriminals. They may have a low level of technical skill; however, they start their careers by learning tools and tradecraft from criminal websites and forums. As they develop and test their skills, their range of options to commit cybercrime expands.

Business Competitor

The marketplace can be a very aggressive environment for businesses, with each placing an emphasis on developing a strategic advantage. One way is to steal the competition's IP through computer hacking to provide an advantage.

Another is to damage the competitor's reputation through a technical attack, leaving existing and potential clients with concerns about doing business with a company under a technical attack.

These strategies may be very successful when a tender involving the victim company is to be decided.

Professional Criminal

The professional criminal's motivation is seeking personal financial advantage. The attack is rarely personal and the attack on the target company is nothing more than a business venture to make money.

A type of professional criminal is the contractor who is available to do the work of a client, and therefore the motivation is financial, with no element of personal grievance against the target. These persons may be located online, including on the dark web, and offer their services (such as hacking) to the highest bidder.

Issue-Motivated Attacker

This is a very personal attack and the victim may be targeted for a political reason rather than any other event. Examples may be an advertiser who is the subject of a consumer boycott or a business providing a product or service that members of the community may disagree with. It can also involve the target making a comment on social media that is perceived as wrong.

Geopolitics

A state actor is a government agency or aligned group who conducts cyber activities on behalf of that government. The motivation may be to seek the IP of specific industries in foreign countries to gain a competitive advantage. Alternatively, they may seek to target the infrastructure of a hostile company or country to cause as much damage as possible.

Terrorism

With the world being connected, the opportunity exists for persons in remote locations to target the critical infrastructure of an entity they wish to cause extreme harm to. A person in a remote location may see their goals advanced by causing a massive security failure in another nation's critical infrastructure—such as power, nuclear energy, or water delivery—that leads to a large-scale loss of life.

The skill set of the attacker may vary; however, with the vast array of network and attack tools freely available online with support instructions available, the threshold in becoming a cybercriminal is very low.

As mentioned earlier, motivations may make no sense to the complainant or investigator. In fact, some motivations may never be uncovered. What is important is that to the attacker, the motivation made such sense as to commence a criminal offense.

While the nation state and criminal contractor may be perceived as actors, they still have specific motivations to conduct the attacks.

CYBERCRIME CASE STUDY I

The accountant of a business was directed to create false invoices to be supplied to a financing company, which was purchasing the invoices at 80 percent of their face value.

"Factoring" is a legitimate financing arrangement in which a company sells its accounts receivable to a third party at a discount. In this case, the arrangement was to provide cash flow to the company in question. The remainder of the funds, less a 3 percent fee, was paid to the company once the invoice had been paid by the debtor.

The company was in poor financial shape and the factoring company had not made a thorough investigation into the financial health of their new client prior to agreeing to structure the factoring agreement. Within several months of the financing agreement, the company was creating fake invoices to sell to the factoring company. It was also attempting to produce false invoices for the investors as well as government tax offices.

As the company books were required by many sources, including the finance company, the owner directed the accountant to create different sets of books for different audiences. When the frauds were identified, the company had five sets of books located on the company network.

The digital evidence included logs showing the false invoices delivered to the finance company that were created by the accountant as well as by the company's owner, who would create them after hours using his unique identifier and password to access the system. He would then create a schedule detailing the false invoices to provide to the accountant the following morning for inclusion in the designated fake set of books. These schedules were located on the company owner's private drive on the network, with logs showing no other party had access to this portion of the storage.

CYBERCRIME CASE STUDY II

A woman met a person on the Internet through a dating site and over the following months a relationship developed. She believed she was in a legitimate online relationship and that there was to be a future with her new partner once he made his way to Australia. He represented himself as an engineer who needed to finalize his work overseas before returning to Australia.

To assist him with his finances, the woman sent sums of money to help him pay for his living expenses, business fees, and personal tax charges he said had to be paid before he left the country. Over the course of six months she forwarded approximately $250,000 to him, which was to be paid back once he made it to Australia with the proceeds of his business venture.

As is the case with this form of fraud, there is always another delay, another request for money, and another problem that can only be solved by the victim sending more money as a "final payment" prior to the journey being undertaken and the couple meeting up. The victim stated that she no longer had access to money to send, as she had sent all the cash she had, fully mortgaged her home, borrowed what she could from friends, sold her car, and obtained money from her pension fund in a hardship claim. Despite this, there were further requests for money from her online partner.

At this time, she was desperate to keep the relationship alive and meet her partner. She was also desperate to recover the money she had lent him. She was also a respected accounting manager in a business that had a significant cash flow.

In desperation, she decided to "borrow" a sum of money from her employer with the internal promise to repay it as soon as her partner arrived with her money. She forwarded the money and was met with further requests for money and regular commitments of love and the future they would have together. After realizing that no one had noticed the $10,000 she'd borrowed, she continued borrowing and sending money until she had fraudulently obtained in excess of $350,000 from her employer.

When the fraud was noticed, she left the company, traveled interstate, and attempted to restart her life. She was located, prosecuted, and sentenced to five years' imprisonment. No reparation could be made.

People becoming victims in online relationship frauds are a very common occurrence and the financial and emotional toll taken on the victims can be extreme. They have been defrauded financially and emotionally and some victims state they do not know which is worse.

For the investigator, the crime scene was the office location where she fraudulently accessed the company's financials and took the money. The log receipts on the device, including the accounting software, clearly showed her activity in creating and authorizing the payments, and the funds were sent directly to the same bank account her pay went into.

There was a secondary crime scene, however: her computer device at home, which recorded all the communication with her online partner, including his requests for money and her provision of the fund transfer identifiers. These were corroborated with the money transfer agent.

In effect, this was a significant fraud with an easily followed line of evidence. The motivation of the victim was to find a partner to share her life, which is a very common activity in an online environment. This relationship was so real to her that she sent all her assets and stole from work. The fraudsters understand the human psychology of loneliness and Internet communication and are ruthless in the manner in which they socially engineer and damage their victims. While she was convicted of a serious fraud, she was also a victim.

Text-based interactions produce a false sense of intimacy between the sender and receiver of communication. It promotes fantasy development due to the reduced availability of sensory information.[1] Online relationship fraud is a clear example of the false sense of intimacy built between the criminal and their target, which is often totally text based, and this false level of intimacy and desperation to recover her lost funds led her to making a series of criminal decisions.

Chapter 4 will introduce some of the indicators a cyber-attack has taken place against a company. These indicators will lead to the investigation team being called in to identify the scene(s) and commence planning their investigation.

NOTE

1. Cameron Brown, "Investigating and Prosecuting Cyber Crime: Forensic Dependencies and Barriers to Justice, *International Journal of Cyber Criminology* 9, no. 1 (2015): 55–109, doi:10:5281/zenodo.22387.

Determining That a Cybercrime Is Being Committed

THERE ARE many forms of warning that a cyber security incident has occurred that need an incident response and possible investigation. These may be technical, nontechnical, or a combination of both. It is highly beneficial for the investigator to be familiar with such warnings as they commence their investigations, as they will provide a pathway to where some of the most valuable evidence will be located and provide direction as to the motivation of the attacker.

The alert may be electronically generated using technology such as a firewall or an Intrusion Detection System (IDS); alternatively, a systems administrator may discover a new systems file they were unaware of in a foreign language. Unfortunately, alerts may be missed due to short staffing of technical teams or because so many alerts are being received from poorly configured software that the genuine alert is seen as a false positive.

The National Institute of Standards and Technology (NIST) describes a security incident as follows:

> A security incident is a violation or imminent threat of violation of computer, security policies, acceptable use policies, or standard security practices.[1]

There are many ways a party may become aware that they are the target of a cyber-attack. The list in this chapter, while not exclusive, covers many of the potential warnings system administrators or users may encounter.

▓ CYBER INCIDENT ALERTS

A list of 27 potential cyber incident alerts follows:

1. An alert from a security application, such as an IDS or Anti Virus (AV). Both the IDS and the AV monitor anomalies on a system and may provide an early warning of an intrusion or intrusion attempt. Just because a warning is generated does not mean the system is under attack. It may mean there is an anomaly needing investigation to determine what is behind the alert being generated.[1] The 2018 *Australian Government Information Security Manual* identifies a series of data sources that may identify a cyber security incident. These include monitoring the logs of the domain name system, email servers, the Operating System (OS), the virtual private network, and web proxies.[2]
2. A firewall identifying a successful intrusion or attempt to gain unlawful access to a network or device.[1]
3. Unusual network activity, such as heavy usage overnight when staff is not working or unscheduled updates being installed across the network.[3]
4. A user identifying unusual activity on their device. A user knows how their device operates in normal circumstances.[1] Signs such as very slow processing or hot batteries on devices they are not using may be indicators of unusual processes operating in the background. Overheated batteries on mobile devices that are not being used are a particularly good sign that apps are operating, and these may include stalking apps.
5. Vulnerability scanners are legitimate applications used by systems administrators to test the security of their networks and websites. The misuse of such software by unauthorized parties may be evidence of a cybercriminal seeking unlawful pathways into a corporate network, device, or website.[1,3]
6. Unusual log-on behavior, which may include unrecognized IP addresses or log-on times outside of normal user times.
7. An AV alert warning that malicious software has been located or is attempting to install itself on a system or device. An example would be AV software identifying unknown software attempting to encrypt a device's database in a possible ransomware attack.[1]

8. Identifying a file name with unusual characters, especially if recently installed without permission.[1,3]

9. Repeated, failed log-on attempts from an unknown Internet Protocol address. This would be evidence of an attempt to break a password using brute force or someone trying to guess a password.[1,3]

10. Gaps or missing logs indicating an attempt to remove evidence. An example would be all logs after a recent date on an established device being wiped.

11. Repeated attempts to log on to sensitive files or folders. This suggests a party has obtained access to the network and is targeting specific data. The attack may originate from inside or outside the network.

12. Unusual attempts to create profiles or increase privileges. Generally as user privileges escalate, access to more valuable information is granted.

13. Unknown processes running or the identification of applications not installed or approved by systems security personnel.

14. The downloading of sensitive files to remote locations, indicating that unlawful access to sensitive data has been obtained and is being removed to a device external to the network. A review of File Transfer Protocol (FTP) logs will confirm the downloading of sensitive files.

15. The identification of unusual activity, such as valuable Intellectual Property being downloaded onto an external drive without authority or just prior to a staff member resigning, through an internal audit.[3]

16. A network outage, which may indicate an external attack or a hardware/software issue.

17. Bounced emails, some of which may contain malicious software or links. This can indicate that someone is trying to guess the syntax of a specific person's email account or that a criminal is using an out-of-date email list containing the details of persons who no longer work for the company.[1,3]

18. A breach of acceptable usage policies. This may identify internal staff downloading inappropriate content (such as pornography) or installing unapproved applications (such as personal cloud computing services). The appearance on corporate networks of peer-to-peer software that is being used to download movies and music should be seen as a serious risk to corporate security.

19. External parties identifying suspicious emails coming from the corporate account.[3] The message may be very different in wording or content from what is normal, suggesting a criminal is using the hacked corporate account to try to breach the security of another company or user.

20. An overt act such as a Distributed Denial of Service (DDoS) attack. A DDoS is a large-scale cyber-attack against a company that attempts to take it

offline by clogging up its web server with large volumes of traffic. This is a direct attack against the ability of the network to operate, causing significant financial and reputational damage.

21. Encrypted volumes, such as a ransomware attack. This is evidence of extortion against a company.

22. A notification coming from an external source, such as a law enforcement agency, the media, customers, or the attacker.[3]

23. A Security Information and Event Management (SIEM) alert identifying logs experiencing unusual activity, such as one or more of the activities on this list. SIEM software processes log entries being generated within a network, looks for anomalies, and provides alerts to suspicious activity.[1]

24. The identification of unauthorized changes by file integrity monitoring software. Application files have a set hash value; when changes are made to the application without authority, the hash value changes and can provide system administrators notice of unauthorized modifications to software.[1]

25. A user logging into valuable corporate intellectual property or files and exiting within a short time without having made any attempt to action the files within the realm of their duties.

26. The corporate website being defaced.

27. A threat from issue-based activists.[1,3]

When the breach is first discovered, the system administrators will not have many facts at hand and will start trying to identify what is happening, whether in fact an attack is underway, how bad it is if there is, what is being targeted, and so on.

If it is identified there is in fact a cyber-attack underway, there will be a wide range of human emotions on display, which may include fear, panic, stress, anxiety, and sometimes anger. Human nature dictates that decisions made in this environment may not always be consistent with best practice. As there will be limited knowledge available and managers will be demanding answers and immediate containment of the attack, the team assigned to dealing with the attack in the very first instance will be operating under a lot of pressure until the IR team is assembled and starts executing their duties.

It is at this time that the decisions made in this high-stress environment may inadvertently destroy the evidence needed by cyber investigators. With the extent and seriousness of the incident being unknown, any thought of evidence identification and preservation may not be of major concern to the initial responders.

To assist in these duties, the cyber investigator may join the IR team in the first instance. Alternatively, they may be brought in once all Incident Response (IR) activity has been completed. The investigator will review all evidence and seek avenues of investigation in an attempt to identify who was behind the attack, their motives, and what potential there is to recover the data stolen. They may also work with the IR team to scope the seriousness and extent of the attack.

As the IR team has been operating at a crime scene, the investigator must take control of the evidence generated and become familiar with the activities of the IR team, their actions, and what they have identified. It is generally not the role of the cybercrime investigator to provide a detailed analysis of the security vulnerabilities and mitigation strategies, as the IR team has predefined skills in this area and is better able to provide this advice to management. The cybercrime investigator will seek to identify potential lines of inquiry from the IR team and commence a full cybercrime investigation.

ATTACK METHODOLOGIES

Understanding the indicators of a cybercrime occurring leads to identifying the attack methodologies being undertaken. Understanding the attack methodology of the offender puts into context their goals and provides some indication of the potential evidence available. It will also provide evidence of the skill level of the attacker and whether it was an attack using specific tools that may be sought in follow-up examinations of an identified suspect's computer. The investigator may use this information to direct lines of inquiry and locating evidence. A list of 12 attack methodologies follows.

1. External/removable media (insider threat).[1] A USB or external drive is attached to the internal network and a file with malicious software (such as a Trojan virus) is opened. This opens a pathway to the downloading of more malicious software that infects devices and networks. The advantage of this strategy to the attacker is that they have breached the security of the external-facing corporate network security without having to attack it directly.
2. Brute force (attrition).[1] The attacker tries to break the passwords used to gain access to a system.
3. Web-based attack/hacking.[1] The attacker destroys or damages a website, or gains unauthorized access to a network or device.

4. Email (phishing/social engineering).[1] A fraudulent email is designed to entice the user to click on the enclosed link or to open a file attachment so that malicious software may be downloaded, giving the attacker unauthorized access to the system. As with the attack that uses external/removable media, this attack breaches corporate security without having to find an unpatched vulnerability in external-facing infrastructure.

5. Breach of acceptable-use policies and the internal threat.[1] Internal policies are designed to keep a network safe and to prevent users from accessing high-risk sites (such as pornographic sites). Many sites restricted by company policies contain material inappropriate for viewing in a work environment or carry a high risk of infecting the corporate network (such as a file-sharing site).

   Improper usage can also lead to malicious software being introduced inside the corporate network by a person using an external drive from home that has been infected by a computer virus.

6. Loss or theft of equipment (USB/computer).[1] USB and external drives contain massive amounts of corporate data. Should one be lost that is not encrypted, the finder will have access to the corporate records.

7. Cloud-computing compromise. Storing corporate data in a cloud-computing environment should only be done with the approval of management and systems administrators. Should an internal or external attacker compromise a cloud service, the corporate data will be at risk. Users often create cloud-computing storage to assist them when working from home, uploading corporate documents to the new cloud account without the knowledge or approval of the system administrators tasked with protecting the corporate networks and data.

   The cloud account being used may be any one of many available on the market, and valuable corporate data may be being stored in unknown legal jurisdictions and being protected by unknown security systems. In the end user license agreement, some examples have existed of small cloud services stipulating that data stored in the cloud service transfers to the ownership of the Cloud Service Provider (CSP) or that a lifetime nonrevocable license to the data is provided to the CSP.

8. Social engineering. Building a personal relationship with a key person in an organization and exploiting that relationship is a common way that corporate data is lost. The relationship does not have to be intimate in nature, but a personal professional relationship where trust has been built over time results in the potential for valuable corporate data to be sent to an attacker.

9. Keylogger. A keylogger is either a physical device attached to a computer or a piece of software installed on a targeted device/network that captures every keystroke or mouse click. This allows the attacker to capture all activity on the device, including reports and passwords.

10. The insider threat. Using a trusted employee with access to a network is another method of breaching the corporate firewall. Employees have access not only to corporate data but also to physical devices. Insiders have their own motivations to commit criminal offenses against their employer, and an external cybercriminal exploiting such a person greatly expands their attack platform.

11. Operating systems and application exploitation. Operating systems and applications need to be updated regularly, as the cybercriminal will learn the vulnerabilities an update repairs. Technical products can undertake port scans to identify current operating systems and applications in use and identify which version they are. With this information, the cybercriminal can develop an attack strategy that seeks to exploit the unfixed vulnerability.

12. Malicious software. The term "malicious software," or "malware," generally covers a wide range of computer viruses, Trojans, worms, and the like. While this form of attack has been present on the Internet for several decades, it is still a productive method of attack for the cybercriminal.

A particularly dangerous form of attack is one that is unknown and stays undetected within the system for an extended period of time while corporate data is being extracted. As discussed in Chapter 2, these are called, Advanced Persistent Threats or APTs. An attacker using an APT seeks to infiltrate a network and have the APT remain undetected while it gathers as much information as possible about the network and its activity. The APT controller will seek to increase their access privileges over time to gain access to the most sensitive corporate data.

APTs are generally associated with well-resourced, organized groups whose aim is for the APT to remain undetected within the network as long as possible. This may be months, if not years.

An advantage of APT exploitation to the attacker is that they gain updated data as it is generated, with the ability to monitor security activity so that they are alerted should their intrusion be detected. Upon realizing that they have been discovered, in some instances APT controllers seek to destroy any potential evidence of the intrusion and their activity, meaning the IR team will have difficulty in identifying the boundaries of the intrusion and its seriousness. This will then complicate the investigation, as valuable evidence will have been destroyed.

Identifying an APT intrusion will give the investigator a very clear indication that the attacker has a high level of skills and capabilities. APT intrusions take significant time and resources to maintain, in some instances including the updating of malware that has been placed on the network to keep ahead of the AV security on the network.

 ## CYBERCRIME CASE STUDY I

A multinational company installed new fraud-detection software in their accounting systems. A systems administrator stated it was a highly regarded product, which when turned on "lit up like a Christmas tree." Over the coming months, the system continually identified fraudulent accounting transactions and provided warnings.

Members of the system operator's team were so annoyed at the constant warnings that they determined the application was working incorrectly and turned it off. Unfortunately, the application was working correctly and each of the alerts was an accurate identification of a suspicious transaction. The total loss to the multinational was in excess of $20 million, and much of that total was lost after the fraud detection system had been installed and turned off. In this case, the technology was working correctly but was not understood by the operators.

 ## CYBERCRIME CASE STUDY II

An employee of an organization was in the process of being disciplined for a range of activities. The disciplinary process was heated, and the employee faced dismissal if the charges were proven.

Late one evening he returned to work and placed a hardware keylogger on the back of the computer of the manager who was investigating him. The mouse and keyboard were attached to the keylogger, which sat between these devices and the device port on the back of the computer. The keylogger captured all the activity on the computer.

By coincidence, the next day the manager cleared his desk and noticed the keylogger. To most people the keylogger would look like part of the infrastructure of the computer and arouse no suspicion; however, this manager quickly identified the device and understood its meaning. A covert camera was installed in his office, which captured the employee returning the following evening and looking for the keylogger, which had been removed.

Police were called and the employee charged criminally. The scene examination of his home identified purchase receipts for the device and bank records showed a payment transaction. His personal computer's web history showed him purchasing the keylogger online. Computer logs also showed the keylogger being tested on the employee's personal computer, providing a direct link between the attacker and the keylogger.

NOTES

1. Paul Cichonski, Thomas Millar, Tim Grance, and Karen Scarfone, *Computer Security Incident Handling Guide*, Special Publication 800-61 Revision 2, August 2012, National Institute of Standards and Technology, United States Department of Commerce.
2. Australian Signals Directorate, *Australian Government Information Security Manual*, 2018.
3. CREST, *Cyber Security Incident Response Guide* Version 1, 2013, https://www.crest-approved.org/wp-content/uploads/2014/11/CSIR-Procurement-Guide.pdf.

CHAPTER FIVE

Commencing a Cybercrime Investigation

The main goals in any investigation are to follow the trails that offenders leave during the commission of a crime and to tie the perpetrators to the victims and the crime scene.[1]

THIS CHAPTER provides guidelines that may be used to investigate cyber events that originate either internally or externally to an organization. It is only a guide and will need to be applied to meet the unique circumstances of each organization, legal environment, type of event under investigation, potential evidence available, and level of investigation required by the client. The investigation plans developed using this knowledge may be merged into an Incident Response (IR) plan or sit parallel to it, with a designated investigation manager working in partnership with the IR lead.

WHY INVESTIGATE A CYBERCRIME?

Conducting a cyber investigation may be initiated for many reasons and not just to find out who the bad guy is and prosecute them. Some reasons include identifying where the weaknesses in systems are, how they were exploited, how to tighten security, and developing training packages for staff to make them more aware of cyber safety. Clients who have their data stolen may want answers as to the severity of the attack, and should the data stolen belong to another party, there is the potential for litigation to follow. A final reason is that cyber insurers may want to know whether there were security failures that allowed the attack to occur or if system flaws magnified the attack.

Of the number of cyber-attacks occurring each year, very few are reported to police or even internally investigated. The main focus is to fix the problem, make sure it does not happen again, and get back to business. While this may make sense to managers, it provides a platform for the near-perfect crime by the cyber-attacker. Break into a company, steal what you want, and do as much damage as you want, safe in the knowledge that the company will never report you to police or even try to find out who you are. There is no real weakness in this criminal business model.

 ## THE CYBER INVESTIGATOR

The role of the cyber investigator is different from that of the IR team. The investigator is like the detective at the homicide scene. The lead detective directs the investigation, including tasking experts to perform photography, scientific examination, area inquiries, forensic examination of exhibits, ballistic examination, interviews, and so on at the scene. The investigator does not have to be an expert in each of these fields, but they must understand the role of each expert, be able to direct the experts, and be able to understand the relevance of the evidence each produces, which will then lead to further lines of inquiry. Whereas on television a cyber investigator may be an expert on everything digital they see and touch, in a real-world investigation this is not even close to reality. There is just too much technology: it is constantly changing and no one person is an expert on everything.

 ## MANAGEMENT SUPPORT

When the decision is made to conduct an investigation after a cyber event, the appropriate levels of management within the organization must provide authority and active support. This will include financing in the case of a civil investigation, as well as authorizing appropriate staff members to provide evidence and statements, and organizing members of the internal/external IR teams to assist in the investigation. The IR team may be tasked with providing copies of notes taken, explaining reasons for actions taken, supplying copies of digital files, and cooperating fully in the recording of a statement for referral to law enforcement or for internal use. This may need to be a part of the terms of engagement between the client and the IR team.

Whether the complaint initially referred is civil or criminal, in planning the investigation the investigator will be operating within the boundaries outlined by the client/complainant. However, these boundaries may change if the investigation reveals that the cyber event is significantly larger than initially believed and senior management believes the investigation should be expanded. If an investigation operating within the initial boundaries defined identifies the cybercriminal as a trusted employee in the organization, there may be strong evidence to support civil litigation or a referral to police.

An investigator operating within the initial boundaries defined must be aware that the terms of engagement may subsequently change, and that the evidence identification and collection strategies may become subject to future scrutiny. Consequently, evidence identified and collected must be always treated as valuable and accountable, even in a so-called "for management information only" investigation.

Digital evidence can be the target of the crime, an instrument of the crime, or a repository of evidence that documents the crime itself. Digital evidence may be highly volatile, and the actions of IR team members, who are required to mitigate and eradicate an attack, may limit the potential to undertake a complete investigation in which all potential evidence may be legally and forensically obtained and seized. In fact, the roles of the IR and the investigation team leads may be regularly in conflict, as the IR lead seeks to protect the network and its data while the investigation lead seeks to preserve and secure evidence to progress post-event investigations. While each event will be different, the understanding of each other's roles and responsibilities, accompanied with respectful communication, will assist in managing a high-stress environment and competing responsibilities.

In an ideal world, the threshold for the form of cyber event requiring an investigation to commence will have been determined by senior management prior to an event occurring. This may be governed by internal policy or by legislation, such as data breach reporting legislation. However, in reality, few companies have made such a determination. Therefore, it is helpful to determine what exactly a cyber event is before we discuss in depth how to investigate it. The United States National Institute of Standards and Technology (NIST) describes it as:

> [An] identified occurrence of a system, service or network state, indicating a possible breach of information security policy or failure of safeguards, or a previously unknown situation that may be relevant to security.[2]

When called to the scene of a cyber event as an investigator, speak to the system administrator to see if a previous documented event has occurred that may be used to provide some direction to the new investigation. A previous incident may show attempts by the attacker to map the system or find ways to break through the differing levels of security and provide evidence of how the crime was committed. It will also be beneficial to the external investigator to understand the nature of the business, where it fits in the marketplace, and the information in the organization that would be most valuable to an attacker.

When an IR team arrives at the scene of a cyber event, they need to assume from the start that the event is continuing.[2] This is more complex in a cloud-computing environment, as access to evidence of the event is restricted by the nature of the service the complainant has. The infrastructure of a cloud platform may be made up of different infrastructure providers, meaning access to evidence may be restricted and therefore time consuming to collect. Cloud-computing investigations are discussed in detail in Chapter 12.

IS THERE A RESPONSIBILITY TO TRY TO GET THE DATA BACK?

A question to be considered by directors is if the company has its Intellectual Property (IP), customer, or staff files stolen, is it a natural or rational decision to attempt to get them back prior to their being exploited? Would a shareholder expect the directors to seek to investigate the matter and try to get the data back before it is exploited, or at the very least refer the matter to police?

Currently there are very few referrals made to police in these instances, as entities typically instead seek to bolster their defenses and ensure the breach does not reoccur. The prospect of investigating the matter and referring the matter to police raises the potential for public disclosure of the breach and the reputational damage that follows. Consequently, the cybercriminal operates within a secure environment where they understand they may attack any corporation they wish and few will make any effort to identify who the attacker is or refer the matter to police. For the cybercriminal, this is truly a best-case scenario.

CYBERCRIME CASE STUDY

Bill (not his real name) was an employee of a web host who was a system administrator as well as being involved in the development of clients' web pages. Bill had a very hostile attitude toward his boss, the company owner, whom he considered to be an inferior program coder. Bill felt he was unappreciated and deserved a significantly higher salary to reflect his importance to the company.

After resigning, Bill went home and launched a series of technical attacks against his former employer. These included using the company's resources to attack other companies—including launching a Denial of Service (DoS)—downloading pornography from the company's Internet address, and deleting all the clients' web pages and the backups from the web server.

The victim of the attacker suffered reputational damage, as their Internet service provider cut their Internet access due to the attacks on other companies. The company was also charged for the excessive data usage used in the attacks.

When arrested, Bill explained he was very angry at his former employer and felt his actions were justified. He pleaded guilty to the offenses in court. An examination of his computers located corroborative evidence as well as Child Exploitation Material (CEM), leading to further charges and convictions.

Chapter 6 will identify and discuss some of the legal considerations the investigation team must understand. The discussion is jurisdiction neutral and covers a range of the major concepts the investigation must operate within. As legal jurisdictions have different legislation and courts have provided different case law for guidance, it is the role of the investigator to understand the laws of the jurisdiction they operate within. This extends to multijurisdictional investigations, as what is a legal investigator activity in one jurisdiction may be a criminal offense in another jurisdiction they are operating in. For specific examples of these hazards see Chapter 12, which discusses cloud-computing investigations and highlights the many legal and technical problems investigations will face when cloud-computing servers and the evidence they store are located across many jurisdictions.

NOTES

1. Eoghan Casey, *Digital Evidence and Cybercrime*, 3rd ed. (Academic Press, 2011).
2. https://www.iso.org/obp/ui/-iso:std:iso-iec:27001:ed-1:v1:en.

CHAPTER SIX

Legal Considerations When Planning an Investigation

ALL INVESTIGATIONS must be conducted with the understanding that the actions of the Incident Response (IR) and the investigation teams may be required to be accounted for in a court of law should a prosecution be commenced against an individual. Even when an investigation is conducted for insurance requirements or for management information only, the investigators must be aware of the potential for a critical review at a later date, especially if the investigation identifies the event is far more serious than was initially thought and the decision is made to refer the matter to police or to sue another party.

The investigation team's actions or lack thereof may be subject to question, as well as the order of actions taken, evidence handling, and examination procedures. For these reasons, investigators must be mindful to operate within the guidelines provided, to keep management informed of progress, and to act consistently with the laws and rules of evidence within their jurisdiction.

It may be that a management team requests that an investigation be undertaken for their information and understanding of a cyber incident and as the investigation develops the breach comes to be identified as falling under the reporting requirements of legislation such as state data breach notification laws in the United States, Singapore's Cybersecurity Act, Australia's Privacy Amendment (Notifiable Data Breaches) Act 2017, or the European Union's General Data Protection Regulation (GDPR). Alternatively, a suspect may be positively identified and the management team decide to initiate civil action or refer the incident to police for further investigation and potential prosecution.

Investigators place their own personal credibility on the line when conducting an investigation, and their actions must be accurate, transparent, and ethical. Their reputation travels with them across jobs and courts. Judges speak to each other behind closed doors and swap notes as much as any occupational group, and if an investigator is identified as playing fast and loose with the rules of evidence they may well become a negative topic of conversation among members of the judiciary.

The following sections provide guidelines as to considerations the investigator must keep in mind during all phases of the investigation.

As mentioned previously, the information provided is jurisdiction neutral and general in nature, as each jurisdiction has its own laws and judicial precedents. It is the responsibility of an investigator to understand the legislation and rules of evidence of the jurisdiction(s) they are operating within.

ROLE OF THE LAW IN A DIGITAL CRIMES INVESTIGATION

While the rules of evidence may differ among legal jurisdictions, they have generally been developed through a process of legislation, case law, and legal convention developed over many years of hearings during which matters have been challenged and judges have provided rulings, a process that in turn has established legal precedents. The rules are there to ensure that the evidence, produced in a matter is consistent and accurate in its meaning, quality, and integrity. This is effectively so that the judicial officer presiding can have the required level of confidence in the evidence before them.

When considering initiating an investigation you will be constantly reviewing the evidence to determine where it leads your investigation. You will instantly decide that some of it is highly relevant and should be presented to the court should your investigation progress that far. However, in many instances you may not understand the full value of your evidence until later in the investigation; nevertheless, it must be preserved as securely as that which you immediately identified as key evidence.

The law is constantly evolving, and it is your responsibility to keep up to date with the law. It is worth having a lawyer who is either a part of your team or easily accessible who is a specialist in digital evidence and cybercrime law to provide expert evidence if required.

PROTECTING DIGITAL EVIDENCE

Digital evidence may be highly volatile and obtained from numerous sources. The infrastructure, storage, and retrieval methods and tools used in seizing the evidence may differ widely across investigations and it is the role of the investigator to understand these nuances during the investigation, not just prior to a hearing. The investigator must take control of the scene and in a prompt manner assess the value of potential evidence and its likelihood of being lost or damaged.

Whether the digital crime scene is a physical or logical location (virtual or network), preferably the evidence should be located in situ (in the original place). All actions involving the crime scene and the evidence need to be documented and accounted for in case of a challenge at a later date in court.

To protect digital evidence, the scene investigator would ideally be a person who has a strong understanding of digital evidence, has practical scene management experience, and possesses an understanding of the ease with which evidence can be damaged or destroyed. A pre-search briefing on the volatility of digital evidence and the existence of strong guidelines regarding the management of this evidence will be of benefit to all investigators, especially those who may not have experience in this form of evidence collection. The volatility of evidence and the order for its capture is discussed in Chapter 10, in the section "Acquisition of Digital Evidence."

Digital evidence may be highly volatile and easily damaged or lost. It is the responsibility of the investigator to protect evidence and account for its state from the time of capture through to presentation in court. Where there are changes, extensive notes explaining what happened and why are to be recorded in a chronologically ordered notebook with numbered pages to negate arguments that notes were created well after the event. When a mistake is made, it should be acknowledged and the reasons for it recorded. Acknowledging a mistake may enhance the perceived integrity of the investigator, as it shows that they are not trying to cover anything up: a cover-up is significantly worse and more damaging than the initial mistake.

The Association of Chief Police Officers (ACPO) in the United Kingdom has made a series of recommendations as to how digital evidence should be handled to ensure compliance with the requirements of the court:

1. No action taken by a law enforcement agency or others should change data, which may subsequently be relied upon in court.

2. In circumstances where a person finds it necessary to access original data, that person must be competent to do so and be able to give evidence explaining the relevance and the implications of their actions.
3. An audit trail or other record of all processes applied to digital evidence should be created and preserved. An independent third party should be able to examine these processes and achieve the same results.
4. The person in charge of the investigation has overall responsibility for ensuring that the law and these principles are adhered to.[1]

When presenting evidence before a court, the party presenting it must prove its relevance to the case and why it can be relied upon. This includes the tools used for evidence capture. For the opposing party, having incriminating evidence excluded under challenge is a proven method for advancing their side of the matter. The onus is on the party presenting the evidence to show it is of a standard the court can place trust in and of a credibility that can be be relied upon. Honest mistakes occur—particularly in live situations, such as when attending scenes—and being transparent when challenged assists your credibility before the court.

For digital evidence, it is not always necessary, practical, or possible to obtain a full bit-by-bit image of a device due to the volume of the evidence. Seek advice from the digital investigator before making any decisions. The decision that is eventually made may be based on a risk assessment or for technical/nontechnical reasons. Account for the reasons for your decisions as you would when seizing any other exhibit.

PRESERVATION OF THE CHAIN OF CUSTODY

The chain of custody is a combination of written statements, reports, and oral evidence documenting the identification, lawful seizure, examination, and movement of evidence from the time of identification through presentation in court as evidence. For example, a computer located in an office may be an exhibit, and the chain of custody would require identification of the person(s) who found the exhibit, seized it, transported it, stored it, transported it for forensic examination, and conducted the examination, as well as how it was secured after examination and other information regarding not only the physical computer seized but also the images created by the examiner.

All exhibits are required to have a person prepare a statement supporting these criteria. Creating a schedule that includes dates and times of custody helps to ensure continuity. By failing to ensure the chain of custody, the potential exists for evidence to be excluded or have a reduced value in court, as its credibility can be questioned.

The exhibits officer is the person designated at the commencement of the investigation to take custody and secure all exhibits seized. They are also responsible for ensuring the chain of evidence of all exhibits, recording where they were found and by whom. The exhibits officer must be able to record the history of the evidence at any given time of the investigation and whose custody it was in at the time of identification, seizure, examination, and so on. A schedule provides a quick, convenient, and transparent method of accounting for the evidence and identifies any gaps in the chain of custody that needs to be investigated.

Of note is that both the physical item and images taken need to be accounted for when dealing with digital evidence. Originals should never be used in a forensic examination. The examiner may obtain the original disk from the exhibits officer and create a series of images. The chain of custody will account for this and the examiner's statements will differentiate between the original and images.

Maintaining the integrity of the chain of custody of the digital evidence is accomplished by creating documentary evidence of all actions involving the evidence from identification to collection or acquisition to present status and location. This may include:

- Uniquely identifying each exhibit you are going to seize and recording exactly where it was found, when, and by whom. Photographs help to support the accuracy of seizure.
- Maintaining a written log of events for each exhibit attached to the exhibit by a tag or label.
- Taking notes to record the time of location, seizure, preservation, securing, transport, logging into your storage facility, and the like. Recording the time is critical to proving that you have had control of your exhibits from identification to presentation in court.
- Signing, sealing, and dating digital evidence seized. In some instances evidence may be stored in bags that can be sealed, in which case you can sign and note the date across the seals to provide a higher level of exhibit security.
- Recording the investigation identifier on the exhibit packaging and log. When you work in a busy office with lots of investigators pursuing their cases, human error may unfortunately mean that some exhibits end up

close to those of another case. While this is not best practice, it is the reality of a detective's office.

- Considering the need for proprietary software to view digital evidence collected from a complainant. Companies create their own software unique to their purposes. While your evidence operates smoothly on their network, it will not operate on yours, as you do not have a copy of the proprietary software. Obtain a copy to view the data and for potential use in court.
- Obtaining a statement for each item that covers from identification to production in court. One investigator may be able to account for 10 items in their statement and another seven items. The exhibits officer will record receiving all 17 from the two investigators.
- Including an exhibit schedule. This is very helpful to your lawyers during their preparation and in court.
- Recording where the exhibit was found and its serial number, model number, hostname, Media Access Control (MAC) address, and Internet Protocol (IP) address where applicable. The MAC and IP addresses are particularly relevant when your digital examiner is capturing network traffic. Photos of devices and serial/model numbers are of great assistance in ensuring accuracy.
- Ensuring you can identify every person involved in handling exhibits. If you have a team member who is resigning and traveling overseas, for example, you can use them to search for the evidence but should not have them physically seize it, as you may not be able to locate them in several years for the court hearing. Obtain statements from everyone at the first opportunity.
- Recording the circumstances of the location of the exhibit. Is it in an open space where everyone can access it or in a secure office? This is an important line of questioning in court and must be covered early in the investigation.
- When storing evidence, record who had access to it and the reasons why it was viewed or moved either in or out of the preservation facility; legitimate reasons may include forensic examination, viewing documents, or photographing evidence.
- Recording all changes or damage to any exhibit, whether digital or otherwise, immediately. For example, digital evidence is highly volatile and seizing it from a network may involve loading new software onto the network. Although it is not damaging the network, it is introducing a change. Also if an accident happens and an exhibit is dropped and damaged (such as a laptop screen being cracked), record the incident.

PROTECTION OF EVIDENCE

While preserving the chain of evidence is crucial, there is also a wide range of work that is required to be undertaken with exhibits to preserve their authenticity. Each person involved in examining, storing, and transporting exhibits needs to understand their responsibilities to their safety and security. Seven considerations for investigation and exhibit officers follow:

1. Chain of custody

    See the previous section, "Preservation of the Chain of Custody," for a discussion.
2. Secure storage

    Securing an exhibit requires that it be placed in an environment where there is no opportunity for it to be interfered with and its credibility tarnished. Law enforcement use designated exhibit storage units and locked facilities whose access is restricted and recorded. Only persons who have a lawful and necessary reason to access an exhibit should be anywhere near it once seized.

    First off, where a device has access to wireless or cellular networks, the device should be placed into flight mode (or similar mode, depending on the device) and/or where feasible, placed into a Faraday bag or similar container that inhibits network access. When a device is connected to a wireless network, you may disconnect the connection. With a cellular device, removing the SIM card will be of benefit. Record notes of your actions involving the device, as they will affect the logs within the device. As a back up procedure a very basic way of helping to stop any potential interference with digital evidence connected to the Internet by a remote suspect or their associate is to place it in a clean metal container with a secure seal and/or wrap the device in aluminum foil.
3. Statements and exhibit schedule

    The statement covering the integrity of the exhibit is an explanation to the court that the evidence can be relied upon as being genuine. Should there be little effort to explain the integrity of the exhibit or should gaps in its preservation be identified, it opens a very large door to the other side's legal team to get the exhibit removed from the case as unreliable.
4. Examination reports

    A digital exhibit may undergo specialist forensic examination by a suitably trained person. Their statement will need to explain their credentials and examination techniques and explain why the court can trust their examination as being of an acceptable standard and its output as reliable.

Sometimes this may involve a technical expert from the company creating the examination software and this will need to be prepared for well before the hearing date.

5. Examination of devices through backups only

Using an image of a copy (copy of a copy) of the device preserves the original for an independent examination at the request of the opposing party. Using an image also allows for an instance of malicious software that is executed involving the copy; in this case, the original and initial image will be both available and uncompromised.

6. Examination using a designated device

When creating an image, using a designated device means using a machine whose sole use is imaging and examination of digital evidence— and which is not used for Internet surfing, checking emails, or streaming music online, for example.

7. How long can you hold the evidence?

Some jurisdictions specify a maximum time for which evidence may be held after the time of seizure that can be exceeded only if an extension is granted by the court. For example, a jurisdiction may specify that police may execute a search warrant but not make a decision on whether to commence a prosecution for up to 12 months in a particularly complex investigation or if another investigation demands priority attention.

It is the investigator's job to understand these rules and ensure that if the evidence is seized by court order, all obligations are adhered to, including any time limits imposed by the courts. Failure to adhere to this may lead to an application by the suspect to have the evidence returned and excluded from the investigation.

 ## LEGAL IMPLICATIONS OF DIGITAL EVIDENCE COLLECTION

When considering seizing any item to advance your investigation, you must ensure that you have the legal authority to obtain it and keep custody of it. This section provides seven areas to consider regarding your actions.

1. Consider the nature and purpose of the digital examination.

When seizing evidence, understand why you are taking that item and be prepared to provide an explanation in court should you be asked. If an item seized is no longer relevant, consider giving it back where lawful to do so, as it will mean less evidence that you have to account for.

2. What are our priorities?

    Digital evidence may be highly volatile, and the investigator needs to understand the many forms of digital evidence, its volatility, and the consequences of not prioritizing the preservation of evidence (it may be lost). See "Acquisition of Digital Evidence" in Chapter 10 for a discussion of this.

3. What are we looking for?

    When seizing a device, know what you are looking for. The courts do not like so-called fishing trips, where large amounts of evidence are taken on the chance that it may prove relevant later on.

4. Work within legally defined boundaries of examination and seizure.

    Particularly when operating under a court order, understand *exactly* what the order authorizes you to do and take. Do not exceed the authority of the order, as the additional evidence you seize or powers executed may lead to that evidence being thrown out and your case tainted.

5. Understand the ethical implications of examination and chance discovery of unrelated illegal material.

    When searching digital devices, you will potentially face stored on the device a wide variety of material a person may locate online. It is very common today to locate many forms of pornography (downloaded or self-made) on mobile or fixed devices that are seized and examined. Alternatively, the digital examiner may locate criminal material, such as fake identities, stolen, Intellectual Property (IP) or Child Exploitation Material (CEM), resulting in immediate ethical and legal obligations. Particularly in the instance of CEM identification, it is recommended that the examiner cease the examination, notify police immediately, seek their direction, and record the actions that led to identifying the criminal material.

    Examination of the device may also locate cryptocurrency wallets with large values stored. These may be seen as cash, and special attention needs to be paid to ensuring that access to these exhibits is restricted. Due to the anonymous nature of online cryptocurrencies, the temptation may be present for someone to access the device and transfer value to their cryptocurrency wallet, taking measures to ensure that such actions cannot be matched to them.

    The same applies to IP that is located. Databases can contain both very valuable and personal information, and depending on the case being investigated, highly personal data may be present, as would be the case if a medical center were compromised. The cybercriminal community places a very high value on medical data due to its capacity to be used in extortion against the patient, particularly when the cybercriminal identifies the patient as a celebrity, senior executive, or high–net worth individual.

6. As previously mentioned, conduct your investigation on a copy of the image obtained from the exhibit. This means the exhibit is imaged and a copy made of that image, on which the examination is conducted. This provides a clear form of separation from the exhibit, so if malware is executed or a power surge causes damage in the course of the examination, the damage is done only on a copy and not the original image. This will protect the integrity of your exhibit and examination.

7. Treat all evidence that may be subject to aggressive legal scrutiny as court exhibits. All parties who are involved in handling the evidence, from identification to production in court, must be prepared to testify in court as to their actions should it be required. Even a document that is thought to contain minimal value on the day of seizure may be found to contain crucial information once more facts of the case unfold.

Should a defendant be facing significant evidence indicating that they are guilty of the crime or civil offense they are accused of, a legal strategy of the defense is to find a weakness with the integrity of the evidence and have it excluded by the court as unreliable. There are a series of challenges a party may make involving the technical side of digital evidence. Several of these are:

- Evidence was not recorded at the scene due to the investigator not capturing Random Access Memory (RAM). Malicious software affecting the evidence may initially be resident within the RAM but be deleted and leave no trace after a forced shutdown.
- Evidence was not collected because of budgetary restraints. An example is the collection of evidence from a cloud-computing account where the legal costs of obtaining data from potentially multiple cloud-computing companies making up the components of the service requires court orders for differing companies in different jurisdictions.
- Failure to account for the chain of evidence.
- Failure to examine encrypted partitions or files.
- Storage devices used to capture digital evidence containing remnants of previous examinations.
- Evidence extracted directly from the device and not imaged by an experienced digital forensics examiner.

CYBERCRIME CASE STUDY

Executing search warrants and civil court orders on commercial premises provides advantages in terms of controlling the evidence, scene, and inhabitants; however, you are in effect hindering the operation of a business. Your presence will have been authorized by the court as legal, but you will need to balance the needs of your investigation against the requirements of a legitimate business to keep operating.

A business was raided by police on suspicion of fraudulently providing financial services. The allegations were that the business was engaging in a combination of cyber fraud, where fraudulent websites had been created showing impressive financial returns over the preceding years, and the social engineering of victims through phone and email communication.

The business claimed that the search warrant hindered its capacity to operate what it stated was a legitimate business and that it was concerned at the loss of trading, its computer servers, and its personal and business reputation. It was also concerned that its employees would no longer work for it should there be suspicions that the company was engaging in a series of frauds.

The investigators understood these concerns when seizing the company servers and multitudes of documents, and also understood that they were effectively shutting the business down permanently. Subsequently, corroborative evidence supporting the seizure of the evidence from the digital crime scene was located, including evidence of the selling of financial services without a license, of employees using fake identities, and of the claims of the financial success of the products being fake. Also, a review of digital printouts located evidence of several phoenix companies, providing a long list of evidence of suspected financial frauds.

Chapter 7 introduces the initial engagement meeting with the complainant, where the boundaries of the investigation are set, resources allocated, and authority delegated.

 ## NOTE

1. Janet Williams, *ACPO Good Practice Guide for Digital Evidence*, March 2012, Association of Chief Police Officers.

Initial Meeting with the Complainant

THE PRE INVESTIGATION meeting seeks to obtain an understanding of the event requiring investigation and set the terms of engagement. This is the opportunity to identify the known extent of the event and what exactly the client wants from their investigators. The initial investigation meeting may cover a lot of ground and needs to be structured to allow a full understanding of the event and the role of the investigator.

People who can be interviewed in this initial stage may include the manager with designated responsibility for corporate oversight of the incident response, members of the legal team (especially valuable when a suspect is identified within the organization), the systems administrator and others responsible for operation of the network (internal and external to the organization), and device users.

INITIAL DISCUSSION

In this initial phase of the investigation, the investigators gain an understanding of the event and the goals of management. These may change throughout the investigation, however, so at the start, the civilian investigators need to have a formal agreement in writing as to the expectations of management.

In general, police do not need such formal written guidelines, as their authority comes with the complaint being received and because of their legislative authority.

Although the investigator may have conducted numerous investigations and attended numerous crime scenes throughout their career, each is different, and the investigators must keep their minds open to unique features of the complaint, scene, attack methodology, and persons they are to interact with. Having tunnel vision in the initial stages of an investigation means the investigator will end up in a predetermined location and miss important facts.

An investigator needs to take full advantage of this interview, as the more senior the manager within an organization, the harder it will be to speak to them again, as they will be involved in running the many aspects of the business. Although they are asking for your assistance, they may designate another person to be your point of contact in the organization after the initial interview.

At the very beginning of conversations, identify any potential safety risks to the investigation team or other persons. This is a critical point, as while the initial interview is taking place, other team members may be dispersing to commence their duties. Details of any potential risks, such as suspects being present, must be immediately communicated to all team members and others whose safety may be at risk.

Examples of questions the investigator may ask in the initial interview include:

- What has happened to your computer network/device that requires an investigation?
- Is the event continuing?
- What level of investigation do you want? The investigation may be undertaken for the information of the manager only, to identify whether the attacker is local, to find out what information you can about the type of person the attacker is, or to do a scoping investigation to understand the nature of what has happened. With law enforcement, it will include locating the attacker and commencing a prosecution.
- Where is the investigation to end up? Is the investigation for a civil or criminal court, or for a tribunal (such as for resolving an employment matter)?
- What is the time available for the investigation and report? Are the necessary resources available to you?
- What is the investigation budget? This is particularly relevant to the civil investigator. Costs will include not only the cost of staff attending the scene, but those related to many hours of evidence analysis, following

up of leads, suspect identification, and so on. A budget may be defined by number of hours spent, by phase of the investigation (to determine whether it is beneficial to continue), or by a fixed budget for a complete investigation and report.

- What information has been disclosed, stolen, deleted, or corrupted by unauthorized parties? Does a privacy commissioner or other relevant government agency need to be notified of the breach? Depending on your jurisdiction, there may need to be an initial report made to your national or state privacy officer (or similar entity) providing details on facts known at that time.
- What system resources did the attacker use? This will provide the investigation lead with knowledge about exactly what resources they need in the first scene phase of the investigation, particularly when they need to bring in third-party support.
- What is the potential impact of the investigation team operating in the corporate workspace? Investigation teams will seek to work with and around the local workforce.
- What is the investigation plan and employee assistance required? The complainant may wish to involve their staff in helping the investigation team to speed the scene work up and provide any assistance available. A manager with authority to make decisions on behalf of the company may be assigned to work with the investigation lead to answer any questions and to provide immediate authorities when required.
- What is the Bring-Your-Own-Device (BYOD) policy of the company? A BYOD computer is owned by the employee who uses it, subject to the agreement of their manager. Data stored on it is owned by the company subject to any agreement; however, there may be no express or implied authority to examine the device without the authority of the employee in the event of a cyber security incident.
- Is there approval to obtain data and documents from the Incident Response (IR) team? The IR team may be external to the organization and there may be a cost involved in interviewing them. The complainant will carry this cost; however, this conversation needs to take place in the initial stages of the preliminary interview and approval obtained from the client.
- Is there approval to interview staff and to make arrangements to interview IR staff as required? Unless there is a specific reason not to, ideally a senior manager will provide a staff briefing that explains what has happened and why the investigation team is present. Obtain approval for these interviews. Where law enforcement is present, they have their own protocols in these

matters and will provide guidance to management, including potentially briefing staff themselves.

▪ Is there approval to obtain client Human Resources (HR) documents as required? Obtain approval to access these documents. This is particularly relevant when dealing with a BYOD or an internal employee is considered to be a suspect in the event, including instances in which an employee may be suspected of being negligent in their duties and exposing the company to a cyber threat through activity such as accessing peer-to-peer networks from the corporate network.

Once the general outline of the investigation is complete, the next phase is to record details of the complainant and their liaison officers for the investigation.

COMPLAINANT DETAILS

The complainant is the person making the referral for investigation. In a corporate environment, the entity may be the complainant and the officers formally making the complaint or seeking an investigation may be collectively seen as the informant. Regardless of the structure of the organization or whether the complainant is an individual, key details need to be obtained at the beginning. These include:

▪ Full details of the complainant company and authorizing person, including their role.
▪ If an individual, their name, address, date of birth, contact details, and employer.
▪ Name in which the complaint made.
▪ The contact person, their details, and their levels of authorization. Authorization level is a major consideration, as sometimes decisions need to be made quickly, especially when an event is ongoing.
▪ Means of contacting this liaison when you need a question answered or increased authority. Ideally you will obtain a 24/7 phone contact.

EVENT DETAILS

The event is the breach of security that needs investigation. In this phase of the initial interview, the investigator gains an understanding of the breach and obtains whatever facts are available. This may be a dynamic environment the investigation team is operating in, as the cyber event may be continuing during the initial interview.

Understanding the event provides a direction for the investigation, as identifying the form of event provides direction as to the location of evidence, offender motivation, and possible suspects.

People to interview may include the systems administrator, the device user, the person who identified the incident, and members of the security team responding to the event. Questions to ask may include:

- What do you understand has happened?
- When did the event occur?
- How was the incident detected and by whom?
- What evidence is available? Is the attacker's Internet Protocol address available? Is there knowledge of the tools used by the attacker?
- What knowledge do we have as to suspects, motivations, and the like? Has there been any previous suspicious activity?
- Have the systems privileges of any user been increased recently? This may indicate an attacker has operated within the network over a period of time, gaining higher levels of access to data as they slowly compromise more devices and managers' accounts.
- Who has remote access to the network and specific devices? Do they still have this access?
- Have there been any system updates or new applications installed recently?
- What are the consequences of the event to the entity?
- Who has administrator access to the network and was this form of access required to commit the attack?
- What evidence is there that this was a targeted attack versus a random one?

CYBER SECURITY HISTORY

Understanding the history of cyber security of the victim organization may provide an understanding of the nature of the event. Evidence of footprinting will show that the event is not a random incident and that the offender may have been preparing for the breach for a period of time.

- Discuss the history of cyber incidents and security events.
- What log files are available for analysis of past events if the history is unknown?

- Have there been any threats to the security of the entity?
- Is there any evidence of footprinting, where an attacker seeks to gain an understanding of the network from a remote location?

SCENE DETAILS

The cybercrime scene may be physical, virtual, multijurisdictional, or a combination of any or each of these. The crime scene is where elements of the offense occurred and may include the computer network, local area network, metropolitan area network, wide area network, or cloud services. The crime scene also includes the device where the offense occurred and locations surrounding it, such as an office. For a large event, there may be multiple crime scenes.

- Define the physical and virtual boundaries of the investigation.
- Identify the legal jurisdiction of the event and evidence (are cloud services involved?).
- How many crime scenes do we have?
- Are staff members aware of the event?
- Who will brief the staff on the event and investigation team's presence?
- What is the subject device?
- Where is the subject device?
- Again, identify any potential risks to your team and any other party. This is a continual process involving all team members. Communication among all team members is essential.
- In a corporate office, cover logistical issues, such as independent access for the investigation team, building emergency measures, the location of bathrooms, and after-hours access (including elevators, after-hours lighting and air conditioning, and so on). These are all small issues that if not addressed may cause unnecessary problems.

In some instances there will be little-to-no initial scene management involved, as when you are called in to begin an investigation several weeks after the event and all the subject devices and evidence collected by the IR team are secured for your collection. In this instance you may still be required to understand the dynamics of where the attack occurred, network topology, and related issues.

IDENTIFYING OFFENSES

Offenses are specific to jurisdiction. It is the responsibility of investigators to understand the elements of offenses at a civil and criminal level to particularize in their reports to management. The initial interview should provide a clear direction as to offenses the investigation team considers throughout their investigation.

- Understand the alleged/suspected offenses (civil/criminal).
- Understand the ingredients of each suspected offense.
- Understand the requirement to link the evidence located to the ingredients of the suspected offenses.

IDENTIFYING WITNESSES

A witness may be any person having any knowledge of or association to the suspected offense. A witness may include the person reporting the offense. Identifying the witnesses in the initial interview can provide valuable assistance in planning the order of interviews, as some witnesses may be about to go on leave, attend courses, or leave the business.

- Identify the person who discovered the incident.
- Record contact details for all witnesses.
- Obtain signed statements for each witness at the earliest opportunity.
- Record qualifications and experience for witnesses involved in technical evidence identification, capture, and storage.
- Record addendum statements as necessary. Addendum statements are secondary statements from witnesses that are recorded due to new information being located or a new line of questioning, unexplored at the time of the initial interview, being asked of witnesses.

IDENTIFYING SUSPECTS

Identifying a suspect at the initial interview provides a strong direction as to the form of investigation. Should the suspect be present while the initial interview is taking place, they may be warned and destroy evidence. Should a cyber offender identify that they have been discovered through digital communication among management team members, they may destroy evidence remotely as well.

- Identify potential suspects (internal/external) and any suspected motivations for the attack.
- As per previous discussions, constantly review safety threats for team members and other persons present.
- Obtain HR records in the instance of an internal suspect.
- If the suspect is an internal employee, determine the location of their office/ desk, what their duties are, when they are present in the office, whether their digital activity is stored on the device or on the company server, whether they use a BYOD computer, whether they have remote access to the subject device/network, the number of people using that device, and the nature of their recent behavior.
- If the suspect is an internal employee, seek permission to remove their access to the network, locally and remotely, as well as their access to the physical premises.

IDENTIFYING THE MODUS OPERANDI OF ATTACK

Understanding the modus operandi (MO) of any attack provides direction to the investigation and to the locating of evidence. It also provides an understanding of the attack and potential data stolen. The initial interview may provide limited information at first, as there may be a limited understanding of these details while the breach is ongoing. In this instance, the investigator must operate with the information they have and begin with evidence identification and seizure in partnership with the IR team.

- What was the target of the event: data, system privileges, Intellectual Property, resources, or something else?
- What were the actions of the attacker while in the system? Did they go directly to the target or did they have to navigate the system to find it?
- What tools were used: a vulnerability scanner or individual tools?
- What commands were used? These will provide evidence of the skill set of the attacker. An attacker who uses command line attacks may be seen as having a different range of skills from an attacker who uses a commercially available vulnerability scanner.

- What was the vulnerability identified and exploited and how long has it been known? If a vulnerability is new, the attack is known as a zero-day attack and indicates a highly skilled attacker.

EVIDENCE: TECHNICAL

The initial interview may provide direction as to the technical evidence involved in the breach and what may be seized as evidence. Areas to be covered in the interview include:

- What systems, networks, and assets have been attacked/compromised?
- When was the system security first breached and how long was the attacker in the network?
- What passwords are associated with the device?
- Was a specific device or database targeted?
- What security measures are in use on the device or evidence captured by the investigators that they need to examine? For example, does the company use proprietary software, meaning the device/evidence will not be able to be reviewed back in the investigator's office without a copy of the application?
- Under what user account was the vulnerability exploited? Does this account include administrator privileges? Had the privileges been upgraded without authority?
- What are the details of the compromised device, including the subnet address? This may be asked in the initial interview but is more likely to be asked of technical staff.
- Are the Security Information and Event Management (SIEM) logs available for analysis?
- If files/records were altered or changed, are there copies of the originals for comparison?
- Is the device compromised critical to the operation of the business?
- Has packet capture identified the attacker's Internet Protocol address?
- What are the activities of and the contact details for the IR team and how they can be located?
- What tools have been used for IR and evidence capture? Are these proprietary or industry standard?
- What evidence did the IR team obtain? Did they reach any conclusions about the attack, its methodologies, damage caused, and suspects?

EVIDENCE: OTHER

Evidence must be treated with respect, as it may be required to be presented in a court of law. The initial interview phase of the investigation will provide direction as to evidence known to date, where it can be located, and the people associated with it.

- What is the legality of having custody of the evidence due to privilege, such as for a doctor, attorney, clergy, psychiatrist, and the like? Beware of any suspicion of a device or network containing Child Exploitation Material and seek immediate police advice as to what action they require.
- How much space will be required for digital storage of evidence? Keep in mind that the amount needed for device capture may be very different from that needed for network capture.
- Has the chain of evidence for all physical and digital evidence, including that obtained from the IR team, been ensured?
- Is there a common logon for the device suspected of being compromised or does everyone have a unique identifier?
- Who has access to the subject device? Do they (or anyone else) have remote access for working from home or when traveling? This is critical for evidence preservation, as remote access by a suspect or their associate may destroy your evidence before you get the opportunity to preserve it.
- Have there been any changes to the network recently, such as a system upgrade or the installation of new devices?
- Do you have any suspects? Obtain details about them, including their personnel file, their duties, any possible motivations, where their desk is, and the like.
- Is everything documented?
- What are the consequences of the breach?
- Will a referral to police be made on behalf of company?

 CYBERCRIME CASE STUDY

A large company discovered that a senior manager was involved in stealing parts during the construction of industrial electrical switchboards. The manager, who was extremely good at their job, was often required to purchase air conditioners for the switchboards due to the heat they generated. He would often purchase two, install one, and keep the other to sell online. The weakness in the process was that the manager designed the switchboards, ordered the parts, oversaw construction, and approved payment for the parts. He jealously guarded his workspace, even from the company owner.

The initial complaint to police from management was to investigate 20 instances of fraud totaling approximately $50,000. The police investigation identified three other fraudulent methodologies. The company owner stopped the scope of the investigation at approximately $450,000 due to the stress it was causing the company, even though there was thought to be many more instances of fraud.

The digital records of the company's accounting system revealed that they had been manipulated to hide the activity. These digital records showed the senior manager to be the person who created the fraudulent documentation, who provided the false descriptors of the purchases on the accounting application, and who authorized the invoices for payment as legitimate expenses related to the building of the switchboards.

A search warrant executed on the senior manager's home located corroborative evidence of large-scale spending significantly in excess of his legitimate income, and a large quantity of objects from the interior of the home (electronic goods, fittings, furniture, etc.) were seized as proceeds of crime. The tax return of the suspect was located and corroborated that the lawful declared income was significantly less than expenditures.

Once arrested, the senior manager pleaded guilty to the fraudulent charges supported by the technical evidence. His wife was also charged and pleaded guilty to fraud, as she had knowingly participated in the accounting for the family finances and was aware her husband was committing large-scale fraud against his employer.

Chapter 8 introduces activities that are undertaken by the IR team to mitigate and eradicate the breach. This introduction is provided for the information of the investigator, so they will have an understanding of the role of members of the IR team, as their evidence will be incorporated into any potential court matter. It will also provide an understanding of the duties and actions of IR team members, so evidence identified and secured can have its origins understood.

CHAPTER EIGHT

Containing and Remediating the Cyber Security Incident

THERE ARE many high-quality guides available to describe in detail the duties of the Incident Response (IR) team, including those provided by organizations such as the SANS Institute. It is not the intention of this chapter to repeat their lessons, but rather to make the investigator aware of what the IR team is doing while the investigator undertakes their duties, as their roles may be seen as complementary.

The US National Institute of Standards and Technology (NIST) has identified an incident response framework for the IR team. It lays out the IR stages as preparation; detection and analysis; containment, eradication, and recovery; and post-incident activity.[1]

The containment and eradication stages reference the capture of evidence and its subsequent handling. In this capture we will identify several of the opportunities for the investigation team to work in partnership with the IR team in obtaining evidence, a partnership that can be used to advance your investigation.

CONTAINING THE CYBER SECURITY INCIDENT

Containing the cyber security event is generally the role of a specified team that has been designated prior to the event. The IR team may be made up of internal staff members or be a team of experts brought in from outside the organization. The investigation team may be requested by the IR team manager to participate in event management when there is evidence of a civil or criminal offense that will require investigation after mitigation.

The goal of the IR team in the containment phase is to restrict the damage that can be done to the system, whether this is the loss of confidential corporate data or damage to the integrity of the network. This phase also allows for the capture of evidence.[1] If the attacker is still within the network, the IR team will seek to restrict any further exploitation and remove them from the system and devices. At this time evidence may become available as to the network vulnerability identified by the attacker and how it was exploited. This should be communicated to the investigation team as a line of inquiry for your investigations.

There are a series of actions the IR team may take that can produce evidence for you at the start while they are containing the attack. This may not always be the case depending on the logs recorded and damage done to systems by the attacker; however, be aware the potential exists for evidence to be found by the IR team that you can use toward building a foundation at the beginning of your investigation. NIST identify examples such as:[1]

- The identification information on the compromised devices
- Location where the evidence is found
- Chain of custody procedures
- Details of an attacker's IP address
- Attack methodology as determined

Ensure the IR team understands your role and its requirements. As you are all in effect working toward the same goal, having a shared understanding and respect of each other's tasks and how they intersect is essential. Large-scale professional IR teams will understand your requirements; however, small in-house team may not until you tell them.

Other examples of potential avenues of inquiry the IR team can provide include:

- Preserving authentication logs that show attempts to log onto the system. These records will show successful and unsuccessful attempts to gain access to the system or the locations of valuable intellectual property. For example, the evidence may show that the attacker gained immediate access to the corporate database on the first try using the compromised credentials of a legitimate employee or that they used a brute force attack in an attempt to crack a password. This information will be of interest to the investigator, as it provides an understanding of whether the attacker is an insider, an external person who has somehow compromised legitimate credentials (another line of inquiry), or an attacker who has no previous insight into the corporate network.

- Obtaining a copy of any malicious software used by the attacker. The investigator may refer to online resources to gain an understanding of the malware, or if the attack is a zero-day exploit (which, as previously discussed, is the exploitation of a previously unknown vulnerability in an Operating System (OS) or application), the investigator will become aware that they are dealing with an experienced cybercriminal with significant technical skills.
- If passwords are compromised, identify whether there are multiple passwords or just one belonging to a single user. Initial inquiries may involve identifying the access privileges of that user and their position in the company, meaning the investigator may start working on understanding how the attacker gained those credentials. Investigating the profile of the user credentials exploited may provide some guidance to the IR and investigation teams as to the initial point of compromise in the device or network.
- If damage has been done to the corporate website in an issue-motivated attack, ensure the IR team keeps a copy of the damaged site as a foundation for your investigation. Should you locate a suspect, you will seek to show the court the damage they have done, especially if the content displayed under the company name is malicious.

The IR team will be covering many different areas of potential compromise and may have few answers to your questions until they have had the opportunity to review logs, understand the attack methodology, and clarify the nature and extent of the attack. Depending upon the circumstances of the attack and size of the complainant entity, this may take several hours or days. In some cases this can extend to weeks. Be aware that the IR team will be operating under great pressure.

Several other areas the IR team will be concentrating on which, depending on the circumstances, you may find as sources of evidence include:

- Closing ports where data comes into and leaves the network. If a port is activated and has no function within the network, this may have been a pathway of compromise. As different ports are used for different forms of digital traffic, identifying which ports are the subject of compromise may provide a small step forward in your investigation and knowledge of how the attack was initiated. For example, port 80 may be for web traffic, whereas port 25 may be related to email traffic. The IR team will be able to provide you with this information and an explanation of its meaning.

- Identifying and removing compromised or suspect devices from a network where feasible. This is of particular interest to the investigator, as you will want to work in partnership with your digital investigator to image the devices and identify evidence of the compromise. A problem may occur if the compromised device is critical to the organization, such as the database where all the corporate records required for day-to-day operation are stored. Taking this database offline may mean that the company will cease to function. An example of this situation would be an online company whose web server is damaged and needs to be taken offline. This would mean that the company is not able to trade until the server is secured or an alternative host is located.

An example of a conflict between the IR and investigation teams would be where a virtual machine has been infected by malicious software (malware) and the IR team wishes to shut it down and reboot a new instance of the machine, eradicating the malware. While this may prove very effective in containing and eradicating the attack, it also would destroy valuable evidence that will not be able to be recovered and that the investigation team would be interested in. This action may be favored by management, as it is a quick and clean way of eradicating malware; however, your evidence will now be gone and will not be able to be recovered.

While containment is the prime responsibility of the IR team, the cyber investigator may be included in this process to oversee evidence collection and initiate new lines of inquiry. A valuable part of your evidence is to seek the notes of members of the IR team to understand what they saw, what actions they took, the reasons for the decisions they made, and the consequences of containing and eradicating the event. These notes can be used in the preparation of statements by IR team members, and in the instance where a suspect is identified and prosecuted, will be part of the evidence of the prosecution.

ERADICATING THE CYBER SECURITY INCIDENT

As with the containment phase, the IR team is responsible for eradication of the threat and the cyber investigator is responsible for providing investigation and evidence collection support. The investigator will continue with investigations after the IR team has completed their duties.

Eradication involves removing the threat and securing the exploited vulnerabilities after the attack has been contained.[1] The containment and eradication processes may be completed within several hours, or in the cases of large corporate networks attacked by very experienced and well-resourced cybercriminals, weeks or even months.[1] Prepare for the possibility of the latter case, as logistics will take careful planning and resourcing. Also, continual communication with management is essential, as they will be concerned about costs and disruption to the day-to-day functioning of the business.

While you will have collected valuable information during the containment phase, the eradication process has the potential to destroy valuable evidence, which will not be able to be recovered. As mentioned previously, closing virtual machines is an effective manner of eradicating malware, but it also eradicates value evidence you may require from within the virtual machine.

Listed below are examples of some of the processes the IR team undertakes in the eradication phase, which may be of interest to the investigation team:

- Identifying any other devices that may have been compromised.[1] The investigator will be interested in examining these devices, as they, too, may contain new or corroborating evidence to support information gained in the containment phase.
- Reinstalling the OS and pertinent applications. Once the OS and applications are reinstalled, potential evidence is overwritten. Ensure you have all your evidence from the OS and pertinent applications before reinstallation.
- Reinstalling trusted copies of the database, OS, and other applications, which will then be monitored. The IR team will be aware the experienced attacker may still have remote access to the network, which has not been detected in the detection and eradication phases. Alternatively, the attacker may have left malware that has not been identified or activated. It would be of benefit to keep in contact with the IR team and system administrators over the days following reinstallation to confirm there have been no further compromises of the network.
- Conducting testing to ensure the vulnerabilities exploited by the attacker have been fixed.[1] You will be interested in this information as additional confirmation of the attack vectors used by the cybercriminal.

There are many processes the IR team undertakes in the containment and eradication phases. The examples listed here are meant to provide insight into their duties and how their work can be used as a foundation for your investigation. It is strongly recommended that where practical you communicate with the IR team prior to the start of incident response to an event—or immediately upon being brought into the event, should you be a party external to the entity under attack.

 NOTE

1. Paul Cichonski, Thomas Millar, Tim Grance, and Karen Scarfone, *Computer Security Incident Handling Guide*, Special Publication 800-61 Revision 2, August 2012, National Institute of Standards and Technology, United States Department of Commerce.

CHAPTER NINE

Challenges in Cyber Security Incident Investigations

G AINING AN understanding of the crime under investigation is more complex in a cyber environment than in a physical domain. As much of the evidence is digital, it may be very volatile and subject to loss or damage should prompt action not be taken to ensure its preservation. Also, with distributed data servers—such as cloud computing—becoming more common, the evidence the investigator is seeking can be spread across multiple jurisdictions and be lost very quickly due to the suspect remotely deleting evidence of their crime. Alternatively, Cloud Service Provider (CSP) resource maximization policies may result in key log evidence being overwritten.

In the initial phases, the investigator may be unaware of the extent or boundaries of the investigation—or even the precise crime under investigation—when commencing action. As we discovered in Chapter 8, evidence may be slow in being obtained as the (Incident Response) IR team seeks to contain the threat and build their technical understanding of the attack, sometimes with limited consideration of the requirements of the cyber investigator. You may also find weak management support, with some managers just wanting the problem to go away so that they can get back to business as usual, albeit with a higher standard of security so that the problem does not reoccur.

The crime scene in a cyber investigation differs from that of a traditional, physical crime scene in which the investigator has control of the scene from the start, provides direction to all inquiries, and can ensure the scene and exhibits are not contaminated. As discussed, the first responsibilities of the Incident Response (IR) team may be to mitigate and eradicate the attack, with event investigation and the collection of forensic evidence being important responsibilities—instead of premier features—incorporated into the response.

For a traditional crime, the detective examining the scene will want to start their examination with the scene in as close to the state the offender left it in as possible. That means controlling access to the scene, protecting it from damage from events such as weather in the case of an outdoor scene, photographing the scene and evidence, and so on. The investigator will be working in a very different environment in the case of a cyber-attack, with different consequences to scene management and evidence protection.

Whether the cyber-attack is continuing when the cyber investigator first attends or has been remediated, the scene and evidence will look very different from when the crime was first identified, and they will need to look retrospectively to account for all actions taken after the identification of the cyber event in partnership with the IR team. These are dynamic investigations, and the decision to seize valuable evidence later during the response may be a decision later regretted.

This chapter will discuss in brief a series of the unique challenges the cybercrime investigator may discover when compared to other crime types.

UNIQUE CHALLENGES

Defining Investigation Boundaries and Management Objectives

As the extent of the crime may be unknown, the initial direction from management as to the objectives of the IR investigation may change throughout the investigation. The initial direction may be to provide a report for the information of management only; however, the investigation may find significant evidence to identify the attacker or may find that the attack was far greater than initially thought, resulting in the management then wishing to begin legal proceedings against the identified attacker and/or report the matter to police and/or the data privacy officers within your jurisdictions.

Tip: Define the boundaries of the investigation broadly and narrow them as the situation becomes clearer. It is easier to start wide and work inwards than the opposite, as evidence outside your investigation boundaries may be lost or destroyed. Always be prepared to have your evidence and investigation processes challenged in a court of law, even when the initial instructions provided by your client are to provide a report for management only.

Identifying Potential Offenses (Criminal and/or Civil)

In understanding the crime, the investigator needs to ensure that they are aware that there may be more than one action by the attacker in the cyber event. For example, a Distributed Denial of Service (DDoS) attack may be initiated against the web server of the target company for the purpose of diverting the attention of the security team from the real target of the attack: the stealing of corporate Intellectual Property (IP) from the database of a separate server.

Tip: While the obvious attack must be addressed, being aware of the potential for it to be a diversion attack is important. Having a member of the system security staff continue to monitor other activity across the network is an investment the attacker may not be expecting.

Identifying Compromised Data and/or Resources

Systems records may not always be available to the investigator, as mitigation and eradication actions may have permanently deleted data the investigator would use. Also, in many instances logs are not kept due to the expense of maintaining large volumes of log data from previous months from the many operating systems and applications.

Tip: An IR plan should be devised to incorporate the role of the investigator. This will also teach team members about the value of each other's role. Also run IR training events across a variety of attack scenarios, during which the value of various logs can be identified and incorporated into the log preservation policy.

Identifying Suspects and Motivations

Offenders may be located literally anywhere in the world and be hiding behind anonymizing applications and other technology. Offenders may also be located in the organization under attack, so the insider threat cannot be discounted. They may also destroy the evidence of their presence before an event is even identified.

A cybercriminal who is experienced at computer crime has the capacity to make it incredibly difficult for an investigator to locate them. Even identifying the international region they are in is a significant challenge in itself. Using technical resources such as Virtual Private Networks (VPNs), proxy servers, encryption, anonymizers, fraudulent identities, and cloud services destroys evidence as it is created; with an attack potentially crossing many legal jurisdictions, the response time may be significantly behind the progression of the offense.

> Tip: There is no fast and easy method of mitigating this problem. Involving one of the large IR companies may provide some valuable assistance, as these companies have international resources, visibility, and extensive awareness of cybercriminal behavior.

Identifying Exploited Vulnerabilities

The methodologies of the attacker are only limited by their skill and imagination. While they may apply successful general methodologies, skilled attackers modify their attack strategies to fit the circumstances and to reflect the environment they are operating within.

The investigator must understand a broad range of attack methodologies and, if possible, identify the motivations of the attacker early in the investigation in order to understand how they moved around the network and evaded security.

> Tip: Pre-event training of system security staff and access to experienced IR teams brings the knowledge of current attack methodologies into your IR and investigation teams. Often you may not have the skills required to successfully defend the network and you will require expert external assistance. This information can be shared with the investigators to provide direction as they commence their inquiries.

Securing Evidence

The primary roles of the IR team are to contain the threat, mitigate it, and return the company to a higher standard of security. To accomplish this, the IR team has to work quickly and make rapid decisions, which may conflict with the wishes of the lead investigator. We previously explained the example of the IR team deciding that shutting down a virtual server and rebooting it in a safe state would best eradicate a threat coming from a cloud server that has been infected. While this action may be the best option for containing the threat, valuable log data, which may provide evidence of the suspect and their activities, will destroyed and will not be able to be recovered.

In the course of the IR team's operations, the thought of commencing a post-event investigation to locate a suspect may not surface. However, once the extent of the breach has been identified, the decision may be made to begin an investigation and refer the matter to police. Unfortunately, as stated previously, valuable evidence will have been destroyed and will not be able to be recovered.

The cyber investigator should seek all available evidence from a multitude of sources. However, evidence may not be always available without external cooperation, as in the instances where third parties, such as cloud-computing providers, control systems hardware/software.

The investigator needs to be aware of all the different sources of evidence that can be generated by computer devices and ensure that these are promptly secured.

> Tip: Pre-event training exercises highlight the role of the IR and investigation teams and how their objectives may complement or conflict with each other. Building the roles and duties of each party into a response plan will help to preserve evidence. A direction from management to the IR team that evidence is to be collected as a part of their duties will assist the investigator.

Where a live event is occurring and there is no IR plan in place, communication and respect for each other's role is required, with management providing direction to all parties.

Understanding the Legal Jurisdiction Where the Incident Occurred and the Evidence Exists

As a cybercriminal may reside in a country separate from their target, the law of that country may be very different from that of the victim's country. What may be a serious criminal offense in the victim's jurisdiction may not be an offense at all in the attacker's country, and may in fact be a legal activity.

Tip: If you have identified the attacker as being in a foreign jurisdiction where they have not committed an offense by attacking your network, define your objectives. Liaise with law enforcement to determine whether they are able to conduct their investigation and identify a suspect. In the event of a major breach where the suspect is in a legal jurisdiction beyond the reach of an investigation, law enforcement may be able to obtain an arrest warrant that provides for the suspect being arrested if they leave their local jurisdiction.

Locating Digital Evidence in a Timely Manner

The investigator will need to work in partnership with the IR team or system administrators to determine what devices contain evidence and to ensure its accountable capture.

Digital evidence may be lost very quickly after an event, as evidence such as log data is regularly overwritten. Also, the attacker may still have access to the system and start destroying evidence once they identify they have been compromised.

Criminals have also been known to remotely wipe their phones after having been seized by police if the phone was not put in flight mode or stored in a Faraday bag. Mobile phones may also be used as a listening device, meaning that should you legally seize the device, the owner may have the capacity to remotely turn on an application and listen to your conversations while you conduct your investigation.

Tip: Determine early in the investigation the order of volatility of evidence and respond accordingly. This is discussed in Chapter 10's section "Acquisition of Digital Evidence."

Maintaining the Chain of Evidence across Multiple Jurisdictions

Because digital evidence may be located in international jurisdictions, as may be the case with cloud servers, the responsibility of the investigator to maintain the chain of evidence becomes more complex, although no less important.

Tip: This is a basic component of your investigation. Understand the process of obtaining your evidence across international jurisdictions and the persons who are involved. Obtain statements immediately, as obtaining them a year later will be likely met with a mixed response. Map your evidence pathway from source to courtroom so that you can be thorough and accurate in your evidence.

Understanding the Complexity of the Evidence

Digital crimes can be very complex, as a unique technical language will apply. Remember that technology is designed to function according to specification, not with the requirements of the court to understand it in mind.

Tip: Plan for the complexity. Consider bringing an independent person into the court to present overtly technical evidence. In the investigation phase, designate a technically minded person to research the technology and its processes.

Synchronizing the Time on Event Logs across the System Architecture

With the many different components being built into computer architecture, manufacturers of hardware, operating systems, and applications may not always use the same formats for recording logs. Some are not readable by humans. The time recorded on logs may be spread across different time zones, meaning that a translation process will be required before the log analysis can commence. This process may also need to be explained to the court.

Tip: This is very important, as logs do not always operate in the same time zone. Ensure all logs are in or converted to a designated time zone and record the process in which this was done. Also look to confirm that times from logs are consistent, as even a one-second difference between different sets of logs will confuse your investigation.

Understanding the Cost of Multijurisdictional Investigations

Obtaining evidence across international boundaries is particularly difficult and expensive for civilian investigators. Whereas criminal investigators may benefit from using Mutual Legal Assistance Treaties (MLATs) to assist their investigations, civilian investigators have no such formal support. Costs can escalate very quickly and having a defined budget at the commencement of the investigation can provide the investigation team with some clarity.

Tip: With a civil investigation, set a budget and monitor it with regular reviews. The cost of investigative and legal support across international boundaries is very expensive, and the cost of the investigation can quickly exceed the cost of the cyber attack.

Assessing Impact Costs

An investigator may be employed to provide a report to management to support a cyber-insurance claim. With the dynamic nature of digital evidence, assessing the extent of the crime and its associated cost may prove difficult.

Tip: When submitting a cyber-insurance claim, there may be a requirement to provide expert evidence to support the claim. This also applies in court, where should you win your case, the judge will be interested in obtaining an assessment of the cost of losses so as to determine their options, including damages to be awarded to the complainant.

Be prepared for the estimate of losses to be challenged by the defendant, as their future sentence or punishment will be determined by factors that include the cost of their actions. Use qualified expert support from legal representatives, investigators, and/or assessors who can provide expert evidence to the court about the cost of losses.

Understanding these challenges is a skill learned by experience only. Lessons learned will be incorporated into the updated IR plan, but also into the collective knowledge of the investigation team. With this information, investigation of subsequent cybercrime scenes will be undertaken.

CYBERCRIME CASE STUDY

A marriage breakup was followed by contested hearings in court over marital assets and associated issues. The wife was experiencing difficulty in court on top of the normal stresses involved in a marriage breakup.

She had been communicating with her lawyer and personal support network through her webmail account. As time progressed, she noticed that her soon-to-be ex-husband seemed to know what she was doing and who she was associating with, as well as details about her communication with her lawyer.

The level of knowledge he had became very specific and applied across different conversations she was having. She suspected that he might be hacking into her online email account, which he had set up years previously. She changed the password but this made little difference as to the information he knew about her activities.

Inquiries were made with a friend who had technical skills, and he checked the settings on her email account. It was found that the husband had a redirect on the account, meaning that all email correspondence in and out of the account was forwarded to him.

A consideration when police reviewed the complaint was which jurisdiction had the responsibility of investigating the complaint: Australia, where the suspect and complainant were resident, or the United States, where the computer servers were located. It was determined that because of local legislation, local courts had jurisdiction even though the computer servers were located in the United States, as the husband and his activity were based in Australia.

Digital evidence included the Internet Protocol addresses used to access the account as well as evidence of the redirect email account belonging to the husband. Computer logs on the husband's computer identified log-on activity and time stamps of his logging onto his Hotmail account, where the redirected emails were sent.

Upon the court hearing the matter, the husband was convicted and sentenced to a noncustodial sentence.

CHAPTER TEN

Investigating the Cybercrime Scene

LTHOUGH A cybercrime event may occur in a digital environment, the location of the device or network affected is in effect a crime scene. It is where the offense occurred and/or evidence resides. The crime scene where the investigator gains lawful access via consent or a court order may be commercial premises and/or the suspect's home address. It may also be a public place where a suspect has joined a free Wi-Fi network and used unverified access as a means to anonymize their activities.

This chapter is particularly relevant to law enforcement investigators but will apply to civilian investigators as well. For example, the scene management involved in investigating an allegation of an internal theft of Intellectual Property (IP) will differ from that involving an external Distributed Denial of Service (DDoS) attack, and the contents of this section will apply based on the circumstances as well as the experience, knowledge, and requirements of the investigators of the day. Care of exhibits should be at the same standard for all cybercrime scenes; however, activities such as photographing the scene may not be as relevant in the example of the DDoS attack.

Crime scenes differ in size, and a single crime may have been committed across multiple locations. Your cybercrime scene may be a large commercial office or a small office where a manager who committed fraud against their clients worked. Alternatively, you may be required to attend to a business and collect a single device for investigation with little scene work required.

For example, the offender who is an employee of a company may have committed offenses against their employer at work through the internal network, as well as from their home address where they had remote log-on access. Crime scenes may cross local and international borders, with law enforcement and industry cooperating to locate suspects whose locality when they committed the crime in turn becomes a crime scene. The legality of lawful access to the crime scene(s) will depend on the circumstances and be determined with qualified legal advice.

It is the examination of the crime scene and evidence that leads to follow-up inquiries that may in turn lead to identification of the offender and the evidence to conduct a successful prosecution if required. The experienced investigator will understand that the investment of time and effort in examining the scene will show its true worth several years later when being cross-examined about their work by the defendant's lawyer. The word "investment" is specifically used, as your work at the crime scene and evidence identification/seizure/collection will prove to be valuable parts of the foundation to your investigation.

Management of the crime scene is a skill many detectives spend significant periods of their career learning, as each crime scene may differ. While a digital crime scene will obviously look very different from a homicide scene, the principles surrounding the rules of evidence remain the same and the evidence must be dealt with at the standard the court demands. Although a computer is a different piece of evidence from a bloodied knife next to a body, it does not mean the applicable rules of evidence have a lower threshold of accountability.

Should the scene and evidence be poorly handled, the evidence may be excluded or admitted reluctantly, with a consequent weakening of its value. Many cases have been weakened in court because the crime scene and exhibits were poorly managed and their integrity could not be explained to the standard required by the court. This may lead to the awarding of costs to the benefit of the defendant, particularly in a case being heard in a civil court or tribunal.

A high-quality, complete examination of the crime scene gives the opposing party's lawyers an insight into the capabilities of the investigators. Should they review the examination and conclude it was poorly managed, with evidence unaccounted for or documentation that is incomplete, their view will be that the rest of the investigation was of a similar standard. This may make the difference between a lawyer recommending that their client admit the charges against them and the lawyer challenging the evidence, your investigation, and the accusations of guilt.

At a scene detectives use the saying "Control the people and you control the scene." This means that people at the scene and their actions are one of the biggest risks to the integrity of scene management, and the digital crimes investigator must ensure that only those persons who are required at the scene are present, that their presence is documented, and that their actions are recorded in notebooks, which may become evidence in its own right. This may be difficult in a commercial scene where the day-to-day business is continuing, but the burden remains on the investigation team to work within this environment and preserve the scene and collected evidence to the standard required by the local courts.

A pre-event plan records many aspects of responding to a digital event, and the scene manager is in effect the detective who has control over the event from the start. The pre-event plan will be discussed in subsequent sections of this chapter. The investigation manager and team members need to understand the crucial role of evidence preservation and have the preapproved authority to manage the event as they deem necessary in the circumstances. This may involve the authority to tell senior members of the organization to stay away from the scene while emergency action is being taken and to provide briefings in a separate location on a regular basis or when new information comes to hand. Should a senior manager of an organization start telling the investigators how to do their job, the senior manager may be required to attend court in the trial of a defendant, explain the reasons for their directions, and detail their experience in scene management and evidence preservation, as well as take responsibility for any negative consequences arising from their directions.

As a final thought before we progress into the investigation processes, understand that your job at the scene is not necessarily to solve the crime within the first hour, although that is a great result if you can. One of your key tasks is to lay a solid foundation for the main investigation phase through scene management and evidence collection.

This chapter discusses the many different aspects of scene management. It will take a very generic view of evidence identification, collection, and seizure, as the laws in each legal jurisdiction will vary. It is the responsibility of the investigator to understand the rules of evidence and scene management in their jurisdiction while using this chapter as a supporting document. The principles of this chapter may apply to searches at a complainant's premises as well as those of a suspect, where you attend the scene with a court order. Note that Figures 10.1 through 10.8 are re-creations for the benefit of the reader. These images have been included in the book to add relevance. The original images from the crime scenes are not available, as they are the property of the relevant law enforcement agency.

First we shall examine the makeup of the investigation team.

 ## THE INVESTIGATION TEAM

The members of the scene investigation team are some of the most critical components of your investigation, as these are the people who will collect the evidence that much of the remainder of your investigation will rely upon. Law enforcement spends significant time training their officers in scene investigation and management, which reflects the fact that these are skills that are continually being developed and adapted, as all scenes are different in some way.

How Many People Do You Need?

This will be determined by the circumstances of your investigation and the amount of time you have available. Be aware that circumstances can change very quickly on location as more information about the investigation is discovered, and having extra staff available is invaluable. While it is preferable to have exactly the number of people required, having an additional person available during the initial phase of the scene examination until you have a full understanding of the dynamics of the situation may be of benefit. If you find you have too many people at a location, they can always be released to other duties.

Determine the Skills Required

Digital investigators are highly skilled individuals and having one on your team is recommended unless you are collecting evidence to deliver to the digital investigator that has already been preserved. Understanding the skills of your team in areas such as interviewing, evidence location, exhibits management, and general searching is required pre-event.

The cybercrime scene may range from a laptop computer to a suite of corporate offices. At the physical location, the lead investigator is responsible for maintaining the crime scene and the lawful, orderly discovery, seizure, and preservation of evidence. As each scene is different, the resources required will differ and be managed according to the experience and requirements of the scene manager as well as the local rules of evidence.

At the beginning there may be three levels of authority: the lead investigator, who has total authority of the investigation; the scene manager, who will execute search warrants/court orders; and the exhibits officer, who will secure the exhibits seized and maintain the chain of custody. Also present will be the search officers, who conduct the physical search/examination of the location. The scene manager will be a person designated by the lead investigator to control the search and evidence-collection phase. Depending upon the scene size, number of people in the location, and resources and skills available, the lead investigator and scene manager may be the same person. Having a separate exhibits manager takes a significant workload off the lead investigator and scene manager.

Each person at the scene, such as searchers, digital investigators, exhibits officer, and others, will have specific responsibilities. Ensure that people understand their duties and have the equipment required prior to arrival at the scene.

A brief explanation of who the members of the scene examination team are is as follows:

■ **General Searchers:** Persons who physically search for evidence and locate it. They will work closely with the exhibits officer and record what they find, where they found it, and what time they found it, and provide a description of the exhibit. An example of their notebook entry after finding a Dell laptop might be:

> Item 1: Located one Dell laptop computer, model ABC, serial number 12345678, on the desk of Joe Smith at 09:17 a.m. Laptop was turned off. Silver in color with black Dell carry bag. Leads to laptop in bag secured as well. Scratches observed on the base of device.

■ **Exhibits Officer:** Appointing a designated exhibits officer helps reduce the workload of the lead investigator; they are responsible for making sure they have everything they need to manage the exhibits.

This person is responsible for accounting for all evidence seized. They will have the exhibits delivered to them by the general searchers and take responsibility for preserving the chain of custody. An example of an entry in their field log might be:

> Item 1: Received one Dell laptop computer, model ABC, serial number 12345678, from Mary Jones at 09:22 a.m. Silver in color with leads in a black Dell carry bag.

Examples of devices with unique identifiers are illustrated in Figures 10.1 and 10.2.

■ **Scene Manager:** The scene manager is responsible for the team working the scene. They will liaise with the investigation lead, who may, depending on the circumstances, be the same person. They will draw or have drawn a sketch map of the location and be able to identify exactly where each item of evidence was located.

For example, the sketch map prepared and associated notes will show the Dell computer located by Mary Jones was from the desk of Joe Smith, which is the first desk on the right-hand side of the main room next to the doorway. In a large office, the room would have its own designation, such as "main office" or "telemarketers' call center."

The scene manager will appoint a person to prepare a receipt for each evidence item owner, accounting for every item seized. Usually this person will

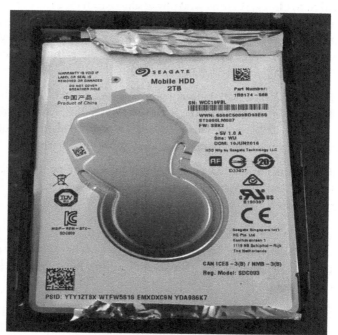

FIGURE 10.1 Hard drive showing serial number as a unique identifier.
Source: Photo © Graeme Edwards.

FIGURE 10.2 Computer printer showing serial number as a unique identifier.
Source: Photo © Graeme Edwards.

be the exhibits officer, although a member of the general search team may be tasked to assist the exhibits officer in this duty once they have completed their other duties.

- **Photographer:** The scene manager will also ensure that a person is designated to take photos of the location and exhibits as they are found and before they are moved. Upon first arriving at the scene, have the photographer record the scene via photos or video so that it can later be seen exactly as it looked when the investigation team arrived.

The photographer will take photos of exhibits as they are found. Depending upon the circumstances, general photos may identify information that later becomes important, such as sticky notes on the wall above a user's desk.

When Mary locates the laptop on the desk of Joe, she would call the photographer over to take a general photo of where the desk of Joe is located in the office, the exhibit as it was found, when it was removed from the carry bag, and any unique identifiers, such as the serial number. If the computer is running, they will take photos of the screen and of the open windows.

To prevent claims that the scratches on the laptop were caused by the investigation team, the photographer would take a photo of the scratches on the base of the laptop at the time it is found and Mary would record this in her notebook.

To corroborate that the desk is Joe's, the photographer may also take photos of personal items on the desk, such as handwritten notes, family photographs, a wallet, personal documents, and the like.

The scene manager will also find the photographer invaluable when exhibits of value, such as cash, are found. Filming the finding of the cash and the amount by electronically recording the serial numbers of each note provides a level of security to the investigation team against accusations of theft being made against them. Also, if the cash is seized as an exhibit, recording the serial numbers ensures that if there is a miscount, the recording can clearly show it was only an error and nothing dishonest.

▪ **Digital Investigator:** As has been discussed, this person will have specific skills and knowledge and will be responsible for overseeing the capture of digital data, especially from devices that are operating.

As their evidence will ultimately be crucial to an investigation, when assembling your investigation team ensure that they are technically competent for this duty, with the capacity to deliver their evidence in court if required. They will need to be able to produce independent evidence of their qualifications and training, prove that their skill sets are current, and prove that the digital tools they are using are suitable for the tasks they are undertaking and they are qualified and competent to use them.

▪ **Interviewer:** The person assigned the task of interviewer may be any member of the team who has the proven skills. Alternatively, they may be assigned this task if you have (a) specific person(s) in mind.

As the investigation team will attend to the scene while the Incident Response (IR) team is operating, the reality is that they may have limited knowledge of the event apart from a brief initial outline. This is the case in many police investigations when investigations are begun with very limited information, and important decisions are made in this environment.

While there may be no conscious decision to interview a suspect when at the scene, circumstances sometimes overrun this plan and a suspect may be identified during a routine conversation without any preplanning or warning. In effect your initial interview will commence and having a digital voice recorder (where your jurisdiction allows) will be of great benefit. Details about suspect interviews are covered in Chapter 16, "Suspect Interviews."

In summary, the basics of investigation team membership need to be established prior to attending any scene. Also allow for team members who have holidays upcoming, training courses, and other Human Resource (HR) considerations that mean they may not be available at a specific time or for follow-up investigation. To alleviate these potential problems, having staff able to cover a multitude of positions is recommended, as well as having multiple options available for the specialist position of digital investigators. Over time, where possible and practical, rotate staff to different positions on the investigation team as it helps keep them motivated and develops their skills.

Now that we have an understanding of the people who make up the membership of the search team, we will examine the equipment they may need at the scene.

RESOURCES REQUIRED

There are a lot of items scene examiners may take to a scene to assist them seize and secure evidence. The list that follows covers a lot of material, and the experienced scene examiner will add to or delete items as their experience and the unique circumstances of each scene dictates. The digital investigator will have an additional list of requirements.

- Containers for carrying a large volume of exhibits. These may be cardboard boxes, specific storage containers, carry bags, and the like.
- A notebook with numbered pages. Never tear out the pages of a notebook, even if a mistake is made, as defense lawyers will want to know if anything is being hidden. Cross out mistakes so they can be read. Honest mistakes and misspellings occur.
- A master exhibit register to record all items seized and the movement of exhibits.
- A receipt book or document to provide a receipt to the party you are seizing evidence from so that they are aware of exactly what has been taken. This document will also be of value when recording the chain of custody. An example is included in Figure 10.3.
- Labels to attach to items seized, such as computer devices, hard drives, and the like. Also tags to attach to leads and cables so that they can be uniquely associated with the device they were located with/connected to.

- A camera/video recorder/GoPro camera or similar device. Do not use your personal phone unless absolutely necessary, as defense lawyers may ask to examine it. A GoPro camera or similar device may be very useful if dealing with a large number of people or if there may some conflict involved in your attending the location. It may also record the level of professionalism of the investigation team and prevent accusations from being made against you. Check the laws in your jurisdiction as to the recording of interviews and related matters.
- A Faraday bag to restrict external access to live mobile devices. This prevents an external party from remotely interfering with the mobile device, such as deleting evidence. If a Faraday bag is not available, an empty (unused) metal container is sometimes a suitable substitute, as is using aluminum foil to wrap the exhibit. While these latter methods may seem unsophisticated in a digital world, as long as they work there is no need to discount them when a Faraday bag is unavailable.
- A laptop. A laptop is useful for many reasons, including for Internet access, recording exhibits, having a copy of portions of the investigation file, and so on.
- Digital recorders to record conversations as required. The laws of your jurisdiction will determine the legality of recording conversations.
- External hard drives for securing evidence with the assistance of the digital examiner. Use new or reformatted devices to prove that the evidence located is not contaminated by previous investigations.
- A series of computers for recording statements.
- A portable printer to print out statements to sign if there are no facilities available where you are.
- Preprinted labels and forms for recording exhibits and the team member locating them. These support the notebooks of the investigation team.
- Stationery and materials for writing and marking items, including pens, pencils, marker pens, and related items.
- A bag of small tools, such as a flashlight, a pair of scissors, screwdrivers of various sizes, and the like.

This is not a definitive list and scene managers/exhibits officers will add further items as required. Technology management is also expanding and consideration of the need for developing technology will be required. Some of these items are similar to those used by the digital investigator and may be included in the investigator's kit bag as a backup to the digital investigator in the event a larger volume of digital evidence exists than initially thought.

Figure 10.3 shows an example of a scene property schedule. This is a template figure you may review and modify to suit your requirements.

Property Schedule   No: 123456

Person whom property seized from:

Name:..

Address:...

Contact Numbers

Cell: ....   Business: ....   Home: ....

Relationship to property

Owner   In possession of   Finder   Other

Authority for possession

Consent   Court Order   Found   Exhibit

Location of taking possession

Residential premises   Commercial premises   Government premises

Public place   Other

Item Number	Description	Damage (Y/N)

Reporting officer:

Name:...Rank:..............................
Station:...Phone Number:.....................
Signature:..

Location exhibits to be secured:...

I agree the items described in this document are an accurate representation of the items taken by the reporting officer

Property owner/finder/person in possession of

Name:...   Date:........................
Signature:..

FIGURE 10.3 Example of a scene property schedule.
Source: Photo © Graeme Edwards.

The scene property receipt is a very important document, as it is a record of what you have taken as agreed to by the property owner/custodian. The receipt may be evidence in itself, and a copy is provided showing not only what is being taken but by whom and where it is to be secured. Note also on the top right-hand corner of the receipt is a receipt number, which assists in the credibility of the document.

AVAILABILITY AND MANAGEMENT OF EVIDENCE

This section identifies and discusses examples of the forms of digital evidence that exist. There is no definitive list covering every possible example of digital evidence available, as technology evolves daily; however, this section will provide investigators with an understanding of what technology is included in crime scenes and may hold evidence.

Digital evidence may be defined as:

> Any data stored or transmitted using a computer that supports or refutes a theory of how an offence occurred or that addresses critical elements of the offence such as intent or alibi.[1]

This is a wide-ranging definition; however, it is very accurate as the technology available today will be very different from that available when Casey made this statement. Casey also states that digital evidence must be of a probative value and collected in a manner acceptable to a court of law.[1]

The evidence you are seeking must be relevant, reliable, and sufficient. That is, the evidence must be relevant in proving ingredients of the matter being investigated, reliable in that it is what it purports itself to be, and sufficient in that the evidence seized must allow the matter being investigated to be fully investigated.[2]

With technology evolving on a daily basis, the forms of digital evidence the investigator may consider are restricted only by the limits of their imagination. Digital evidence may come in traditional forms, as with computers, USB drives, routers, switches and phones, and wearable devices, such as iWatches. Smart devices reside in homes and on business premises and they may assist in informing the investigator as to who was in a specific location or conducting the defining activities at the time of the suspected offenses. The Internet of Things (IoT) has created numerous technology items in our lives, and home devices gather data, which may progress your investigation.

For technological evidence, look around your scene and record all the technology you can see. Understand what it is for and question yourself to understand what data it is collecting and where it may reside. The data may be held in the device itself, on a local server, or in cloud-computing databases. Understanding the technology you see and what it does may lead you to new avenues of inquiry or to finding definitive evidence that links a suspect to a specific location at a time they denied being there.

For example, a suspect may deny being in the office at the time data was downloaded from a computer to an external hard drive. An examination of the router in the office may show, however, that at that specific time the Media Access Control (MAC) address of the suspect's mobile phone was recorded leaving its unique identifier as it attempted to connect to the router. That means that the suspect's phone was present in the room at the time of the data theft, which, while not 100 percent conclusive, means that the suspect was there as well, placing you in a strong position as your suspect list is narrowed down and strong evidence for a follow-up interview is built.

The lists that follow provide examples of technical, nontechnical, and physical evidence that may be used to advance an investigation. Due to the nature of particular items, some may appear on more than one list. These lists are not exhaustive and the development of new technologies will expand the lists. The explanations provided are to give the investigator an understanding of the potential value of each item of evidence.

TECHNICAL ITEMS

- *Event logs.* These logs are like a CCTV camera recording what happens at a scene during a crime. The logs that were recorded and are accessible will tell you what happened in the system, when it happened, in what order, and by whom. Refer to Chapter 11 for more information on event logs and the many other forms of logs available to assist in your investigation. While a skilled criminal may modify logs to cover their activity, this may also prove evidence of intent and the criminal's skill set.
- *Application whitelisting schedule.* Application whitelisting is a service available from the system administrator that allows only preapproved programs to run on a system. Its purpose is to ensure that programs that have security vulnerabilities or that leak data are not able to run on the system and create new security vulnerabilities. If an application is on this list without the approval of the system administrator, then the criminal may have

been able to gain administrator privileges, which is valuable evidence in its own right.

- **Antivirus logs.** **Anti Virus** (AV) logs provide information on the operation of the AV system. Evidence available shows when the AV application was installed, when updated, when scans were operated, and their results.
- **Proxy logs.** A proxy server acts as an intermediary between an endpoint device, such as a networked computer, and another server, such as a web server. It records the activity from the endpoint device and may possess evidence of interactions between the endpoint device and an external device, such as the transfer of files.
- **Virtual private network logs.** A Virtual Private Network(VPN) provides an encrypted pathway from the local device or network to the Internet, where the details of the connection are not recorded on the normal log files. Look for who initiated the VPN session, time of connection, where the VPN service connected to, how long the connection was open, and whether the time frame for the connection coincides with the time frame for the event you are investigating. A suspect who uses a VPN may have evidence of it located on their device, in which case you can compare connection times from the suspect's device to those on the device or network compromised.

    In some instances you may be able to make contact with the VPN service and obtain log records from the suspect's account. This is not an option in all cases, as many VPN services do not record client logs because of client confidentiality or host their services in locations where foreign court orders are not honored. However, like all investigation options, if you do not ask, you will not find out, and in this instance, your making the inquiry proves your investigation was thorough.
- **Domain name server logs.** Domain Name Server (DNS) logs show the service your computer connects to when seeking the address of websites being searched for on the Internet. If the computer is going to a regularly visited website, it does not connect to a DNS as it will already have the address of the site it is seeking. However, if the user is looking for a website not previously visited, the computer will connect to the designated DNS server and locate the address of the website, which is then sent back to the client's computer, who then commences to make a connection with the website they wish to contact. These logs are particularly useful when seeking connection pathways and associated times for websites created to receive data taken from a complainant.
- **Dynamic Host Configuration Protocol logs.** Dynamic Host Configuration Protocol (DHCP) is the process by which Internet addresses

(192.168.***.***, or 10.***.*** *** in a very large internal network) are allocated to computers on an *internal* network. Internal networks are called subnetworks, or subnets. A DHCP address will start with 192.168 or 10.***, as these numbers represent the internal addressing system within a network. If you have an Internet Protocol (IP) address for a company but do not know which computer on its network was involved in an event, DHCP logs retrieved by the system administrator will tell you which computer on the network you are looking for.

The alternative to DHCP is if the system administrator designates every computer and device on an internal network by a specific IP address within the dedicated range.

An investigator may seek this information, for example, if they have an Internet Protocol (IP) address that links to a large corporate office from which an employee has been making threats to another person. The investigator has the evidence to point to the company, but does not know which of the many people in the organization is the person behind the threats. Speaking to the system administrator and providing the website in question and the time the threats were made provides the opportunity to check the internal network logs to identify who in the company was logged onto that website at the time the threat was made.

The system administrator will be able to see that the activity was generated by a person on their network with address 192.168.213.57 and will be able to identify the terminal the threat originated from. From there, suspect inquiries can be made, such as interviewing the person, conducting a digital examination of the device, and asking the victim if they know the person who was logged onto the device.

- ▪ **Cloud service providers.** Cloud computing is discussed in depth in Chapter 12. In general, a complainant or suspect may store evidence on a cloud server owned and operated by companies such as Apple, Dropbox, Amazon Web Services, Microsoft, and Cisco. Storage may be located throughout the world and the evidence sought may be spread across many data centers in different legal jurisdictions.

   Cloud-based evidence may include logs, documents, audio recordings, and the like. Subscriber details may include IP addresses used to log on and access cloud accounts, credit card details, and more.

- ▪ **Webmail accounts.** Webmail providers such as Gmail, Hotmail, and Yahoo offer free services to customers. Webmail accounts contain a large amount of data, including registration details, sign-up and log-on IP addresses, communication content, and address lists. For paid services, credit card or other payment details may be located. Accessing and seizing this evidence may be possible technically; however, if the service is hosted in foreign legal jurisdictions secured by different legislation, consent of the account owner, a court order, and/or the authority of the service provider may be required prior to accessing and seizing digital evidence, especially if the account belongs to a suspect. Obtain legal advice prior to downloading webmail accounts, especially those belonging to suspects.

- *Mail server logs and content.* A mail server records data on the internal email network and may contain evidence of the sending/receiving of emails from a network computer. Email accounts show relationships between parties, and the content of the communication may provide background for a line of inquiry. The metadata in the accounts may show information such as when an email was received, when it was opened, and who read it.

- *Privacy applications.* Look at the anonymity programs a person is using and determine whether they are consistent with their lifestyle and position. It may be that a person just wants to communicate with friends anonymously, but these programs are highly valued by criminals as a means to prevent law enforcement from monitoring their communications.

- *Device forensic examination.* A device may be fixed (desktop computer) or mobile (phone/tablet). Device forensics is the digital imaging of a physical electronic device containing potential evidence and the detailed examination for evidence of that copy of the image taken. A highly qualified and experienced person should be the only person to undertake this form of examination.

- *Network capture and forensic examination.* Network forensics captures data as it travels over a network the investigator has access to, particularly an internal corporate network. The connection will usually be wireless or via Ethernet connection (the blue cable attached to the back of a computer). The data captured may include evidence of an offense in progress, such as valuable files being removed over the network, or a suspect navigating through the network.

- *Internet of Things identification and digital forensics.* The Internet of Things (IoT) includes the many devices connected to a computer. Examples include the multitude of devices in a smart house or building connected to the network. Cities are now becoming highly connected, with numerous infrastructure devices such as traffic lights, street lighting, and road sensors being connected. Each of these devices may capture evidence of an offense, and the evidence available is only limited by the knowledge of the investigator as to what connected devices are in the crime scene, how they operate, and the evidence they collect.

Smart devices collect data and may send it to central servers. Commercial and residential buildings are being retrofitted to be managed by smart devices, which are sources of evidence. As a cybercrime scene may be anywhere technology is resident, the investigator may find that digital evidence may be gained from part of a city's infrastructure.

Wearable technology generates data, as do the smart devices. It may identify the activities of a person at a specific time. An introduction to the IoT is included in Chapter 13.

- *Proprietary applications and operating systems.* Not all applications are commercially available. Some companies develop their own software to suit their needs, and it is not used outside of their company or industry. When conducting a search, ask the complainant whether they are using proprietary software, and if so, obtain a copy of the application, which may be installed on the devices being examined back at the forensic laboratory. This will allow evidence to be viewed in its native form.
- *Instant messaging logs and content.* Instant Messaging (IM) logs show communication between parties that is recorded on the device. Suspects often communicate freely using online services, and an examination of communication logs may provide evidence of their involvement in an offense.

  Applications such as Skype are very popular. In some instances people record their conversations. Fraudsters often use these services without the use of the webcam and converse using written text. A detailed conversation may provide evidence of an offense, information about a suspect, or time logs for a conversation that link a person to a location at a specific time. Ensure that you know the time zone the chat logs are recorded in when comparing them to suspect activity. There are numerous forms of online chat applications available, many of which use encryption.
- *Online browsing history.* Internet history shows the web pages a user of a device has visited. It may also show Google searches and identify what the user of the device has been looking up. Homicide investigators have located such search queries as "How to kill a person" and "How to dispose of a body" from suspects' computer devices.
- *Documents.* Documents and spreadsheets may be stored in many places on a device. When using forensic software, open the pathway to the Documents folder, where you will find saved documents, spreadsheets, and the

like. Word and Excel documents will also be stored in other locations on the various drives internal and external to the network architecture.

Some criminals change the file extension of documents in the hope that should there be a search of their device, having a file extension different from the usual extensions of .doc or .docx for Microsoft Word documents will fool the forensic software and their criminal documents will not be located. For example, the default extension for a Word document would be identities.doc, while the criminal may manually change it to identities.exe.

The metadata in a document may show who created a document, when it was created and last accessed, and whether it was modified using a program such as Photoshop. This is particularly useful when people create or modify documents and deny doing so.

▪ **Multimedia.** Images and videos may be relevant to an investigation. They may also show evidence of the time a device is being used. On some occasions, metadata may be available to provide evidence of the date of creation of a document or when/where a photo was taken.

▪ **Online chat services and applications.** In chat rooms, people hide behind a user name and tend to speak very freely. If you can link a suspect to a user name, a chat room may provide very valuable evidence.

▪ **Peer-to-peer programs.** Peer-to-peer networks allow data to be shared among users from around the world. Examples of data shared include movies and music. These are generally illegal downloads and are often infected by malicious software, as this is a simple way to infect a person's computer.

▪ **Log evidence.** The number of logs available and how they may be used in your investigation is covered in Chapter 11. Several examples are also included in the beginning of this section.

▪ **Registry examination.** The registry contains data from the hardware and programs that operate on a Windows device. Examples of available data include settings and the software version being used. The registry is structured as a database.

▪ **Wireless access points.** A Wireless Access Point (WAP) is a place where a device can connect to the Internet. These are located in homes, businesses, coffee shops, libraries, and many other places. A WAP records details of the MAC address of a device with the wireless turned on. The MAC address originates from the Network Interface Card (NIC) on a user's device and is a unique identifier of that device connecting to a network. A device may have separate MAC addresses for wireless and Ethernet connections.

- **Bluetooth.** Mobile devices using Bluetooth leave behind unique identifiers, such as the MAC address. As is the case with a WAP, this identifier may prove a connection between devices and specify times of relevance to the investigation.
- **Geolocation data.** Location data may be built into a device or applications. It is common to find this form of evidence embedded in photos and communications. Applications may record all Global Positioning System (GPS) data, which can place your suspect at a specific location at a defined time.

  If you are using an online service such as an EXIF (Exchangeable Image File Format)finder, be aware that you are uploading that photo to an external service and are subject to their End User License Agreement (EULA), meaning that you may be losing control of that image subject to the EULA. Photoshop has a capacity to identify geolocation data and this can be examined within your device.
- **Online payment methods.** Details of connections to web payment services, such as money transfer agents.
- **Encrypted evidence.** Obtaining access to an encrypted folder or drive will be a priority for the investigator. Access codes and passwords may be obtained from a suspect at the beginning through a court order directing the device owner to pass over the password, through finding passwords written down on notepaper, or by other means. Locating passwords is a crucial activity to be aware of when conducting a search.
- **Computer coding.** Computer programmers develop distinctive traits in their programming. Some keep copies of blocks of their favorite code to use across multiple projects or because the code is very complex and took a long period of time and testing to make it work. In the comments fields of lines of code are unique comments from the programmer to explain what a line or block of code does, and these comments may be used to identify the creation of a block of computer program source code.
- **Open source, including social media accounts.** Social media is a goldmine of information about the activities and location of a person. Depending on the service, activities, associations and locations, and communication may be recorded. Through comments made, the state of mind of a person at the time of an offense may be shown.

  Accessing open social media networks of individuals may be allowed as evidence within your jurisdiction. Accessing locked data on social media may require legal advice prior to search and capture. Open source material is examined in Chapter 14.
- **Cryptocurrency accounts.** Many cybercriminals use cryptocurrency accounts, such as Bitcoin accounts, to assist in their trading or to move

the proceeds of their crimes. Be careful if you seize such an account resident on a device being examined, as the contents of the account can be of great value. Consider whether there is a need to have the password to the cryptocurrency wallet. Unless there is a specific need and you have a court order authorizing the seizure of the wallet, use caution, as you do not want any allegations from the suspect that the wallet was interfered with in your custody.

▪ **Networking hardware.** Networking hardware records a lot of user information and will provide the digital investigator with direction. The smart device a person carries connects to wireless routers, leaving the MAC address as a unique identifier.

Nontechnical and Physical Items

▪ **Device/network user names and passwords.** These are especially critical in obtaining access to devices and encrypted folders. These may be written down in a book, on a piece of paper, on a sticky note attached to a device or under a desk, and elsewhere. Taking the time to locate all passwords, not only the ones the device owner volunteers, will save you the time and stress later of finding a device without a password or a drive partition you cannot access.

▪ **Receipts.** These may be used to identify who purchased the specific device being examined, which will assist in proving ownership of the device.

▪ **User names.** User names will identify all of the different people who may use a specific device. For example, people on different shifts may use the same device; over the course of a week, five people may have used it. Identifying user credentials helps to narrow down activity on the device and the identities of users.

 User names are also used on online sites, including for social media and in chat rooms. As discussed previously, people may have an online user name that's used across many sites, providing you with a source of inquiry to identify their online activity.

▪ **Phone numbers.** Obtain all phone numbers associated with the scene and suspect. This may include mobile devices connected wirelessly to a network. Landline numbers are often used in cybercrimes to provide a level of legitimacy to the fraud. Obtaining an office contacts list will be of assistance.

▪ **Physical computer devices.** Physical computer devices include standalone computers, laptops, tablets, and other hardware devices. Also look at gaming consoles, which provide Internet access as well as storage capabilities.

- ▪ ***Mobile phones and devices.*** A mobile phone will often be the major way a person communicates online; therefore it will be one of the most significant sources of evidence for an investigator.
- ▪ ***External storage devices.*** External devices carry extensive amounts of storage. Often copies of backups are forgotten by the criminal or available in the deleted space on the disk. Figure 10.4 shows examples of different external storage devices that may be located. Note that at a scene, there may be many of these devices and each will need to be able to be uniquely identified and the location found documented, as you do not know which one may contain evidence.
- ▪ ***Printers, photocopiers, and cameras.*** Modern printers and photo-copiers contain internal hard drives that scan an image onto the drive before printing it. The scanned image may be recovered from the printer or photocopier.

This may help you obtain a large volume of documentation that has been printed or scanned. This is an often overlooked source of very valu-able evidence, which depending on the size of the hard drive and frequency

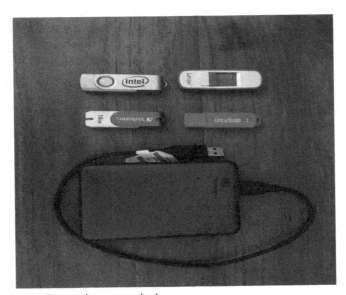

FIGURE 10.4 External storage devices.
Source: Photo © Graeme Edwards.

FIGURE 10.5 Printer.
Source: Photo © Graeme Edwards.

of use can show a timeline of activity in a subject organization or by an individual. While a suspect may have deleted all copies of the incriminating evidence, they may not have realized that the photocopier will have a complete history of their crime stored.

Figure 10.5 is an image of a photocopier/printer. Although this model does not contain an internal hard drive, when dealing with suspects, a photocopier is a very good place to seek evidence.

▪ ***Rubbish bins and confidential document collection bins.*** These contain documents discarded by the suspect and may contain valuable information. The criminal throws evidence away and may forget that it has not been collected for destruction or that the weekly trash has not been collected. Although going through someone else's trash may not be the most pleasant of tasks, it is worth it to locate a valuable piece of evidence that links a suspect to the crime and to develop new lines of investigation. Figure 10.6 shows examples of the extent to which you will be required to search for digital and physical evidence.

▪ ***Account registration details.*** Obtaining the registration details of account holders helps to identify who has been involved in setting up an account and may have continued access to it. For example, the person registering an account online cannot deny knowledge of it if they have had personal data such as that from a driver's license or credit card details

FIGURE 10.6   Rubbish bags containing potential evidence.
Source: Photo © Graeme Edwards.

submitted as a part of the registration process, unless they are going to claim identity theft.

- **_Financial account details._** Trace the money and you find the person behind the crime! Financial transactions today are carried out by many means, so include any details of the use of traditional banking services, money transfer agencies, PayPal, and other online payment services. Even the use of gift cards has become a very common method for criminals to transfer the proceeds of their crimes across international borders. Linking credit card details to the crime and activity seen on the card may provide evidence of further offending or of spending the proceeds of the crime. This may be used to seek seizure of tainted assets.

- **_Associated accounts._** A credit card may be linked to an online account providing direction to who the owner of the account is.

- **_Company organizational chart and phone list._** When dealing with a company that is suspected of conducting fraud, obtaining a company organizational chart will help to formally place each person within the organization, so that if a person you are interviewing states, for example, that they are merely a line manager and have no responsibility for decision making, the organizational chart will confirm or disprove that statement.

  The phone list provides a schedule of contact numbers of everyone in the organization and may provide phone numbers linked to your suspect that you were unaware of.

Evidence Capture and Handling

Digital evidence capture is the art of lawfully seizing evidence from a digital device in a manner that will be accepted by the court for its relevancy, completeness, and accuracy. Evidence is captured for the purpose of providing direction to an investigation, and when relevant, proving an ingredient of the charges before the court. Once digital evidence has been captured, it must be preserved in such a manner that the court can be assured of its authenticity and reliability. Should the evidence be captured and preserved in a manner that is not consistent with the laws of evidence of that jurisdiction, the risk exists that the court will not accept the evidence or accept it reluctantly and with reservations, downgrading its value.

As each legal jurisdiction has its own laws and precedents, this chapter will only provide a general overview of evidence capture and handling. It is the responsibility of the investigator and scene examiner to understand the laws and precedents of any jurisdiction in which they are operating.

The International Organization for Standardization (ISO) and the International Electrotechnical Commission (IEC) has produced standard ISO/IEC 27037:2012, Information Technology—Security Techniques—Guidelines for Identification, Collection, Acquisition and Preservation of Digital Evidence, which identifies the initial handling processes for digital evidence.[2] These processes relate to the:

- Identification of potential digital evidence
- Collection of potential digital evidence
- Acquisition of potential digital evidence
- Preservation of potential digital evidence

This ISO/IEC standard identifies four procedures to ensure that the integrity and reliability of potential digital evidence is maintained by following a series of fundamental principles.[2] These are:

1. Minimize the handling of original digital devices and digital evidence.
2. Account for any changes and document any actions taken.
3. Comply with the local rules of evidence.
4. The investigators should not take any actions beyond their level of competence.

As you review these procedures, you will notice that they are very similar to the ACPO principles introduced in Chapter 6 under "Protecting Digital Evidence."

We have discussed that the location of a cyber incident may be viewed as a crime scene by the court that ultimately hears a prosecution. The rules of evidence require that the digital evidence be treated with the same care and respect as evidence from a homicide scene, as the legal rules of evidence for both crime types are the same, although the offenses are obviously very different in nature and seriousness. Whoever presents evidence in a court is required to account for it to the required standard, with the integrity of the evidence being of critical consideration.

All data capture and handling must be consistent with the local rules of evidence of the relevant legal jurisdiction(s). Due to digital evidence potentially being resident across multiple legal jurisdictions, as is the case with cloud servers, there may be many jurisdictions, requiring that local rules of evidence and laws of evidence seizure in each instance be adhered to. As the potential exists to be questioned in court regarding the legality of the data capture methodologies used, the digital crimes investigator will need to make inquiries with lawyers to ensure that the laws of each jurisdiction are respected.

The cybercrime scene will provide both digital and physical evidence. A schedule of the potential evidence the investigator may locate was discussed earlier in this section, and illustrated in Figure 10.3. The digital evidence may be captured from a device, network, or through online sources. Each will potentially provide evidence and further avenues of inquiry.

The IR plan prepared by an entity pre-event will cover many components of the response to an incident or perceived threat. As previously mentioned, the first priority of the IR Team may be to mitigate and stop an attack, but such an approach may likely involve the destruction of valuable digital evidence that may be required for the review phase of the IR plan, management briefing, or prosecution once a suspect has been identified. In this instance, the IR team lead, who makes such decisions, must document the reasons for taking particular actions that destroy potentially valuable evidence and the environment that existed at that moment the decision was made. In hindsight their decision may turn out to be correct, but it needs to be accounted for in case their actions are challenged.

As the investigator examines the scene and potential evidence, special care and priority must go to understanding the volatility of the digital evidence, especially as the cybercriminal may still have physical or remote access to the device or network and begin destroying the evidence once they realize that they have been discovered. Also, as devices are shut down, potential evidence in memory will be lost. Depending on storage capabilities, logs may also be overwritten.

Digital investigators undertake specialist training in how to seize digital evidence in a forensically sound manner. They will also generally have a strong understanding of the rules of evidence of their jurisdiction and its requirements to account not only for the possession of the evidence but how it was obtained and preserved. The lead investigator must confirm the skills and qualifications of the digital investigator to ensure that they are qualified to undertake the tasks designated. As there are many forensic tools available for digital evidence capture, ensure that the digital investigator is qualified to use the tools they're using and will be able to account for their expertise should they be required to in a court of law. Examples of digital examination tools include Forensic Toolkit, EnCase, and those from Cellebrite.

In larger corporations or even cloud services, the forensic tools used may be proprietary to that corporation in that they have been designed internally and have never been subject to independent peer review. Identify whether the forensic software used has been independently validated against proprietary infrastructure, such as cloud servers.

It is preferable to have a qualified digital investigator present when seizing digital evidence, but this may not be the case in every instance. For example, you may attend to a scene where the evidence has been collected by the system administrator and stored on an external device. Alternatively, the investigator may be at a scene of a traditional investigation where there was no perception that digital evidence was going to be seized, when digital evidence they were unaware existed was located at the scene. This can extend to chance discovery when investigating an unrelated offense, such as a drug possession matter in which information related to the importation of drugs from a vendor on the criminal markets is located on a computer.

To assist with the capture and handling of digital evidence, ensure that the digital investigator is provided with a full briefing of the facts of the case before their attendance at the scene, thus ensuring that they know what they are trying to achieve and the investigation boundaries they are likely to encounter.

Having introduced the principles of evidence, the following section discusses how these principles should be identified and managed using the ISO/IEC 27037:2012 framework as a guide.[2]

Identification of Evidence

Identifying what may be an exhibit is not necessarily always clear cut. Cybercrime scenes come in many shapes and sizes, and exhibits do as well. Earlier in this chapter we identified examples of the different types of digital evidence that may exist; however, it is rare that all these will be relevant to all investigations.

Members of the investigation team will be briefed before entering the scene not only about the event that has brought them there but also which exhibits may contain evidence. However, as any experienced scene investigator will explain, chance findings or leads followed up on the initial lead may lead to further exhibits being located that were originally thought to be irrelevant or not thought of at all. Understand what you are able to seize by consent or court order.

Investigators must keep their mind open while conducting the scene investigation and identification of exhibits. While a court order may restrict what exactly can be taken from a suspect involved in the complainant's scene, evidence may be taken with the consent of the owner. However, beware if the suspect is an internal employee, as seizing their personal property (such as their mobile phone) or conducting a search of their desk may require legal consideration and direction from the company lawyers. Bring Your Own Device (BYOD) policies are particularly troublesome, as the device itself is owned by the employee with data and potential evidence belonging to the corporation resident upon it. If the suspect has committed the alleged crime using a BYOD computer, seeking early legal advice would be very advantageous to the investigation team. Looking in the employment agreement with the user may provide some guidance as to managing BYODs and the corporate data on them.

The evidence identified may be physical, such as a computer device, or logical, such as data captured over a network communication channel. For computer devices, identify and record the time on the devices, including time zones, as this will allow for synchronization of digital evidence, especially logs.

Once evidence has been identified, it must next be collected.

Collection of Digital Evidence

As we have discussed, evidence collected from a cybercrime scene must be relevant to the investigation, legal to possess, and seized with lawful authority (such as a court order or consent). An example of evidence that it would not be legal to possess would be a computer that has evidence of the crime being investigated (such as data theft) that later is identified to have Child Exploitation Material (CEM) stored on it. In this instance, contact police *immediately* for their advice and action. Should a device or other potential evidence not be seized, note the reasons.

Be aware of staff member safety when conducting a seizure of evidence, including when dealing with electrical devices. The physical location may pose a hazard, such as might be the case with the room in a suspect's home where the subject devices are being seized. As mentioned previously, cases exist of offenders hiding weapons in their rooms. Also electrical leads may be in poor condition, leading to the potential for a team member to be electrocuted or the room having loose flooring.

As exhibits are collected, understand the competence and experience of investigators in the roles they are undertaking. The role of exhibit manager, for example, is critical to any investigation, and the control of evidence from the commencement of a search to presentation to the court relies upon the competence and accuracy of the exhibits officer.

Once evidence has been seized, it is the responsibility of the investigation lead to maintain its security and integrity. The next topic is acquiring digital evidence from a network or from an operating physical device, such as a server or desktop computer.

Acquisition of Digital Evidence

Acquiring evidence involves capturing a logical or digital copy of the evidence from a network or physical device. A suitably trained and qualified person who knows exactly what they are doing should be the only person who does this.

The European Convention on Cybercrime allows for the capture of digital evidence that is in plain view online (check to see what your local legislation allows).[3] An example is the capture of a web page that is not restricted to view. This may be recorded and used as evidence using a program such as Microsoft's Expression Encoder or a web browser plugin. Once captured, it becomes evidence as much as any other item seized and should be documented and preserved.

As with a member of the IR team, the role of the digital examiner is a specialist role, and this book does not seek to define it in detail; many other books and courses can provide such a definition.

While investigators would like to seize every piece of digital evidence available, this may not be possible as the IR team contains and eradicates the attack threat. As cyber events come in many different forms and levels of severity, it is not possible to provide a working template to cover all the needs of the IR team and investigators. Communication and mutual respect for each other's roles will smooth any conflicts in this area. Be aware that you may be operating in a highly volatile environment in which corporate data is being lost and networks further infected by malicious software, meaning your requirements as an investigator may be placed behind protecting the network by the corporate decision makers.

Plan also to prevent the evidence from being altered in any way. This is particularly relevant to volatile digital evidence such as that in Random Access Memory (RAM) and Virtual Machines (VMs) where the evidence cannot be recovered. Discuss this activity with the digital investigator prior to leaving for the scene. Evidence may also be lost if a device is closed and the data sought was in an encrypted volume or device.

Identify the Order of Volatility of Digital Evidence

Digital evidence may be lost through routine events, such as logs being over-written and memory being shut down. A web browser that does not record logs will lose any trace evidence should it be shut down, including what the user had been looking at. Identify the evidence that may be subject to such a loss and plan its early capture with your forensic examiner.

An example of an order of volatility as provided by the Australian Computer Emergency Response (AusCERT) team is:[4]

1. Registers and cache
2. Routing tables
3. ARP (Address Resolution Protocol) cache
4. Process table
5. Kernel statistics and module
6. Main memory
7. Temporary file systems
8. Secondary memory
9. Router configuration
10. Network topology

A suggested process of electronic evidence capture is:

1. Photograph the evidence in situ (where it is), including capturing any images on screen.
2. Identify the order of volatility and follow guidance from the digital inves-tigator.
3. Allow the digital evidence investigator to secure the volatile evidence.
4. Keep the communication flowing from all sources, such as the IR team, scene manager, other searchers, and any other involved personnel.
5. Locate passwords and the like from the device or network owner/operator, sticky notes on walls, notebooks, and other locations. The ability to view data on suspect's devices may rely upon your work at the scene.

6. If the device is on, do not turn it off without the direction of the digital investigator. If it is off, leave it off and secure it as a physical exhibit.

7. Where appropriate, remove network access from the device being seized if it is on so remote action cannot affect it.

8. If there is a suspicion that a device is destroying evidence based on a command given by a suspect, external party, or other condition, seek the advice of the digital investigator; otherwise, crash the device by removing the power. This is a decision that can only be made in the individual circumstances.

9. Record all identifiers on devices, such as serial numbers, model and brand numbers, existing damage to the device, and even other identifiers (such as personal stickers) that can later be used to confirm the device was found at a specific location and under the possession of a specific person.

10. Keep devices away from anything that can damage the integrity of the stored data, such as water, electromagnetic discharge, and remote network access.

11. Cords and manuals are also valuable, as they will assist the digital investigator when back in their laboratory.

12. Document all your actions and ensure that the exhibits officer is aware of all evidence being taken. Each item is to have a unique identifier attached to it.

Once evidence has been collected and captured, it must be preserved to be able to maintain its integrity and prove its authenticity.

Preservation of Evidence

Preservation of evidence—protecting it from loss, damage, or tampering—is a key responsibility of members of the scene team. This is everybody's responsibility. Whatever activity is taken regarding the exhibits from the time of discovery through to presentation in court must be recorded. The team must also be able to explain to the satisfaction of the court why the evidence can be relied on and is in the same state as when discovered by explaining the maintenance of its integrity and authenticity, including the chain of custody.

A key task is to record the team member who located the exhibit, where it was found, and who seized it. The person locating it may be different from the person formally seizing it for examination, and it may help in smaller searches if one team member is designated as an exhibits officer who seizes all the evidence the scene search team locates. This assists in ensuring that the minimum number of people have access to exhibits and that they are appointed to be responsible for maintaining their integrity.

Once the decision has been made to seize an exhibit, take a photograph of it in situ, so that several years later you can recall exactly what the scene looked like and where that specific piece of evidence was located if necessary. Place a label on the exhibit recording the data, time of seizure, investigation identifier, person locating, and person seizing. Attaching an exhibit running sheet to the exhibit will help maintain the chain of custody.

The running sheet may also record:

- A unique identifier, such as a model and serial number. This can be linked to the item number on the property receipt register issued at the scene when the exhibit was first seized.
- Who accessed the exhibit, and the time and location at which it was found and seized.
- Who has had custody of the exhibit throughout the time it has been held.
- Where the exhibit has been stored, especially once it has been taken away from the scene.
- Who checked the evidence in and out from storage, and when and why it was done.
- Specialist examinations conducted on the exhibit (if any), such as fingerprint or digital examination, along with the details of the person moving the exhibit.
- Who returned the exhibit to the storage facility and the time it was returned.
- Damage to the exhibit (if applicable), how it occurred, when it was discovered, and who discovered it. Also record the extent of the damage.

From this report, the chain of custody report for each exhibit should be able to be prepared. This will be very handy if you are questioned about the exhibit in court.

 ## SCENE INVESTIGATION

After having discussed the general principles of evidence seizure, the remainder of this chapter introduces and discusses the practicalities of scene examination. First we will discuss initial actions prior to leaving for the scene.

Prior to Leaving for the Scene

In preparation for a successful search, an investigation plan is required so that everyone will understand the circumstances of the search/examination, why they are there, what they are looking for, what everyone's tasks are, and the legality of their actions. Topics that may be included in preparation for attending the scene are covered in the sections that follow.

Staff Safety

Before beginning any scene investigation/examination, consider staff safety, especially when attending at a location where a suspect may be present. People who realize that they have been caught committing a serious offense react in many different ways, and their reaction sometimes includes violence or seeking to physically destroy evidence. Desperate people may make desperate decisions.

Where feasible, when attending to a business crime scene, speak to management and identify whether there are any suspects within the organization and whether there are any potential risks to the safety of the investigation team. This may include staff members who have a history of violence or poor behavior in the workplace, or a history of abusing alcohol, prescription medication, and/or illegal drugs. The time spent making these inquiries may be seen as an investment in the safety of your team, yourself, and any others present.

Are There Weapons Present?

The definition of a weapon is very broad and can include any object a person could use to cause injury to a member of the IR team, investigation team, or any other person. It could also be used against any person present as the suspect tries to leave the scene.

Suspects know their homes and workplaces well and occasionally will position weapons where they can reach them if necessary. When searching homes, for reasons unknown, many conversations are held in kitchens where knives are present. Ideally, move any conversation away from locations where weapons are visible and remove any obvious temptations; for example, place knives in a drawer or the dishwasher, or secure them with the investigation team as circumstances and experience dictate.

In a law enforcement environment, police will usually have the authority under a court order to restrict the movement of persons at a location where they are executing the search warrant. A civil search and seizure order may not contain such authority, requiring search members to ensure their personal protection through observation and using their communication skills. If there is a potential threat of violence in the execution of a civil search order, consider asking police to attend to ensure the safety of all concerned.

Pre-search Briefing

Conduct a pre-search team briefing so everyone understands all the circumstances of the event under investigation and their roles. Present any safety risks and mitigation strategies. Share intelligence about the location, search, evidence, and individuals, as well as the known facts of the cybercrime.

Legality of Attendance

Understand and explain the legality of your attendance at the location and your actions. This may be by court order or consent of the party under control of the location and evidence. Ensure that you and your team understand the powers that court orders provide.

Each country has their own laws regarding search and seizure of evidence, and such legislation will provide guidance as to the legality of your actions. For example, in the United States the Fourth Amendment to the Constitution provides society with safeguards against unreasonable search and seizure.

Is the Suspect Likely to Be Present?

In the initial stages of an investigation, you will most likely not know who the suspect is or even whether that person is an internal employee. Many police investigations have interviewed the offender in the initial interview phase and did not identify them as a potential suspect until weeks later. This is not a failing, as it highlights the fact that in the initial stages of an investigation you will have very limited knowledge of all the different individuals and relationships you will be dealing with. You will also likely have limited evidence to direct your investigation to who the suspect may be or to what the exact details of the offense may be.

If a person is named as a suspect with evidence supporting this claim, the civilian investigator may wish to consider their options. If you are dealing with an investigation likely to be referred to police, an option is to leave the suspect interview to police, who are highly skilled at suspect interviews. Alternatively, you may interview the person if a member of your team has the skills, but remember that you will be conducting a suspect interview in a serious matter with limited information, which may mean many valuable questions will not be asked. Although this is not always the case, suspects usually only interview once and the skilled investigator will want to make sure that they have all the information they need. Interviews are discussed in more detail in Chapter 16.

Plan for Evidence Control and Capture, and for Preservation of Its Integrity

As not all scenes you attend will involve an IR team, plan to prevent any person from interfering with the evidence. Control the movement of people in the scene and you will go a long way toward controlling the preservation of the physical evidence. When dealing with a situation in which the suspect is possibly present, even apparently innocent action such as a person using their phone may hinder your evidence capture, as they may be sending a prepared code to an associate to destroy potential evidence. Ensure the suspect has no direct or indirect access to digital devices, including remote access via mobile devices.

When devices are cloud based, any person can access the service with a mobile device. Therefore, while you and your team are at a scene, a suspect or their associate could use cloud-based services to delete the crucial evidence you are seeking. Mobile phones may contain a remote wiping service through features such as Find my iPhone.

Plan also to prevent the evidence from being altered in any way. This is particularly relevant to volatile digital evidence, such as that in RAM and VMs, that cannot be recovered. Discuss this activity with the digital investigator prior to leaving for the scene. Evidence may also be lost if a device is closed and the data sought was on an encrypted volume or device.

Evidence may also be damaged by innocent actions such as storing digital devices near liquids or electromagnetic sources. Static electricity may damage digital evidence, and securing devices in bags, boxes, or Faraday bags will assist in the preservation of the integrity of the evidence. Prevent the potential for electromagnetic discharge damaging the digital evidence by touching a safe metal object to remove any static electricity on your person prior to picking up the digital evidence. In a perfect situation, there will be no changes to the status of the evidence obtained; however, if there is, document it immediately and explain the reasons why changes were made.

Some suspects especially concerned about the potential of being identified build a kill switch into devices, so if law enforcement or another investigator seeks to seize the device as evidence, they can press the kill switch, which will delete the data or encrypt the device. This is in effect a panic switch of last resort, used when the cybercriminal has no opportunity to manually defend their device. Depending on the circumstances of your search and whether you are attending a scene where a suspect is likely to be, this may be a very relevant consideration.

What Time of the Day Will the Scene Search Be Conducted?

The investigation team called into a corporate environment will often attend during business hours. This is when the bulk of the employees are present and attempting to do their daily tasks. The attendance of an IR and investigation team will likely cause great concern to employees as they see a lot of activity they may have only previously seen on TV, such as computers being imaged and friends being interviewed, and the general dynamics of the IR and investigation teams going about their business.

There is no set answer to the question of whether you should conduct your investigation of a corporate crime scene during business hours or after, as circumstances such as working with the IR team and the availability of witnesses to interview will drive this decision. However, management may request that certain activities, such as interviews, be conducted after hours so that witnesses will have a mind clear of the distractions of their daily duties. This is examined in more detail in Chapter 16. Other issues, such as the need for a prompt response and resources availability, will influence law enforcement searches.

Can the Scene Be Isolated from Bystanders?

In your preparation to conduct your investigation and examination, you will plan for a clear environment in which to work. However, this is not always possible, as you take your crime scenes as you find them. Removing everyone away from a location so that your digital investigator can image devices and other items can be seized may be considered best practice, but when a company needs to keep operating, you may have to plan to work in the environment as best you can while recording notes of the circumstances in which you are operating. The civilian client invites the investigation team into the workplace, and although you are in charge of working the scene, management may require that the scene not be entirely shut down as you would wish. Law enforcement officers responding to a complaint may require a location to be shut down and this would be a separate discussion.

Prepare for the Possibility of People Arriving at the Scene during the Search

Crime scenes are dynamic, and it is not an uncommon occurrence for a search to be undertaken and for people to walk into the scene partway through the search. Generally this is not a problem, as notes recorded will account for this occurring. Particularly in a corporate office, people may arrive from meetings elsewhere totally unaware that an IR and investigation team has been working in the office for the past two hours, and they will need a short briefing as to what is happening. Prepare for this possibility and have a designated officer tasked with meeting and recording their details.

Be Aware of Any Natural or Other Physical Hazards, Such as Exposed or Damaged Electricity Connectors, Rainwater, Leaking Pipes, and the Like

Not all crime scenes are in professional corporate offices, and the circumstances of your investigation will dictate where you work. Suspect's homes are highly variable, and we have discussed potential safety hazards. Be aware of loose or damaged wires and other routine hazards, including items spread around a room, insecure flooring, and so on. Water leaks are their own danger and magnetic devices may be a hazard to digital devices.

Have a Provisional Understanding of the Scene Boundaries

Document the provisional boundaries of the scene to be examined and provide a briefing to team members on the nature of the offense, the evidence being looked for, the known risks, and those that may occur, and identify the scene exhibits officer as well. This briefing may include what evidence is being seized, which will be governed by whether the search is by consent (as in the case of a complainant) or under the authority of a court order (such as when searching a suspect's resident or location of business).

Designate Team Roles

As discussed previously, ensure that all team members have been briefed on the safe way to handle digital evidence; alternatively, have team members locate digital exhibits and the designated exhibits officer (who is trained in digital evidence seizure) physically secure exhibits. Ensure they have the resources to undertake their duties.

Identify an exhibits officer who will handle evidence from inception to presentation in court. This may be their only duty on a large team, or this responsibility may be delegated in conjunction with other duties on smaller teams. Do not neglect the potential consequences of poor evidence-handling procedures.

Understand and Obey the Rules of Evidence

Even if this is a regular feature of your work, ensuring a competency in updated legislation and case law is advantageous.

Work within the Boundaries of Your Knowledge

No one is an expert on everything, so do not be afraid to ask for assistance. It is not a sign of weakness to ask others, even more junior staff, for advice. As you engage specialists to assist in the search/examination, allow them to do their jobs without a need to display authority. This applies to briefings as well as attendance at the scene.

Plan for Dealing with Large Volumes of Online Data to Be Seized

For example, downloading terabytes of data from cloud servers takes a very long time, even on high-quality networks. To ensure the chain of custody, an experienced digital investigator will be required to be present, or have a methodology available to prove that no person had the capacity to interfere and denigrate the quality of the evidence. This question can be decided in discussions with the complainant using the benefit of your experience. Note the reasons why evidence was not collected and be prepared to be challenged in court should potential evidence not be collected because of the cost involved.

Live capture should be used to record data as it moves through a network without shutting the network down. This is particularly valuable in circumstances in which a business needs to continue operating while the IR and investigation teams operate.

Any examination of digital evidence should be by a qualified digital investigator. There have been many cases where investigators have had a "quick look" at a device to see if evidence is there, which changes log files within the device.

What Evidence Not to Collect

There is a cost to collecting digital evidence, and it may take significant time, resources, and expense to collect evidence lawfully from cloud servers. A decision about how much evidence should be seized and what to leave behind and not capture needs to be made. This is a very difficult balancing act, as what you leave behind may be the very evidence defense counsel decides was the crucial evidence that would clear their client. Having team members on site incurs significant costs, especially with experienced digital investigators.

Once you have planned for the search/examination, the next process is attendance at the location.

Scene Action by Investigators

The actual scene examination covers the principles and strategies included in the preceding section; however, we now look at the actual examination the lead investigator will direct. As we mentioned earlier, the location where a criminal offense occurs is a crime scene, so should the event ultimately end up in a court of law you will be held to the same level of accountability regarding evidence location, seizure, collection, handling, and examination as any detective.

While we think that the cybercrime scene will be an office, it could be a person's device if an employee was working from home. It could also be a location external to the business if the company has outsourced their information technology to a specialist company. As another option, the scene could be evidence located in a vehicle placed there by a suspect. As we discuss in Chapter 12, the crime scene could be a cloud-computing service. In these cases, your response may be guided by the legal contracts and service agreements with the third party and/or cloud-computing provider.

Should your search be at a large corporate office, break the search area into components and assign these components to your team members, recording who is assigned to which component. One way of searching a designated area is to search in a clockwise direction after designating a specific point as the location to commence your search. This may be the left-hand side of a specific desk and covering all the area to a specific filing cabinet, where the adjacent search team is commencing their search.

While searching desks and cabinets, do not forget to search floors, under desks, and the floor area under cabinets and the area above these items. It may be that because it makes no sense for valuable data to be stored in a particular location (such as the one under a filing cabinet), it may make perfect sense to the person who was in possession of the incriminating data and looking for a place people would not bother looking at because it was unlikely or difficult to move. Remember, the motivation of the person hiding the evidence may be greater than members of the search team to find it, as they are facing a potential term of imprisonment should the key evidence against them be located.

Evidence identification and preservation are primary considerations and respect for the rules of evidence of the jurisdiction(s) you are working in must be a primary goal of the investigation. The end game for initial action at a cybercrime scene or when seizing a digital device containing potential evidence is a court where the rules of evidence will be applied to your actions. You will be held to the same standards as those for the investigation of a serious crime, in which a qualified detective locates, preserves, seizes, and examines evidence.

From the beginning, the cyber investigator will have many duties to perform to gain an understanding not only of the event they are investigating, but the crime scene, its dynamic nature, witnesses, and locations of potential evidence. The initial interview with the complainant, as detailed in Chapter 7, may provide some of this information, but it is just as likely that the manager providing the briefing has little understanding as to what has taken place. As the investigator takes control of the scene and commences the crime scene management, it is worth remembering that every action they take and every decision made may be subject to questioning in court several years later should a suspect be identified and prosecuted in a civil or criminal court. In this instance, the volumes of notes recorded during the examination will be a very valuable source of assistance in refreshing your memory as to what was done, when, why, and by whose authority.

On-Scene Safety Assessment

As has been mentioned previously, safety is a paramount consideration through all aspects of the search/examination. The team leaders as well as all team members present will be constantly assessing it. On scene, safety assessment does not start and finish when you arrive at the location. It is to be constantly evaluated through the search and it is not a responsibility solely owned by senior members of the team but by all team members.

From the start, you will ensure the safety of staff at the scene. While digital crimes may not carry the same perceived level of threat to investigators as a drug raid, risks may still exist. As we have mentioned, cornered suspects sometimes make panicked decisions. For example, should the cybercriminal be discovered to be an internal staff member unlawfully stealing IP, there is no telling what their actions may be, including potentially assaulting members of the investigation team, once they see they have been identified.

Also understand when attending at a suspect's address with a court order to search for, locate, and seize evidence, they will commonly feel threatened. Being in their home is invading the location they feel most secure and a search team arriving may be seen as very threatening and challenging. A house is full of potential weapons and the suspect knows where they all are, ranging from knives in kitchens and other rooms to firearms hidden through the house.

Introduce Yourself and the Team to All Required Persons

If attending by the authority of a court order, ensure it is present and is available for viewing, as required by the laws of your jurisdiction. As required, provide safeguards to suspects, such as a right to silence, access to legal advice, and the ability to contact their union representative. These will be also be guided by the legislation in your jurisdiction.

If present by consent, meet with the person who invited you. Chapter 7 identifies areas of interest to discuss with the complainant and Chapter 16 discusses areas to discuss with suspects and witnesses. Continue to conduct threat analysis at all stages as long as you are present at the location.

Control Activity

When arriving at the location, control the scene, people, and access to evidence. As discussed previously, this will vary depending upon the circumstances of your presence, as you will not be as direct with the staff of the complainant as you would be with a suspect.

Photograph the Scene and Evidence Located

Taking a series of photographs of the crime scene when it is first located allows a potential judge and jury to understand the layout of the scene and where the evidence was located. It also serves as a memory prompt to the investigator should they be required to give evidence in a future court hearing.

As further evidence is located throughout the search, photograph it in situ (where it is) before moving. Link all evidence seized to the exact location it was found. This is a valuable investigation tool and shows suspects before they have time to react to what is happening.

Avoid using your own phone, as in some jurisdictions defense may subpoena your phone to extract their own copy of the images.

When dealing with a suspect device, recording what is on the screen may be a valuable source of evidence. Should it be a suspect's computer, seeing what windows are open and what can be seen without clicking on links may provide direction to an investigation and to the location of future evidence. For example, a suspect's computer may be open to a webmail account that no one knew about or a victim's computer may show a ransomware demand.

List what is attached to a suspect device, such as Ethernet cables, a mouse, a keyboard, and storage devices. If necessary, draw a configuration diagram showing how devices are connected to the network. Record unique identifiers for devices, such as make, model, and serial numbers.

Photograph all cords and connections to the devices. Seize the cords and chargers, especially when the device is uncommon. The digital investigator may need to charge the device back in the office and not have the required charger. Tag all devices so you can remember which cables belong to which device.

Fingerprinting of Evidence

Depending on the case, evidence may be need to be fingerprinted. This is a specialist process in law enforcement and specialist officers undertake these duties. At the scene, if an item of evidence needs to be fingerprinted, use gloves and pick up the item by the edges at the places least likely to have been touched by an offender. Secure the item so that no other team member can touch it and mark the bag with a label such as "Exhibit to be fingerprinted" prior to securing it in order to alert all team members that the exhibit should be treated with particular care.

Document All Activity

Crime scenes can be very chaotic places, with decisions made on the run as to preserving evidence, interviewing witnesses, and controlling the scene. Decisions made in the heat of the moment may be correct with the very limited information available, but later prove to be incorrect once more information becomes available. While everyone has 20/20 vision once an event is under control and all the information is available, the scene investigator does not have the luxury of postponing all decisions until all information is available and has to work with what they have and balance that against their experience.

If a decision made in the heat of the moment proves incorrect, documentation recorded at the time will show it was made with limited information and in good faith, and that it may have been a prudent decision at the time given the limited information available. Should detailed notes not have been recorded throughout the decision-making process, justifying what time shows to have been an incorrect decision leaves the investigator open to claims of incompetence or of deliberately destroying evidence.

Understand the Requirements of an Investigation

In the initial briefing with management, understand exactly what they want you to do and the boundaries they want you to operate within. While there is always the presumption an investigation may end up in a courtroom, a manager should be able to tell you exactly what they want investigated. For example, they may only want you to investigate the intrusion against the web server and not to spend any time looking at the email server, which, they believe, was not affected in an attack.

As a civilian investigator, the initial terms of engagement document should present the boundaries of the investigation and related information, such as time available, internal support available, and so on.

Managerial Support, Including Human Resources and Legal

At a corporate scene, having the support of management eases the pathway for the investigator. They can provide prompt decisions, allocation of resources, access to key staff, and redefine the boundaries of the investigation as the need dictates.

As the search is being undertaken, make the effort to keep communication channels open between managers and the investigators undertaking the search. They will be interested to get any feedback regarding the value of evidence they are seizing and whether there are any new avenues of inquiry originating from the search. This also helps in keeping the searchers motivated, knowing their work is valued and contributing to the overall investigation.

The HR department and legal officers in the organization have access to very valuable information when you are investigating an incident involving an internal suspect.

Allow for the Continuation of the Business of the Client while Evidence Is Being Collected

Few businesses will want to close down while the cyber investigation is undertaken, as being offline costs money. Also, internal investigations can be very intrusive and disturbing to staff members, who may have concerns to the future of the company. It is the role of the investigator to discuss these matters with a senior manager to plan a response to allow a company to continue trading while the investigation is undertaken.

Explain to the staff what is going on and the need for their cooperation. Explain why certain activity, such as the imaging of computers, is going on. If you do not explain to staff what is happening and why, rumors will start, and people will develop their own theories and their level of cooperation may be reduced.

Confirm the Location of the Offense within the Larger Scene

Confirm exactly where the crime scene is. It may be a physical location, such as a computer on a desk in an office, an internal network, or a cloud server located in a foreign legal jurisdiction.

In some locations, the area to be searched may be a large office containing a series of offices along a hallway. Each needs to be treated as potential locations of evidence and defined as such. An action as simple as that included in Figure 10.7 clearly defines an office on the scene map and can be linked to evidence located within it.

Just because you are conducting a high-tech investigation does not mean a low-tech solution cannot be very effective. Use it when necessary.

Methodical Search

Methodically search the location and find the evidence and record details of the search and exhibit seizure.

FIGURE 10.7 Identifier of hallway office.
Source: Photo © Graeme Edwards.

Computer as an Exhibit

If you are seeking to examine a computer, at first leave it where it is and call in the digital investigator. If the device is turned off or locked down, do not turn it on. If the device is on, photograph the device and what is on the screen, even if there are no tabs open. Some jurisdictions will allow you to open the tabs on the device for viewing and photographing, although you will need to balance that against the need to have minimal interaction with the device before the digital investigator begins their work.

If the evidence you are seizing has any damage, photograph this before it is seized so that no allegation can be made that the damage was caused by the investigation team. Your entry in your notes and property schedule could read: "iPhone seized with cover. Home button damaged."

Figure 10.8 is an example of a device showing damage that was present when located.

Digital Evidence Order of Volatility

Create an order of volatility of digital evidence. This is discussed earlier in this chapter, under "Acquisition of Digital Evidence."

FIGURE 10.8 Image of damaged iPhone.
Source: Photo © Graeme Edwards.

Encryption

Without keys, encryption will cause problems. As the scene investigation is undertaken, locating any potential sources of passwords will assist the digital investigator back at their laboratory as they attempt to gain access to the device and evidence. Keys may be provided by a device owner/controller, or located on pieces of paper, in a notebook, or on a sticky note stuck under a desk.

If a device is operating, the forensic examiner may conduct a live acquisition of the RAM as keys may be resident in plain text.

Sketch Map of Scene If Required

A sketch map of the scene and evidence located may be very valuable when identifying exactly where evidence was located. This will support the scene photographs.

Who Is Present at the Scene?

Scenes may vary greatly and knowing who was present at a specific time allows the investigator to understand the scene: who belongs in it, who is a visitor, and who was not present.

Identify Potential Suspects (Are They Present?)

Identify suspect(s) to reduce the potential for them to damage evidence. Remember that digital evidence may be remotely wiped. As an example, a person in the office may phone a colleague who is at a client's office to let them know an investigation team is looking at their computer, unaware that the person they are calling is a suspect. As previously discussed, upon being alerted the suspect may be motivated to remotely wipe the drive using a cloud-based application.

Locate Passwords

As with looking for encryption passwords, these may be stored in notebooks or on sticky notes attached to a device. USB devices can also contain sets of passwords. You may also ask the person operating a device for the password.

Identify Potential Witnesses and Availability (Digital Recording Where Local Laws Allow)

Some witnesses may need to be interviewed at the time of initial engagement. For example, a key witness may be about to leave the following day with no contact possible for the following month.

Who Is Not Present We Need to Interview?

Key witnesses may not be present and may need to be contacted urgently. For example, the system administrator may be on leave and have valuable evidence regarding the network, its design, and previous security events.

How Do Workers Access the Scene?

Should a device be present at a scene where there is concern that the attack was initiated by an internal employee, obtaining electronic records of staff entering the scene at the subject time may assist in confirming who was present at the time of the event occurring. A physical key may be required for access; however, a Radio Frequency Identification (RFID) swipe card will be very useful for the investigator, as there may be a log entry of swipe cards gaining access that will show whose card was used and the time access was gained.

For example, if logs show data was removed from a device in the early evening, security logs may show who was still present at the location. Also consider CCTV footage showing persons entering and leaving the premises; this can be read along with device/network access authentication logs.

Obtain an Employee List

Having a full list of staff and where they work helps to identify potential suspects and witnesses.

Identify Subject Devices

In a network attack much of the corporate infrastructure may be touched by an attacker. There may be initial confusion as to which device(s) have been compromised and this will need to be managed at the scene with system administrators and the IR team.

In some instances, the subject device may have been removed from the network and secured awaiting the arrival of the investigation team, meaning the hard work of identifying the breached device has already been done.

Who Has/Had Access to the Scene and Subject Devices?

Computers are usually accessed by passwords; however, it is not uncommon for staff to share passwords or for a device to have a generic password. Should a device have a shared or generic password, identifying a suspect may prove very difficult. If the password is left on a piece of paper next to the device, your list of suspects extends beyond those authorized to access the device.

Record Witness Comments and Details Regarding Who They Are, Access, Job Title, and the Like

Identify who is the usual user of a subject device and whether anyone else uses it. For example, some offices are becoming focused on hot desking to reduce costs.

User/Administration Access

What level of access to a subject device does a user have? Do they have administrator or general user access?

Evidence Preservation and Seizure

Treat all items seized as potential evidence in court and obey the rules of evidence for each item, regardless of its initial perceived value.

All evidence is to be tagged and secured with unique identifiers. Use antistatic bags and record who secured the exhibit, when, and where.

As discussed, property receipts are to be issued for all evidence seized and the exhibits officer's receipt and the receipt of the person from whom the property is being seized should both show a full and accurate description of the property and should agree. Providing a copy to the property owner is good practice.

Where there are numerous exhibits in a series of locations (such as a suite of offices) it is possible for exhibits to be overlooked or left behind when you leave. This is a logistical mistake caused by human error when people are under stress or involved in numerous matters, as scenes can be a volatile location. To prevent this from occurring, brief the exhibits officer to exactly detail every item they are seizing with the person from whom it is being seized prior to leaving the location. Cross-reference the exhibits schedule against the property receipt and physically compare it to the physical exhibit or digital capture. This is good practice, as it provides the opportunity to confirm the accuracy of the property receipt you are issuing to the property owner or custodian. Ensure that the original evidence is subject to minimal handling.

Transporting evidence from the location is a further requirement of the scene and exhibits manager. Prior to leaving for the scene, have a designated secure storage facility where all evidence is to go once you return to your office. Once evidence is seized it must be accounted for until presented in court and a decision is made as to what happens to it from there.

Obtain Statements Preserving the Chain of Custody

Preserve the chain of custody of all exhibits by obtaining statements straight off while people's memory is still fresh.

Digital Examination of Subject Devices with External Specialist Support

Suitably qualified examiners must be the ones to make digital investigations of evidence located at the scene. In some instances the subject device may be copied and examined at the crime scene, with mobile forensic devices (such as Cellebrite's mobile software examination device) being commonly used.

Network Records and Time Synchronization

Where evidence is being obtained across a network, record the times and zones of all devices and software operating off of it. This is particularly relevant for investigations involving cloud evidence, where different providers may provide software from across different time zones.

Possession of Intellectual Property

When seizing Intellectual Property the investigator is responsible for ensuring that it is secure and that they do not lose possession of it. Consider encrypting it for safekeeping.

External Storage Devices

Identify storage media that may contain evidence. Identify devices in smart buildings and homes that may record evidence. Speak to the digital and lead investigator to determine whether the digital evidence from smart devices that may assist in the investigation can be legally seized.

Security of Digital Evidence

Keep all electronic devices separate from electromagnetic signals that may damage the evidence.

Notes

Ensure all steps taken by all investigators are thoroughly documented. These documents may be evidence in their own right and be subject to critical examination.

Digital Evidence Examination

The digital investigator will image the devices seized using a write blocker in their laboratory. Never view a device at the scene, as a quick check to see if evidence is there when deciding to seize an exhibit or not will damage the forensic integrity of the device.

Seize Any Backups That May Involve the Suspect's Device

Where a mobile device is seized, place it in flight mode, recording this action in your notes. A Faraday bag is a special device designed to reduce the ability of a mobile device to access a network, preventing an opportunity for a suspect to remotely wipe the device in transport. You can also remove the SIM card.

Identify the location of the evidence, finder, serial number device, model number, hostname, MAC address (where possible), IP address (where possible), time, date of seizure, photo of exhibit in situ, and snapshot of system prior to remediation.

Verify and account for all evidence being seized with the person from whom it is being taken. This may be a complainant, witness, or suspect.

Final Inspection Prior to Leaving

Conduct a final inspection to ensure that nothing has been left behind, such as investigators' notebooks, evidence, personal mobile phones, and so on. All of these items have been left at crime scenes before, requiring a hurried return to the location to recover an item.

Identifying the Network Architecture

When an investigation requires an understanding of the flow of data throughout a network, creating or obtaining a network architecture topology assists the investigator visually understand the system infrastructure. This understanding helps the investigator locate potential points of evidence collection and open new lines of inquiry.

This sort of inquiry would be relevant when the investigator needs to understand how an attacker worked their way through a network from the time of breaching the corporate firewall to locating and removing data.

A network system administrator may have a topology diagram or be able to produce one from network tools or their own resources.

Corporate network architectures can be very complex. The history of the organization may show a series of system administrators building on the work

FIGURE 10.9   Network cabling.
Source: Photo © Graeme Edwards.

of each other. Also, there will be series of switches, routers, and Ethernet cables connecting switches to physical devices through walls and following pathways that cannot be seen.

Figures 10.9 through 10.12 show how complex portions of the cyber scene can be when dealing with a large corporation. While this will not always be what you find and may not even be relevant to your investigation, should you find a scene like this, depending on the circumstances there may be a requirement to have at least an understanding of how the data travels through this network from a switch to a compromised physical device. Remember, this is all evidence and the defense lawyer has the right to ask questions in court about this evidence should they decide to.

This will be particularly relevant in an investigation when a person has placed a physical device on the network with the aim of capturing all data as it travels through the network.

FIGURE 10.10 Ethernet cabling.
Source: Photo © Graeme Edwards.

Figure 10.9 shows a potential starting point should you be required to formally map your network. The network administrator should be able to provide valuable support and direction in this instance.

You may find post-incident that an organization takes the opportunity to invest in their network architecture and cyber security. The corporation that Figures 10.9 through 10.12 relate to took such an opportunity.

The following is a list of questions the investigator should ask the complainant's IT staff to assist in understanding the architecture.

Network Diagrams

A network diagram will show the architecture of a network. The diagram should show all devices; however, in some cases a criminal will attach a device to capture network traffic that is not recorded on any network diagram.

A network map shows the devices connected to a network. Devices connected to a Local Area Network (LAN) identify themselves through the MAC

FIGURE 10.11 Tracing Ethernet cabling 1.
Source: Photo © Graeme Edwards.

address unique to each communication channel on a device. For example, a laptop computer connected to a LAN may have a unique MAC address for the Ethernet connection and a separate MAC address if the connection is through a wireless channel.

As mentioned previously, devices also have a subnet address beginning with the IP address (for example, 192.168.***.***). These numbers are mapped to the router. Within the router is a routing table that connects the MAC address (28:cf:e9:22:e7:b5) and subnet address (192.168 .212.75).

The investigator who is studying the traffic on a network originating from IP address 192.168.212.75 can see it belongs to the device with the address 28:cf:e9:22:e7:b5. Inquiries may then be undertaken to locate this physical device, which may take several minutes or longer depending on the number of devices connected to the router.

A wireless network allows users within a network to access the services of the organization without having to connect via an Ethernet cable. Users

FIGURE 10.12   Tracing Ethernet cabling 2.
Source: Photo © Graeme Edwards.

operate off the internal IP address range (192.168.***.***) and leave the network through a central IP address (such as 207.123.***.***).

Within a network, there are two ways a device within the network can obtain an internal IP address. The first is the system administrator or an equivalent person allocating an IP address to a specific MAC address within the routing table.

The other way is (as referenced earlier) DHCP, where devices allowed onto an internal network are allocated internal IP addresses without the direct hands-on intervention of the system administrator. This is common in large networks where there are literally too many devices for internal addresses to be allocated individually.

These internal addresses travel throughout the network and will be captured by the forensic investigator should they need to examine network traffic. The system administrator will be able to direct you to identify which device a specific IP address is allocated to.[5]

Public IP Address Range

The IP address range is the range of IP addresses the public may use to access the organization. Asking the system administrator or searching domain registration search sites (such as centralops.net) can yield valuable information.[5]

Private/Internal IP Addressing

This is the range of subnetted IP addresses within an organization that external parties do not see or have access to. In the example cited above, this range of addresses would start with 192.168 and the number of addresses will be dictated by the needs of the organizations and the size of the subnetwork created.[5]

Remote Access Point

A remote access point is a hardware device that allows a user to connect a wireless device to a wired network. An example of a remote access point is a router.[5]

Domain Name Servers

A Domain Name Server (DNS) serves as the pathway from a user within a network and the Internet. When a user seeks to go to a website they have not been to before, they do not know the pathway. The DNS server will receive the request, locate the web address the user is seeking, and send a reply with the address to the user's device. The user may then connect to the web address.[5]

Demilitarized Zone Systems

A demilitarized zone (DMZ) is the external-facing portion of a network, such as a web server. The only data that can be viewed is that which the owner has specifically allowed to be viewed, meaning that external visitors cannot directly access private corporate data.[5]

Domain Controllers

A domain controller operates within a Microsoft Windows environment responding to security authentication requests. Examples of requests include passwords and the permissions of a user to access specific resources, including data.[5]

Servers/Databases

Servers and databases contain corporate data of value to an attacker. A cybercriminal may seek to steal copies of the data, delete the data, or modify it. The latter strategy is particularly damaging to a company, as they make decisions based on the accuracy of data stored on a database.[5]

Email Systems

Email systems record email flow into, within, and leaving the network. Evidence may show content of email communications, associations, time stamps, and the like. It may also show an internal suspect emailing confidential IP outside of the business.[5]

Classified Systems

Some servers contain very sensitive commercial material, which senior managers may not want to include in an investigation. This will need to be addressed on a case-by-case basis by the investigator, who will be identifying what evidence the system contains and how it may progress the case. Should senior management deny access to a system the investigator believes may be crucial to an investigation, take detailed notes about the reasons, the identity of the person denying access, and what inquiries you felt were necessary on the system.[5]

Dealing with Fixed and Networked Devices

Devices may be connected to a network by cable or wireless connection. Examples include desktop computers, mainframes, switches, hubs, routers, and the like. Evidence passes through each of these devices and it is the responsibility of the investigator to ensure that all relevant evidence is captured, not just that which is easily accessible. As has been previously discussed, capturing this evidence is a job for the digital forensic investigator as it may provide valuable direction as to the suspect and their attack methodology.

The digital investigator may look to see what activity the device is undertaking on the network, including data moving from the device. The examiner will photograph the device and connections, and where possible physically identify where the device is connected.

Using the network map previously prepared in the investigation of a network intrusion helps the investigator understand how data flows through and out of the network. A wireless signal detector may assist in identifying devices on a network that the system administrator is unaware of, such as mobile devices or a covertly installed server with software allowing it to capture and store network traffic.

Devices That Are Turned On

Digital evidence may be turned on or off when the investigator arrives at the scene. If the device is off, do not turn it on. If it is on, do not turn it off until your digital investigator, who will have triaged the device, gives approval. The only exception to this rule is if you have grounds to believe that the device is in the process of destroying evidence, such as a case of the offender using a remote logon to wipe a drive with incriminating evidence.[2]

While the digital investigator will be the authority on digital evidence seizure, this section will provide an understanding to investigators of what the digital examiner will consider when making their decisions. This information will be valuable when conducting a post-search review, preparing court documents, and when the search team only has a limited number of members.

When you arrive at the scene, there will most likely be devices operating. Sometimes it will be very clear which devices are of interest to your investigation and on other occasions you will have no idea. Your primary interest may be data traveling over the network, with locating and securing devices (such as a desktop computer, laptop, or other devices connected to the network) being secondary. As in the discussion about preserving volatile data, the forensic examiner will make choices about the order of evidence seized from the live network, as identified in the section "Acquisition of Digital Evidence."

After prioritizing the volatility of the evidence, the digital investigator will acquire it using forensically sound tools and methodologies. They will record the times on the devices and date-time settings, which are particularly important when the investigator examines log activity of processes, security applications, and so forth.

Once the evidence has been seized from a live device, the investigator will decide whether they need to take the device or leave it operating. When it is a business-critical device such as a web server, the client may want a digital image of the evidence captured and the investigation will continue using the logical image captured. Document your reasons for either decision should you be asked in court why the device, which later was determined to be a key exhibit, was or was not seized.

The digital investigator will create a master copy of the image of the subject device and then create a verified working copy. While what the examiner will work from is a copy, all copies are potential evidence and need to be treated accordingly. Having a copy image to work off preserves the original and means any problems encountered only occur on the copy of the image.

By taking a forensic image of a live device, the potential exists for passwords to be located in the memory. This is an opportunity not to be missed, as encryption software installed on a suspect's device may prohibit access from ever being gained.

Issues the digital investigator will consider that the lead investigator would benefit from knowing about include:

- Identifying what network or Internet activity is taking place.
- Photographing the layout of the network and devices connected to it where possible.
- Identifying the level of trust in programs on the system. There will be some you are not familiar with and there may be pirated copies of operating systems and applications.
- Using only validated tools that are known and trusted by the courts unless you are required by circumstances to use proprietary tools, such as would be the case on a corporate network with proprietary database.
- Documenting all actions throughout the examination process. Forensic software may contain a documentation-recording process.
- Using the copied image and documenting its hash value once it contains the copied image. This allows a form of accountability throughout the investigation process to prove the images' authenticity.
- Using a wireless detector to locate devices on the network that are unknown. Sometimes on a network there are devices attached that do not appear on the official network map. These may be mobile devices or a server installed by the cybercriminal with the purpose of intercepting all network traffic.
- Instituting a hard shutdown to prevent corruption of the OS and documents. A hard shutdown will also prevent changes to time stamps and prevent changes to file attributes.[5] A hard shutdown is cutting power from the device, such as removing the power cord.
- Instituting a graceful shutdown to help locate network connections.[5] A graceful shutdown is using OS commands such as Cntrl-Alt-Delete-Shutdown. A graceful shutdown may lose some system files and may activate destructive programs.[5] Considering acquisition of volatile data in memory when usage of encryption is suspected. "Acquisition of Digital Evidence" in this chapter provides a suggested order of acquisition by order of data volatility, as provided by AusCERT.[4]
- Using a reliable time source and documenting the time of each performed action.
- Being cautious about the existence of logic bombs or destructive tools installed by the cybercriminal. A logic bomb is a small application or code designed to execute upon a designated event occurring, such as a date or attempt at triage.

- Seizing USB devices. When a USB is used on a device, the serial number is stored. The investigator may assist the digital investigator by ensuring that all USB devices that may be relevant to an investigation are seized and later cross-referenced to the devices seized. This links a USB device to a computer.

Any VM operating on the system when the plug is pulled will be shut down and cannot be retrieved in the state it was. This means any evidence on the VM will be lost. Avenues of investigation that may have originated will now be shut down and any evidence of the offense will have to be located from other sources. The investigator may also face questioning in court as to why the VM was shut down, as a defense lawyer may aggressively argue that the evidence that would have cleared their client was resident in memory or in the VM at the time of the investigator destroying the evidence.

Devices That Are Turned Off

If a subject device is located at the scene and is turned off, do not turn it on even if it is suspected of containing potential evidence.

Secure the device as an exhibit and allow the digital investigator to conduct their examination at the forensics lab using forensically sound tools and methodologies.

Network Servers

On some occasions a storage device may be too large to be completely imaged. Examples include RAID (Redundant Array of Independent Disks) systems and cloud services. A RAID server means a a collection of drives is combined to operate as one, providing a higher quality level of data storage, service, and reliability. In these instances, the digital investigator will discuss this with the complainant and their technical staff to gain an understanding of the most likely places evidence can be found. Alternatively, the system may be too important to the business to be taken offline for a forensic image to be taken, or a court order may only authorize specific activity on the subject device.

Live Capture of Digital Evidence

The digital investigator will commence live capture of data for devices turned on. Record all actions, including using the password and the reason for capturing live data. It is generally not best practice to wake a device from sleep mode and gain access to the device using passwords gained unless there is a particularly compelling reason, such as capturing memory evidence prior to it being shut down for transport. The digital investigator can capture whatever live data they are technically and legally able to. Image the memory and look to see what processes are running, who is logged on, and what the state of the network is.

Where possible, have the digital investigator create an exact image of the devices that are capturing evidence in RAM and VMs.

Once all live data has been captured, unplug the device from the power. This may be done by removing the power cable, or in the instance of a laptop, removing the battery where possible. A reason for crashing the system once the memory has been captured is that some cybercriminals install traps in their devices so when it is powered down in the normal manner, it enacts security within the device, such as deleting data or wiping the drive's slack space.

Returning to Your Location

Upon returning to your location or storage facility, several actions need to be undertaken to account for your evidence and investigation:

- Account for all evidence. This is in effect double-checking the accuracy of your seizure.
- Store evidence in a secure location. If you are reviewing documents, one option is to photocopy originals and work off copies. Secure originals.
- Have a team debrief where everyone is encouraged to present their thoughts and what they learned. The search team members often see and hear things other team members do not.
- Verify that there are no health or safety considerations.
- Collect copies of notes from team members' notebooks. This is important information and obtaining it immediately helps to avoid looking for it months later when team members may be on vacation or gone from the organization, the notebook has been misplaced, and so forth.
- Witness statements will be required from team members and these too should be obtained as soon as possible after the search/examination. The digital investigator will have a lot of work to do once returning to the office and their statement will be a continual work in progress while the examination is undertaken.
- From the information obtained, prepare a schedule of follow-up inquiries. There may be further visits to the corporate offices of the complainant

required to obtain further documentation, statements, and the like, as well as make inquiries based on information learned. New avenues of inquiry may be identified and assigned to team members.

WHAT COULD POSSIBLY GO WRONG?

When human beings are involved, there is always the potential for things to go wrong. No matter how experienced the team, how well resourced, led, or controlled, things sometimes go wrong because mistakes happen, or circumstances overrun your management.

When dealing with suspects in particular, things can go wrong very quickly with little to no warning. The suspect who is cooperative may take advantage of a distraction to destroy evidence, run away, or assault the investigation team. The follow section details instances of things going wrong, which need to be addressed and mitigated as events occur.

The circumstances cover a wide range of offenses that have occurred at crime scenes (not just at financial/cybercrime scenes) and will give you a sample of the volatility that can occur.

Assault of Investigators

When dealing with a suspect, despite inquiries made you will be operating with limited information about their personality and behavior under stress. Even the most mild-mannered individual may behave in an aggressive manner when it has been identified that their criminal behavior has been discovered and they are facing prosecution and the civil forfeiture of their personal and family assets.

Law enforcement investigators are well trained and resourced to deal with these circumstances, whereas the civilian investigator may not be unless they come from a law enforcement background. When attending to a suspect's home address or even their business premises, remember that desperate people make poor decisions when under stress.

Honest Mistakes Being Made

In any investigation, there is the potential for honest mistakes to be made. This may be as simple as misreading or misinterpreting a document, or may involve recording a device's serial number incorrectly, which will cause confusion when attempting to reconcile exhibits.

It is important to understand that no investigation is perfect every time and honest mistakes occur. When they do, it is important to rectify them when possible. Covering them up and denying them when questioned in court is an act far worse than the initial mistake. The cover-up is worse than the initial mistake.

Exhibits Left at the Scene

When you are securing several hundred items at commercial premises it is easy to miss an item and only realize that it has been left behind when doing an audit back in the office. We have discussed the process of physically accounting for every exhibit on an exhibit receipt form to prevent this from occurring. Despite this, occasionally something will go wrong and an exhibit will fall on the floor and be missed when the investigation team leaves the scene after having been present for the past 12 hours. If this occurs in the complainant's office it may not be a major problem and may be able to be easily rectified and recorded in your notebook; however, when it happens at a suspect's address to which you gained access through a court order, there is a very good probability that the exhibit will no longer be there when you return.

Exhibits range in size from large physical devices to small pieces of paper. There are also data storage devices, such as SIM cards, which can easily be misplaced where there are literally hundreds of items to be removed from the premises. The exhibits officer is in charge of these and needs a plan to ensure that all items are accounted for when leaving the premises. One way to do this is for the exhibits officer to personally place each exhibit in numerical order into a large storage container and to tick each exhibit off on their copy of the exhibit schedule. This may be a very slow process that takes place after the investigation team has been at the premises for 12 hours and everyone is very tired, but it is also an investment in the infrastructure of the investigation and the exhibits officer must be allowed to do their job professionally and thoroughly.

Changing Terms of Reference by the Complainant

As scenes and incidents are volatile, the civilian complainant may not have fully defined what is required from the investigation team when asking for your assistance. They are not experienced in the fields of crime scene investigation, management, and follow-up investigations. They also may not have a full understanding of events and their seriousness until you start briefing them.

As you locate information about the cyber security breach, they may subsequently expand the scope of the investigation and require that your investigation be referred to the police, despite originally stating that this was not a consideration. This will in turn affect your methodology; however, as discussed in the beginning of this book, your aim in any investigation will always be to be prepared for your investigation and evidence to be presented in a court of law, even if your initial terms of engagement stated that this was not a requirement.

Poor Record Keeping

With the volume of evidence that may be seized, the number of people to be interviewed, the number of documents to be reviewed, and the amount of digital evidence to be examined, it is easy to let record keeping be ignored as other events take precedence. Notebooks need to be constantly updated to record new information obtained and it is very easy to forget to record some new piece of information or action taken.

When questioned at a later date or when preparing your statement, poor record keeping will leave holes in your evidence, which may be exploited by the lawyers for the defendant.

Loss of the Chain of Evidence

The chain of evidence preserves the integrity of your evidence. Losing track of who was in secure possession of the evidence at any time and being unable to account for its authenticity leaves the evidence open to challenge and to potentially being excluded from your case.

Not Obtaining Statements When You Had the Chance

It is recommended that statements be obtained as soon as possible after interviewing a person. This includes statements from the investigation and IR teams. People are transient in their employment, and the system administrator who is a key witness in your investigation and provided valuable data may take another employment opportunity overseas several months after your interview and may not be able to be located.

Obtaining a statement as soon as possible after an interview will prevent a situation where you have key evidence but no one capable of presenting it in court. If you have the evidence and a statement recorded at the time of interview, even if a witness cannot be located the statement and evidence can be presented to the court and an argument submitted stating that the evidence should be allowed even though there is no opportunity for the witness to be cross-examined. This will be very dependent on the court rules within your jurisdiction.

Being Underresourced

Crime scenes may be very volatile places. Having sufficient team members and equipment is an investment. Taking too many people to the scene is far preferable to taking too few, as excess staff can be released to attend to other duties if they are not needed.

Being underresourced at a scene may be by having too few spare hard drives to capture data or equipment that is out of date for the tasks required.

Careless Comments by the Investigation Team Being Overheard

Should a suspect be identified at a scene, be very aware of what you say. They may have loyal friends nearby who may overhear any derogatory comments made about the suspect, and you cannot assume that their loyalty will be to the company/investigation team.

In today's society, assume someone is recording everything you do and say at a crime scene. The phone left on the desk next to where you are speaking with your staff may have been deliberately left there with the recording feature on to capture your conversation.

Technically knowledgeable suspects may have the capacity to remotely turn on a device you have seized and activate the microphone remotely. This will capture your conversations, including conversations taking place back in the office when you are having your team debrief. The conversation could then be synced into a cloud account, from where the suspect or their associates can listen to you and your discussions. As previously discussed, placing mobile devices in flight mode and then into a Faraday bag or similar container will assist your team security.

The following cybercrime case study provides an example of police attending at a corporate office to obtain technical evidence from within the corporate network after a threatening email had been forwarded to another person with a corporate IP address in the email header.

▨ CYBERCRIME CASE STUDY I

A female sex worker had a client who developed a fixation on her and believed that they were developing a personal relationship, which was obviously false as the worker had made it very clear that the relationship was only a business relationship. The client began to research the worker and identified her true identity and residence.

He began threatening her online and in person that unless she met him and allowed their personal relationship to develop he would contact her family and friends and let them all know what her occupation was. This caused her great distress and she feared for her safety.

The emails were sent from a web email service, and in opening and reading the header the IP address of the sender's Internet Service Provider (ISP) that connected to the web email service was identified.

Inquiries about the IP address with the ISP, identified at the relevant time, revealed that the IP address was assigned to a local corporation.

As the corporation was very large, the IP addresses within the network were generated by DHCP. All devices on the network were connected through the internal network and had a specific subnet address (192.168.***.***). Inquiries with the system administrator identified the specific computer the emails were sent from and the identity of the suspect was confirmed with the complainant. Authentication logs provided corroborative evidence that no other person was using the device at the time emails were sent. Logs confirmed that other activity on the device at the time emails were sent was consistent with his duties.

Network logs were secured with the consent of the corporation and the system administrator provided evidence that the computer of the suspect was logged into the webmail service at the time the threatening emails were sent to the complainant.

When spoken to, the suspect admitted sending the emails and stated that he believed that the affection she had showed him was genuine. He stated that the reason he had sent the threatening emails was to force her into a relationship with him.

Prior to his arrest, due to fears about her safety, the complainant withdrew her complaint and moved overseas. The suspect was fired by his employer for misuse of the computer services provided for his employment.

This case study shows the value of obtaining cooperation from the corporation where a cybercrime was committed. It also shows the necessity of understanding network architecture and the assignment of IP addresses, as well as the role of logs, which uniquely identified the suspect as the person sending the threatening emails.

 ## CYBERCRIME CASE STUDY II

Information was obtained that a member of the community was receiving large sums of money in her bank account from the United States and Canada and forwarding the funds immediately to a series of people in Nigeria. Initially the concern was that she was operating as a money mule and that she was unaware of the fraudulent nature of her activity; however, when initially spoken to she stated that she knew the people in Nigeria and they were her friends.

Inquiries were made with overseas law enforcement to arrange to speak to the series of males in the United States and Canada to identify the reasons why they were sending large sums of money to a person in Australia. Each replied that they were in a romantic relationship with the Australian resident and were planning on arranging for her to travel to meet them. The story each male told was very similar and involved a lot of fraudulently created documentation. Inquiries were made with each of the organizations these documents were represented to be from and each was identified as being an instance of corporate identity theft.

After statements of complaint were recorded with the assistance of US law enforcement, search warrants were executed on the suspect's residential address and significant evidence was located. Email evidence obtained from the US-based webmail provider identified the IP address of the sender, which traced to the suspect's residence.

Financial statements at the scene, which matched bank statements obtained from her financial institution, showed large sums of money being deposited into her bank account. Approximately $14,000 was located in a locked safe and seized, and was ultimately ordered by the court to be repaid proportionally to the victims. Money transfer receipts from various money transfer agencies provided further corroboration of the link between the funds being received and the funds being forwarded to Nigeria.

The scene search was complicated by the messiness of the house, where valuable evidence was located beneath piles of rubbish, and in one instance next to a dead rat. There was also a lack of cooperation from the suspect, including hostility to the search. Also, while the police were at the scene, a suspect in Nigeria became aware of the police search warrant and phoned, trying to plead her innocence.

Search warrants were later executed on the suspect's webmail accounts in the United States via an MLAT and in partnership with US law enforcement. Examination of the accounts identified numerous other instances of offending, and evidence of the suspect communicating with a more experienced cybercriminal about how to get more money out of a victim.

When the suspect was arrested and held in custody, her associates contacted one of the victims in the United States and started making serious allegations about his behavior and made threats to his safety, which were referred to US authorities to provide assistance to the complainant. This series of threats assisted in the suspect being denied bail and being held in custody until she pleaded guilty to the charges. She received a five-year prison sentence.

 ## NOTES

1. Eoghan Casey, *Digital Evidence and Cybercrime*, 3rd ed. (Academic Press, 2011).
2. International Organization for Standardization (ISO) and the International Electrotechnical Commission (IEC), *Information Technology—Security Techniques—Guidelines for Identification, Collection, Acquisition and Preservation of Digital Evidence*, ISO/IEC 27037:2012.
3. Cybercrime Convention Committee, *Transborder Access to Data (Article 32)*, T-CY Guidance Note #3, December 2014, Council of Europe.
4. Thomas King and Phil Cole, "Cyber Incident Handling" (lecture, AusCERT Cyber Security Conference, Gold Coast, Australia, May 23, 2017).
5. Federal Bureau of Investigation, *Digital Evidence Field Guide 2007*, US Department of Justice.

CHAPTER ELEVEN

Log File Identification, Preservation, Collection, and Acquisition

L OGS RECORD events on the computers and the many devices that are part of a network. The activities they record may be valuable evidence to the investigators as they try to understand what has happened, the extent of the activity, and the identity of the person who may be involved. Sources of computer logs include operating systems, applications programs, and the many devices that make up a computer network.[1]

Examples of sources of logs include firewalls, Anti Virus (AV) software, networking equipment (such as switches and routers), proxy servers, File Transfer Protocol (FTP) servers, Intrusion Detection System (IDS) and Intrusion Prevention System (IPS) software, web servers, computer devices, Domain Name Service (DNS) and Dynamic Host Control Protocol (DHCP) logs, and access authentication logs.[1,2,5] Each of these logs records activities on the network, and when combined with other logs can give the investigator an understanding of what was happening at the time of the security event and who may be involved.

Your digital investigator will seek to capture the logs while conducting the forensic image. Alternatively, the system administrator may provide these logs and have access to historical records of log activity prior to the event. They are evidence as much as any other device or piece of paper collected throughout the investigation. A system administrator may be using Security Information and Event Management (SIEM) software, which collates logs from many sources and presents a picture of network activity.[2]

This is a very valuable tool for the investigator, as issues such as time zones and log formatting will have already been addressed, meaning that it will be easier to read evidence.

Of particular interest to the investigator is that logs may be recorded on a separate server away from the device subject to the suspected attack.[2] This will be of value, as while a device may have been compromised or even physically stolen, the server containing the logs of activities on the device may be still accessible, recording evidence of the attack and uncorrupted by the event. Once logs have been generated, they need to be safely stored and secured to preserve their authenticity and integrity, just like any other piece of evidence.

Log files do not generally come in one standard format.[5] They vary among operating systems, applications, and system files. Different vendors of applications may use different formats. Sometimes they are in a format that can be read by a human and sometimes they are not. When a log is generated, it is usually time-stamped.[5] The investigators will need to understand the format and time zone, as these are not a standard feature of log format design. This is where a preconfigured SIEM system is so helpful to the investigator.

LOG CHALLENGES

Some of the challenges an investigator may encounter with log files include:

- Accessing logs in the first place, particularly from a cloud server. Access may be restricted by the service providing the infrastructure and system architecture.[3]
- There will be many different log sources depending on the operating systems and applications used. The investigator will need to discuss with technical support staff the attack methodology and what logs will be required to assist the investigation. If in doubt, obtain the logs; if you later change your mind, they may no longer be available.
- Manufacturers may use different formats.[2,5]
- The data included in the log files may differ across applications.[3,5]
- Time stamps reflect different time zones.[2,5] As you commence your assessment of logs and compare systems to applications, you will want all your logs recorded in the same time zone format.
- The times on the systems that generate the log files may not be synchronized, meaning there will be a variation in the times recorded on different

devices.[2] Where there are many logs involved, if time synchronization is off by a fraction of a second it may affect the investigation and your ability to determine what happened.

- Logs may be held for only short periods of time due to the cost of long-term storage.[3] Businesses that generate large volumes of log records may keep them only for a short period of time, as storage is an additional expense.
- Because of the costs involved in storage, not all logs generated may be recorded.[3] Also, system administrators may perceive that there is no need to record or keep a certain form of log.
- Logs may be very complex to read and be unreadable without specialist applications.[5]
- Logs generated on cloud services may be stored on multiple servers, may not necessarily always be in the same location, and may not be accessible without the consent and assistance of the cloud provider.

Monitoring of logs as they are created may reveal important information about the offense being investigated and lead to the person behind the attack. Although the attacker may destroy log files, if certain logs cannot be located, it may be strong evidence of an attempt to cover someone's activity and should be noted and investigated. This may also show the level of skill and attacker knowledge of the network.

As logs can take up a lot of storage over a period of time, systems generally overwrite logs on a recurrent basis, meaning prompt action will be required by the investigator to secure this valuable source of evidence before it is destroyed. For example, a cloud server may overwrite logs every month depending on client activity while a company having an in-house Information Technology (IT) system may keep logs for six months. The cost of keeping a multitude of logs across many systems is not insignificant and the log data you need as evidence may not have been kept or may have been disposed of as a budgetary measure taken months before the attack.

LOGS AS EVIDENCE

For the investigator, understanding log files is a skill that takes time to learn. There are many forms of logs, and they are confusing and come from many different sources. However, despite this, they provide an excellent commentary on what happened, how it happened, and what the attacker did, and they may also provide direction as to who the attacker is.

To assist the digital investigator, the digital examiner on your team will be skilled in understanding and interpreting logs, and the system administrator of the company whose logs you are investigating will also be able to provide assistance. Communicating with these people will assist the investigator, as they will be able to translate the log data into meaningful data for the investigator to progress their investigation. As technology develops, there are many tools available that are able to collate the log data from many sources and provide a graphical view of events, which makes understanding the data significantly easier.

When examining logs, look for evidence of the incident as well as reconnaissance events over the preceding days or weeks. Logs may even show a so-called dry run or a scoping study of the target before the main attack was undertaken. Experienced hackers will undertake extensive reconnaissance on their target before committing their crime.

In a perfect world, the following information will be included in the structure of the log files seized:

- Time stamp of each activity, to be recorded in a human readable standard format across all applications, the Operating System (OS), databases, and the like.[3]
- A single synchronized time zone.[2]
- Details of the user relating to each activity, such as user details for a log-on authentication attempt.[3]
- Standard format across all logs secured across all sources.[2]
- If authentication fails, the reason why and how many times it failed.[3]
- Session Identifier (ID), which records the activity of a user at a website.[3]
- Details of all activity relating to the access and modification of data and system resources.
- Internet Protocol address of the network user or external party conducting the activity that generated the log.[3]

As mentioned, there are many forms of logs created from many sources. The remainder of this chapter will provide a general understanding of the sources and meaning of the variety of logs an investigator may encounter.

TYPES OF LOGS

Logs originate from many sources, including device operating systems and applications, and across networks. It is not feasible to cover all sources of logs, so this chapter will focus on those originating from Windows operating systems to provide an understanding of what evidence is available from logs and where they can be found. Although an experienced digital examiner will generally undertake this line of inquiry, it is valuable information an investigator will benefit from knowing and having a general understanding of.

Windows devices and servers have multiple forms of logs that may be of benefit to the investigator. These can be located through the Event Viewer. For your general information and understanding, in a Windows 10 OS you may find the Event Viewer through the Windows menu/Windows Administrative Tools/Event Viewer. In an active investigation, you will receive the log evidence from your digital investigator who has already conducted their initial examination.

As you examine the Event Viewer, you will see that there is a standard format containing a set structure across the difference sources of logs. Examples include the date and time of the event, who the user was, the computer the event was generated on, and a specific Windows ID that provides detail on what caused the log to be generated. For example, a file being deleted will produce Windows event identifier 4660, which can be located in the Event Viewer.

Examples of Windows logs include:

System logs. Record events logged by the Windows system components.[4] Examples of system components include applications and utilities, file systems, and startup components.

Figure 11.1 shows an example of system logs in the Event Viewer.

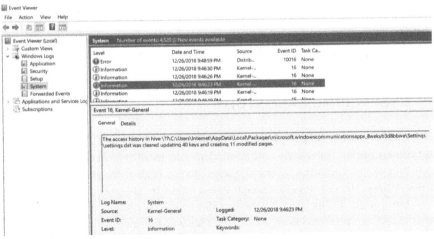

FIGURE 11.1   System logs in the Event Viewer.
Source: Screenshot captured by Graeme Edwards.

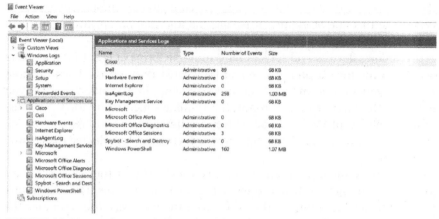

FIGURE 11.2 Application logs in the Event Viewer.
Source: Screenshot captured by Graeme Edwards.

Application logs. Capture information from applications or programs, such as a database.[4]

Figure 11.2 shows an example of applications logs in the Event Viewer.

Security logs. Capture information from different security programs recording data, such as file and directory access, log-on attempts, file modification and deletion, and resource use.[4]

Setup logs. Record activity during the installation of applications.[4]

Forwarded events. Generated by computers on the same network when computers have been configured to forward their event logs to this device.[4]

CYBERCRIME CASE STUDY

A business had a large volume of Intellectual Property (IP) stolen by an unknown party. There was limited evidence to identify whether this was an internal or external attack. The IP was of a very high value and innovative in the industry; the developers stated it was a major threat to competitors.

Early inquiries focused on the log files to narrow down a confirmed time that the IP was removed from the server. This was hampered because the server had multiple people working on it who used a shared user name and password with administrator access. The access details were also known to other parties in the office through weak password protection. The log files were stored on the server and no backups were held.

Further examination of the server identified that log files from a specific date one month earlier had been cleared. As the server had been in operation for several years, it was expected that at least three months of active logs would be found before they were overwritten; however, it was identified at the time of the suspected theft of the IP that the system logs were deleted along with evidence of the time and date of the data theft.

This provided evidence that the attacker knew what they were looking for when accessing the system and had the skills to cover their tracks.

The weakness in the business was that while they were expert at what they did, provided very high-quality service to their clients, and looked after their staff, they did not place a high degree of focus on cyber security. They also did not have an Incident Response plan and their response to the intrusion and evidence preservation was provided largely by the police investigators with the assistance of the company's technical experts.

As computer systems evolve away from storage devices physically accessible to a user, the investigator faces the reality of cloud computing where your evidence may be stored on computer servers across many physical and geographical locations. The Chapter 12 introduces cloud computing and highlights the many reasons investigators need to understand this evolving technology and environment.

NOTES

1. Mark Krotoski and Jason Passwaters, "Obtaining and Admitting Electronic Evidence," *United States Attorney Bulletin* 59, no. 6 (2011): 1–15.
2. Paul Cichonski, Thomas Millar, Tim Grance, and Karen Scarfone, *Computer Security Incident Handling Guide*, Special Publication 800-61 Revision 2, August 2012, National Institute of Standards and Technology, United States Department of Commerce.
3. Raffael Marty, "Cloud Application Logging for Forensics" (PowerPoint presentation, Symposium on Applied Computing, Taichung, Taiwan, March 21–24, 2011).
4. Kate Li, "Event Log—List of evtx Files—Content Meaning," *TechNet* (Microsoft Support blog), January 9, 2019, https://bit.ly/2SpbOqC.
5. Karen Kent and Murugiah Souppaya, *Guide to Computer Security Log Management* Special Publication 800-92, September 2006, National Institute of Standards and Technology, United States Department of Commerce.

CHAPTER TWELVE

Identifying, Seizing, and Preserving Evidence from Cloud-Computing Platforms

A   S YOU read this chapter, you will notice a slight change in the writing style, with more instances of academic referencing. This is because part of the knowledge in this chapter originates from my doctoral thesis "Investigating Cybercrime in a Cloud Computing Environment" as well as the learned practical knowledge of investigating cybercrime in this environment. Whereas the majority of the knowledge included in other chapters in this book originated from many years of conducting financial and cybercrime investigations, as some knowledge originated from academic sources, it is appropriate to reference where the knowledge came from and acknowledge other people's work in this field.

WHAT IS CLOUD COMPUTING?

Cloud computing is the name used for an increasingly common method of storing data of personal and corporate users. Where once all data storage was in devices that were physically accessible, such as computers, external hard drives, USB devices, DVDs, and the like, now storage devices are owned, operated, and secured by external companies who may manage all aspects of the operation on behalf of their clients, usually from foreign legal jurisdictions.

There are many advantages to an entity using a cloud service when compared to buying, maintaining, and operating their own system architecture. These may include cost, time saving, access to highly specialist security staff, and not having to maintain the many operating systems and applications a company may operate. All the traditional issues involving maintenance, security, updating software, and others may be outsourced to the cloud service (depending on the cloud product used), meaning the client can focus their resources on their business, not technology issues.

To the cybercrime investigator, cloud computing takes on great relevance as industry and governments are developing cloud-first policies that dictate that when technical infrastructure needs to be replaced, a very strong and compelling argument needs to be given as to why physical infrastructure and network architecture needs to be purchased, housed, and maintained by the entity and not a Cloud Service Provider (CSP). Consequently, as a cybercrime investigator you will need to become well acquainted with the cloud-computing environment, much as previous generations of investigators needed to understand previous iterations of technology.

There are many forms of cloud services, and apart from providing a brief introduction it is not the intention of this chapter to cover all the possible cloud architecture options an investigator may encounter. We will take the view of an international cloud provider where the client's data is stored on computer servers spread across many local and international jurisdictions (multijurisdictional) and intermingled with data from other clients of the CSP (multitenancy). This is known as a public cloud and the version you will encounter in most investigations.

Cloud computing provides many challenges the investigator does not face with traditional digital evidence and these will be discussed in later in the chapter in "Cloud Barriers to a Successful Investigation." The initial stages of this chapter will provide a general understanding of what a cloud-computing service is, but it is worth the effort to obtain a specific definition of what a particular cloud service is and what the key features of the cloud are. With this information, the cybercrime investigator will be able to relate their investigative strategies to this evolving technology.

In 2014, the International Organization for Standardization (ISO) produced standard ISO/IEC 17788:2014, which identified the six key characteristics of cloud computing. They are:

1. ***Broad network access.*** A feature where the physical and virtual resources are available over a network and accessed through standard mechanisms that promote use by heterogeneous client platforms.[1]

This means that cloud services can be accessed remotely from any location using any compatible device. Your cloud service can be accessed equally easily from your office in Singapore and when you are traveling in New York, Hong Kong, Thailand, Melbourne, or Johannesburg.

2. *Measured service.* A feature where the measured delivery of cloud services is such that usage can be monitored, controlled, reported, and billed.[1]

This means the client uses and is charged only for the resources and services they use and is not billed for excess storage and processing capacity they would rarely if ever require.

3. *Multitenancy.* A feature where physical or virtual resources are allocated in such a way that multiple tenants and their computations of data are isolated from and inaccessible to one another.[1]

This means the cloud provider shares its infrastructure and network architecture with many clients. When stored, the client's data is intermingled to provide the maximum efficiency in data storage.

4. *On-demand self-service.* A feature where a cloud service customer can obtain computing capabilities, as needed, automatically or with minimal interaction with the cloud service provider.[1]

This means the service can be expanded or contracted as required by the client without the need to formally interact with the CSP staff.

5. *Rapidity, elasticity, and scalability.* A feature where physical or virtual resources can be rapidly and elastically adjusted, in some cases automatically, to quickly increase or decrease resources.[1]

This is a service where extra storage or processing capacity can be obtained for the period of use only. The storage/capacity reverts back to the previous configuration once the extra services are no longer required. For example, a business may require extra processing capacity at the end of the financial year and may incorporate this capacity for the several weeks until the accounts are finalized. Once the extra storage/capacity is no longer required the service contracts to its original level.

6. *Resource pooling.* A feature where a cloud service provider's physical or virtual resources can be aggregated in order to serve one or more cloud service customers.[1]

This means you share the architecture and resources of the CSP with the many other clients of the CSP.

For the digital crimes investigator seeking evidence from a cloud service, it helps to understand that they are dealing with a very different environment from one in which they locate a computer on a suspect's desk in an office and get the digital investigator to locate the evidence. In fact, there are no similarities between the two, as with a cloud server the investigator will never get to physically see the cloud cybercrime scene or servers the evidence resides within. Think about this from the perspective of one day having to answer questions in court about where your evidence came from, how it was obtained, international jurisdictions, the chain of custody, and the like.

Cloud computing is a dynamic legal environment with little known legal precedents to guide investigators as to what the court will require. Until legal precedent is established, investigators must be prepared to guide the court on why this form of evidence can be relied upon. Discussions with the CSP should be encouraged in this matter, as they will have the resources to provide the court with assistance in the validation of the credibility of their evidence.

As an introduction to forms of cloud services, there are many products CSP offer their clients. Depending upon their needs, clients generally migrate toward three major offerings: Software as a Service (SaaS), Platform as a Service (PaaS), and Infrastructure as a service (IaaS). The relevance of understanding these CSPs products is that they offer different levels of evidence to the investigator, as each provides different levels of control to the client.

- *Software as a Service.* With the SaaS product the client has no ownership or direct control over the applications making up the service or the infrastructure.[2] Their ability to configure the service is restricted to the options within the application (e.g., Microsoft Office) and the client has little to no access to logs. These are under the control of the CSP and application providers. Access to the applications that make up the SaaS product is via a web browser or app, which may contain evidence in its own right.

  Obtaining evidence to advance the investigation will require the cooperation of the CSP and third-party providers of the service. The End User Licence Agreement (EULA) may provide some assistance in obtaining evidence, but this cannot be relied upon. The data the client is viewing may be provided via a Virtual Machine(VM) that provides its own series of logs that may be used to progress the investigation.

- *Platform as a Service.* PaaS is a product similar to SaaS; however, add-ons are provided to allow clients to create customized applications to suit their needs. As with SaaS and IaaS, the underlying infrastructure is owned and controlled by the CSP. As with the SaaS model, significant assistance will be required from the CSP in the seizure of evidence.[3]

  With PaaS, the customer has the ability to direct how the application interacts with the infrastructure. Logging mechanisms can be implemented and data transferred to a third party.[1] As with SaaS, the logs generated by the underlying infrastructure are under the control of the CSP.[3] The customer, however, does have control of the developed software applications and the associated source code.[3] This last point is of particular relevance to the investigator, as it provides for prompt access to some log evidence you may need to progress your investigation.

- *Infrastructure as a Service.* With IaaS, the customer is provided the basic infrastructure by the CSP on which they can then load their own preferred applications, such as operating systems, databases, and storage systems. The underlying infrastructure is owned and managed by the CSP.[4] This means there are levels of evidence available to investigators to progress the investigation while infrastructure evidence (such as logs) is being sought from the CSP.

This system can provide more information to the client in the event of an incident as they maintain control of the applications they install. The digital investigator or client can take images of their applications as required and store the logs on a separate host.[1] This is easily accessible evidence that can be obtained without seeking the authority of the CSP.

Once you have decided on the type of cloud service you are dealing with, complicating matters even further are the different instances of cloud deployment models. ISO/IEC 17788:2014 explains these as:

- *Public cloud.* Cloud services are potentially available to any cloud service customer and resources are controlled by the CSP.[1]

This is the most commonly used cloud-computing service. Clients join large organizations such as Microsoft, Apple, Amazon Web Services (AWS), or Google for their cloud-computing services (such as SaaS). A common example of an SaaS service on a public cloud is Office 365 sitting on a Microsoft public cloud service.

- *Private cloud.* Cloud services are used exclusively by a single cloud customer and are controlled by that cloud service customer.[1]

A private cloud is a deployment model a large organization may use to obtain the benefits of cloud-computing services while maintaining control over the service. The management of the service may be undertaken by the organization itself or by a third party. For example, a university may operate a private cloud for the benefit of staff and students, and host the service on their premises but contract with a CSP to oversee management of the cloud externally.

Other examples of users of private clouds are governments and industry.[4]

- **Community cloud.** Cloud services exclusively supported and shared by a specific collection of cloud service customers who have shared requirements.[1]

  The infrastructure is provided for the exclusive use of a community of common interests.[4]

- **Hybrid cloud.** May be owned, managed, and operated by the organization itself or by a third party and may exist on or off premises.[1]

  A hybrid cloud uses at least two of the deployment models discussed. There is sufficient compatibility to allow data and applications to be shared.[4]

  An example of a hybrid cloud would be a company that places nonvital information on a public cloud where confidentiality is not an issue, but keeps valuable IP secure on an in-house private cloud.

The following section will provide an introduction to the relevance of cloud computing to the digital crimes investigator.

 ## WHAT IS THE RELEVANCE TO THE INVESTIGATOR?

The cybercrimes investigator is responsible for not only identifying what has happened during a cyber event, but also finding evidence identifying the suspect. This is the same as in any criminal investigation; investigators can depend upon digital evidence playing a role in nearly all investigations today as digital devices become more intrusive in our lives. While most cyber-event responses focus on returning the complainant back to a normal operating environment, there are significant benefits to the company in finding the suspect, obtaining their stolen data back before it is exploited, and prosecuting the offender.

As individuals and corporate entities migrate to cloud-computing services, forensic examination of devices no longer entails seizing a physical device and passing it on to the digital investigator to forensically image, copy, and examine the device for evidence. The cloud-computing server where the investigator's evidence is resident is not physically available except in the instance where the company operates its own private cloud services, which is not the preferred model for many companies.

So in many instances, this leaves the cyber investigator seeking to obtain the digital evidence they require to progress the investigation from an international CSP. As discussed previously in this chapter, depending on the cloud model you are dealing with you may have access to some digital evidence or none. First, consider where the data/evidence is located and what legal authority you have to seize that data. Because it belongs to your client does not necessarily mean you have the authority to download what you want, as data is subject to the privacy laws of the jurisdiction it is resident in and travels through, and government entities such as the European Union (EU) place very strict legal obligations on parties storing Personally Identifiable Information (PII) on a computer resident within the EU. This may include your own corporate data. Reading the EULA and seeking qualified legal advice as to the legality of removing data from the cloud is beneficial.

When placing any evidence before a court, it is the burden of the party producing that evidence to account for it as required by the judge or opposing counsel. This burden extends to proving the evidence was legally obtained and complies with the chain of custody. As this chapter evolves, we shall examine these issues and reveal why cloud-based evidence has not knowingly yet been determined by most jurisdictions' courts.

A further thought considered throughout this chapter is using cloud-based evidence to corroborate evidence located from the physical scene (such as a corporate office). An example of this would be if desktop computer logs showed that a suspect had a history of logging onto a specific cloud server and did so at the time corporate data was stolen.

THE ATTRACTION OF CLOUD COMPUTING FOR THE CYBERCRIMINAL

While cloud computing is highly valued by the business community and increasingly by private users, the criminal community has also seen the benefits of using cloud-computing services. Cloud-computing services may be the target of a crime, used in the commission of a crime, or used to hold information generated during the commission of a crime.[5,6] Hacking as a service is now being offered in criminal communities, and automatic toolkits are being developed to assist those without the technical capacity to target cloud infrastructure.[7] As the criminal community develops new strategies to attack cloud infrastructure and identifies new points of weakness, the volume of attempted compromises can be expected to increase.

Should an incident such as a security breach occur in a cloud-computing environment, it should be of note to the investigator operating in this environment that incident management and follow-up investigations are more difficult than in a traditional client owned-and-operated system.[8] A Service

Level Agreement (SLA) specifies the cloud provider's obligations, and should this not include forensic support, then the client may have restricted access to evidential material. Locating where in the world data was stored at the point of the compromise further hinders effective response and efforts to seek legal redress through the courts.[10] Not knowing exactly where the data was stored means that there may be a need to identify which legal jurisdiction(s) are responsible for conducting an investigation.

The challenge for investigators from a law enforcement and civil perspective is to obtain, store, examine, and present evidence in a transparent manner, which a court can rely upon as being an accurate representation of the data stored in the cloud at that time it was seized.[5]

WHERE IS YOUR DIGITAL EVIDENCE LOCATED?

First, where in the world—literally—is your evidence? Due to the dynamic nature of cloud computing, your evidence may be stored in several legal jurisdictions. While researching my doctoral thesis, I had the opportunity to speak to the chief security officer of a Silicon Valley–based IT provider (who cannot be identified due to the provisions of the ethics consent) specializing in cloud-computing storage. When asked where digital evidence I might seek in a cloud environment would be located, they stated that it could be located on one or all of the twenty-three data centers they have in fifteen different legal jurisdictions, and that they would not know the precise location until they looked.[10] Obviously, if the CSP does not know where data is located, it will be very difficult for the cybercrime investigator to be able to work this out unless the EULA provides for the data to be stored in a specific jurisdiction.

So, where is your evidence? Cloud-computing data moves by the microsecond, meaning it is not resident in one place, as the CSP will move data because of latency, cheap electricity providers, and other considerations. Although the EULA may be with a company based in California in the United States, the company may not store all or any of their client's data in that state.

A further complication is that cloud services may be made up of different companies, each providing specialist services. Some cloud services do not own the physical architecture they operate, but instead lease services from companies such as Amazon Web Services (AWS). This means that even asking the leasing CSP for specific architecture logs through a search warrant or court order will not be successful, as they do not have access to this evidence. The investigator may need to consider the practicalities of serving a request or court order on the CSP leasing space on AWS for specific evidence and a separate order on AWS seeking architecture log evidence.

LAWFUL SEIZURE OF CLOUD DIGITAL EVIDENCE

As the data you seek is on your client's cloud service, the presumption is that it can be accessed and downloaded any time required. The CSP will have considered the legality of data transfer within the jurisdictions they locate data centers; however, laws change and legal precedents are created by the courts that do not always become public knowledge. While the EULA may provide guidance in this instance, privacy legislation in each jurisdiction will have priority over an EULA. As mentioned, the EU is very strict about the removal of PII from their legal jurisdiction and should the data you seek be identified to be resident in the EU, it would be recommended to obtain specialist legal advice before downloading it, even if it is your client's data and you are operating with their consent. If the data you seek were on the suspect's cloud server, it would be very good to consider obtaining legal advice about your options.

To emphasize this point: a CSP interviewed for my thesis stated that there was an incident with a computer they had in France and they wanted to conduct remote diagnostics to determine what the problem was. From their California office they remotely logged onto the device that contained their corporate data, using their own computer, their own office, and their own staff, and transferred the contents to the United States for diagnostics. They were contacted by French authorities and told that they were committing a serious criminal offense under French law—the removal of PII without informed consent of French authorities—and that should they repeat the action, criminal charges would follow. The CSP concerned is one of the largest IT companies in the world and many readers would be very familiar with it (their name cannot be disclosed due to the thesis ethics consent agreement).[10]

Another CSP interviewed stated that if they had problems with computers in the EU, they would fly their staff from London to examine it on site rather than run the risk of violating EU law. When planning their flights, if they had the PII of EU citizens in their possession, they would examine the flight path of all flights they were traveling on while carrying EU data to ensure that at no time did they leave the EU carrying PII subject to EU data and local privacy legislation. While this may seem extreme, these persons interviewed are very experienced operators in cloud-computing services and digital forensics and have a very strong understanding of the multijurisdictional nature of the laws and penalties in different countries and regions.[10]

To assist the investigators, legislators in some instances have created court orders that may be available in your host jurisdiction where the court authorizes you to log onto a cloud server and download the required data. And while this may be legal in your jurisdiction, the search and seizure may actually need to take place across many foreign legal jurisdictions that may not recognize your domestic court order or search warrant unless there are mutual recognition agreements. To emphasize this: Would you go to a court in the United States and obtain a search warrant or court order to search and seize data from a Microsoft Azure cloud service in Sydney, then fly to Australia, hand over your court order, and demand that Microsoft hand over the data? In effect, this is what you are doing.

So while you may have the protection of the law in your jurisdiction in this case, you would nevertheless be conducting a search and seizure of evidence in a foreign legal jurisdiction without local legal authorization. The inverse of this would be if an Australian company complained about being hacked by a foreign law enforcement service, and when challenged the foreign police office provided a local search warrant that they said authorized them to conduct the search and seizure in Australia. With the cloud, you are operating in potentially many different legal jurisdictions and what may be legal in one jurisdiction may be a very serious criminal offense in another.

Should you be fortunate enough to have the CSP within your jurisdiction the process of securing evidence will be far easier, as you will be dealing with domestic court orders.

CSPs interviewed for my doctoral research were unanimous in their opinion that if you want data from a cloud service and have any questions about the legality of obtaining it, first ask the advice of the CSP lawyers and they will provide prompt direction to assist you in continuing your investigations in a legal manner.

Lawyers and forensic examiners for the CSPs interviewed stated that they would appreciate the opportunity to assist when cloud data is required for investigations. This is to ensure that the correct evidence is obtained and the wording of the order is correct. One lawyer at a CSP interviewed stated:

> We get a court order directing us to do things that do not make sense, direct us to breach another piece of legislation, or request only a fraction of the information that is available. I suggest that any investigator, criminal or civil, who seeks information from a CSP to contact that

CSP's legal department first and ask for their assistance in drafting the requested order so that it makes sense, does not direct us to breach another piece of legislation, and to make sure the investigator obtains all the evidence that is available to them. At this time, I do not believe we have ever had someone ask for our assistance in obtaining data from our servers before serving a court order on us and that causes problems for them and us.[10]

The chief security officer of the CSP stated:

People do not understand the law when they are requesting data. I have had a request to supply everything about a specific (MAC) Media Access Control address. Please speak to a legal officer before making a request![10]

They have also given consideration to allowing external parties to download evidence from their cloud services. As discussed, this will depend upon the EULA as well as the laws in the multiple jurisdictions. Of further consideration is that CSPs have reservations about allowing clients to conduct invasive digital forensics on their cloud services, which will be discussed later in the chapter, under "Remote Forensic Examinations."

PRESERVATION OF CLOUD DIGITAL EVIDENCE

As the cloud is a very dynamic environment, evidence such as log data can be lost very quickly. Also, if a suspect has access to the cloud service, they may remotely access the service and destroy all the evidence you are seeking.

Law enforcement has the option of seeking a preservation order, where an image of the sought-after data is made by the CSP forensic examiners and held pending a court order through an MLAT. These orders are generally not available to civilian examiners. Civilian investigators may make personal requests through existing channels of communication, legal or otherwise.

When seeking to preserve cloud evidence, contacting the CSP and asking for a preservation copy is a way of ensuring that the evidence can be preserved as close to the time of the alleged offense as possible. The CSP will tell you what they can preserve and how you can legally obtain it. For example, obtaining a copy of suspect's emails when the evidence is resident in the United States can only be done through a law enforcement search warrant. However, the CSP may be able to assist in other matters, such as Internet logs, subscriber details, payment methods, and the like through a legal request.

If the client has an IaaS cloud product, the user has visibility and control over the virtual servers storing the data. Subject to the terms of the EULA and appropriate legal advice, the forensic investigator may be able to obtain a digital copy of the evidence that they seek.

FORENSIC INVESTIGATIONS OF CLOUD-COMPUTING SERVERS

The following sections will discuss evidence from cloud-computing platforms and some of the considerations involved in identifying, collecting, acquiring, and preserving digital evidence from the cloud.

Identification of Evidence

The Cloud Security Alliance (CSA) states that the first challenge of cloud forensics when compared to traditional forensics is the identification of the location of potential evidence. The CSA explains that physical disk devices may be virtualized and presented to a cloud user to match cost, reliability, and performance requirements. The virtualized logical units may be transported from location to location depending on networking issues. [3]

> With the advent of storage networking and virtualization, mapping storage devices has become more complex and this complexity increases in the cloud. [3]

The international and complex nature of obtaining data from a CSP may impact an investigator's ability to obtain an image of sought-after evidence. For example, an investigator will generally not be able to personally obtain a complete image from the cloud server and must rely instead upon the services of the CSP. [11]

Collection of Evidence

As access to storage becomes cheaper and easier, the volume of data an investigator may need to access and obtain is expected to increase to the point that it will become practically impossible for an examiner to conduct a full investigation. [12] FBI digital laboratories have recorded a significant increase in the amount of digital evidence located in each examination. Whereas in 2003 the average case involved 84 GB of data, [13] in 2013, when the last figures were made available, the average case involved 821 GB. [14]

A digital forensics examiner for a CSP commented on the volume of data they have to image to comply with legal requests for evidence:

> In an investigation, we do not touch servers. I had one example where the server had 16 hard drives on it and that was the smallest one we had. We did not even bother to try and image it. A forensic image on an IaaS is just too big. If over a terabyte, it would cause problems. In the real world, it is just not practicable.[10]

A lawyer for an international law enforcement agency stated:

> I currently have an investigation that has 50 million lines of non-content data. This needs to be stored, processed, and understood.[10]

Along with obtaining the evidence is the cost of the action. While a law enforcement agency may be able to rely upon the support of Mutual Legal Assistance Treaty (MLAT) partners, the civilian investigator will need to rely upon the support of the CSP and legal representatives in your home and the target jurisdictions. This comes at a cost and will need to be budgeted for, along with any other expense associated with the investigation. This expense extends to the cost of storing and preserving large volumes of digital evidence.

Along with planning the collection and storage of evidence, it must be accounted for from the time of collection to presentation in court. As discussed previously, this is known as the chain of custody.

The purpose of the chain of custody is to identify the access to and movement of the evidence throughout the custody process.[15] Mark Taylor and colleagues explain that the chain commences when an investigator takes physical control of the evidence and documentation continues throughout the investigation process.[5] The ISO provides a slightly expanded time frame, holding that the chain of custody commences at the identification stage.[15]

Cloud-based evidence provides unique challenges that the investigating party must plan for and address to ensure that the integrity of the chain of custody is maintained and recorded.[16] The CSA has acknowledged the importance of the preservation of the chain of custody and recommends that as a part of a CSP incident response plan provided to their clients, the CSP provides full forensic support—including preservation of the chain of evidence—to support any potential legal action resulting from the security incident.[3]

Once the planning phase of evidence collection has been undertaken, the next phase is the process of acquiring the evidence. Considerations when the evidence is on cloud servers may consist of legal and technical barriers that must be addressed. The following section introduces and discusses these issues.

Acquisition of Evidence

Traditionally, electronic evidence in an investigation has been able to be physically accessed by an investigator. Examples of electronic evidence sought include items such as computers, USB drives, external storage devices, and mobile phones. In a traditional investigation, a specific physical address where the potential evidence is located can be identified, and once the search warrant has been executed and the evidence obtained it can be taken to the forensic laboratory for examination. As electronic evidence changed to include web and email servers, the methodologies of obtaining the evidence were modified to include making applications to foreign corporations to obtain the evidence under a local court order in the jurisdiction where the sought-after evidence was resident. With the multijurisdictional storage of data in cloud computing, this methodology has become more complex.[17]

Acquiring data in a cloud environment may be complicated, as the data is moved from location to location to take advantage of factors such as load balancing and the cheap supply of electricity in different locations. Also, many CSPs do not store metadata for significant periods of time due to the costs involved, and therefore valuable evidence may be destroyed before an investigator is aware it even exists.[19]

An investigation must be conducted in a timely manner to ensure that evidence is not lost.[5,18,19] Deleted data is an important source of evidence that would be examined in a traditional infrastructure. Should data be deleted, the storage space is available to be overwritten by newly stored data.[20] A forensic examination may not be able to access data remnants or unallocated disk space that may be sources of evidence.[21]

Because the client views their data in a virtualized instance, the closing of a virtual instance destroys the evidence stored, which cannot be recovered once a new instance has been initialized.[5] Consequently an investigator needs to ensure that efforts are made to secure evidence prior to a virtual instance being closed or logs overwritten.[9]

In multitenancy environments resources are shared among a multitude of clients, and common resources (such as the recording of logs) may be overwritten prior to an investigator gaining access. Important evidence—such as file creation, modification, and access times—may be lost prior to an investigator gaining access to it.[8] The evidence sought from the network components may be difficult for an investigator to obtain, as a CSP may not log such data.[2] If the CSP saves a limited number of logs or none at all, there is limited opportunity to obtain these pieces of forensic evidence. Subsequently, there may be some difficulty in identifying the extent of the incident under investigation.[2]

New challenges will be created for forensic examiners, as the capacity to obtain, preserve, and analyze potential digital evidence is a critical path of business and the investigative process. The CSA argues that customers of CSPs and law enforcement investigators tasked with obtaining cloud-based evidence will be increasingly asking for CSPs to provide forensic support, and those organizations that are not prepared for these challenges will be at a distinct disadvantage.[3]

Dennis Stewart argues that CSPs often lack the support staff to assist in the forensic examination process.[20] Of further concern is that disk images cannot be validated because cryptographic hashes cannot be validated, and this can potentially reduce the value of the evidence in court.[16]

The volatility and elasticity of cloud computing makes the task of recovering deleted data from a cloud device a more challenging task than in a traditional recovery, such as with a USB or hard drive. However, one potential benefit to an investigator is that there may be instances where evidence may be recovered because the client of the CSP does not have any access to the device to ensure that deleted data is totally destroyed.[11] Of further difficulty to the examiner is that potentially valuable evidence, such as registry entries and temporary Internet files that are traditionally written to the Operating System (OS), may be lost when a virtual instance is deleted.[5,8]

The size of a cloud data center may prohibit a full seizure of all drives, as an examiner would be unlikely to have the storage available to conduct a full bit-by-bit analysis of target computers in a traditional manner. If they did, this would carry significant cost.[8,11] The logistics involved in such an examination would be extensive and require the involvement of significant financial and personnel resources. Stewart argues that as the data of a client can be stored over multiple servers across different physical locations, the ability to seize the sought-after evidence without interfering with the data of unrelated users is rendered very complex.[20]

If a digital investigator could obtain physical access, the data-distribution technologies used in cloud technology would require an investigator to be reliant upon the assistance of the CSP and their technology to access the data and comply with the chain-of-custody requirements of the court.[6] Virtualization in cloud computing may store the sought-after data on many different physical servers with an interface being present between the physical and logical data;[11] it would subsequently render seeking physical access to the servers as a less viable data collection methodology.

Forensic examination tools such as Forensic Toolkit (FTK) and EnCase are commonly used to examine data. The recovery of deleted data, file search techniques, and a timeline showing the process of a crime being committed are common features of products that are used in the examination process.[11]

Once evidence has been identified and seized, there is a requirement that it be preserved in a manner that ensures it is acceptable as evidence, meaning that it has not been manipulated, damaged, or treated in a manner such that its forensic integrity can be challenged. The following section discusses the preservation of evidence seized from a cloud platform.

Preservation of Evidence

Taylor and colleagues state that evidence to be presented in a court is the responsibility of the person presenting it. Consequently they must prove it was obtained in a legal manner using methodologies that show the integrity of the investigation, evidence collection, and storage. Should this be unable to be proven, the evidence may be given reduced weight or be ruled inadmissible.[5] Consequently the acquisition and preservation phases of evidence collection can be seen as crucial to the credibility of any investigation.

The preservation of evidence from cloud-computing environments is as important as when evidence is obtained from traditional infrastructures and for other forms of digital evidence. Although the cloud environment may be more complex for an investigator to navigate, the burden on the investigator is not diminished from that discussed throughout this section.

The following section discusses the potential to obtain evidence from cloud-computing platforms using forensic computer examination techniques between a remote physical location and the data servers where the potential evidence resides.

 ## REMOTE FORENSIC EXAMINATIONS

Should an incident occur and an investigation be required to identify the facts of the incident, a forensic investigation of the cloud services may be considered to obtain digital evidence. This involves a digital investigator remotely accessing a cloud server and conducting the examination instead of having physical access to the device as they traditionally would.

A definition of cloud forensics is:

[The] process of identifying, labeling, recording and acquiring forensic data from the possible sources of data in the cloud.[9]

Although the Association of Chief Police Officers (ACPO) provides guidelines about the manner in which forensic evidence is to be obtained in traditional examinations where access to the electronic storage device is achievable,[41] it does not provide specific guidelines as to the collection, analysis, and presentation of data secured from a cloud environment. Specific case law and rules of evidence directly attributable to forensic computer examinations and the collection of evidence in a cloud-computing environment are still evolving, providing limited judicial direction to examiners and investigators.

The CSA has stated that conducting forensic examinations in the multi-tenanted, highly virtualized environment that is cloud computing is a complex matter and current forensic techniques are immature. It also states that strong links exist between the practice of digital forensics and the legal system, as established rules of evidence place restrictions on the acceptable manner in how digital evidence is obtained and presented. A paper from its Incident Management and Forensics Working Group titled "Mapping the Forensic Standard ISO/IEC 27037 to Cloud Computing" surveys the issues relating to forensic examinations being conducted in cloud-computing environments.[3]

There will be increasing security challenges to users of the cloud due to the distributed, virtualized nature of the cloud. This will in turn create new challenges for digital investigators, especially as the capacity to obtain, preserve, and analyze potential digital evidence is a critical path of business and the investigative process.

A CSP representative stated that should a client's digital investigator cause damage to a virtual server and interfere with other clients while they are conducting a remote digital examination without express permission, the CSP would retain its rights to sue the party conducting the examination and their client. This is because the servers are finely configured for functionality and stability and are not designed for digital investigators of various standards to use any of the multitudes of forensic tools on the market. A further consideration is that previous instances have been recorded of persons conducting such a digital examination inadvertently obtaining the data of other clients.[10] This requires further consideration by anyone thinking of conducting a remote forensic examination, as the burden on them is not only to obtain the evidence in a forensically sound and legal manner but to ensure that they do not damage the virtual environment in which they are operating.

As in the previous section, we will now break down remote forensics examinations of the cloud into the phases of identification, collection, acquisition, and preservation of evidence.

Identification of Evidence

Prior to an investigation commencing, the data owner needs to identify that an incident in their platform has occurred. They may identify the incident through reporting by the CSP or through their own resources, such as an Intrusion Detection System (IDS) being activated or from review of application/OS logs.[11,23] In some instances the discovery of a crime may not be identified for several years after the event.[8] This will have a potentially significant relevance to the quality and volume of evidence available.

As has been discussed throughout this chapter, obtaining evidence may often require the cooperation of a CSP. The issue of obtaining evidence about an incident may be easily resolved by the terms of the EULA agreed upon prior to the migration of data to the cloud or be resolved post-incident. Should the incident involve the security of the CSP being breached the CSP may not wish to provide any assistance, so as to prevent the business community from becoming aware of a breach of their security, or alternatively the CSP may not wish to devote the resources to assisting their client. Alternatively, they may be very supportive.

Should an event occur where the offense is committed by a person who is a client of the CSP and the victim is not, then the victim may have even less opportunity to obtain evidence without a court order or the cooperation of the CSP. The CSP may have no contractual responsibility to assist the victim and may have even less interest in being involved.

Collection of Evidence

As the act of physically collecting evidence from a cloud server is highly unlikely, this section looks at considerations for the investigator and examiner when laying the foundation of evidence acquisition, primarily when collecting evidence from a foreign jurisdiction(s).

Jurisdiction is very relevant to investigations that involve cloud-based evidence, as CSPs have data centers in many different international and domestic legal jurisdictions. The technical structure of cloud computing moves data regularly across the Internet based on considerations such as load balancing, data optimization, and cost sharing; this practice has evolved into an international phenomenon and is growing at an unprecedented pace. The Internet has evolved into an interconnected storage and data platform.[20] To the investigator, this means your evidence may not be in a location that is the same as the one in which the offense you are investigating occurred.

In the evidence collection and seizure process, failure to comply with local laws where evidence resides may leave the data owner or members of the investigation team liable for criminal or civil prosecution.[23] As previously mentioned, the EU restricts the removal of content data from their jurisdiction except through provisions such as the granting of court orders.[24]

The data stored may be mirrored across different servers to provide backup should an incident occur.[8,9] Data held by a CSP may be stored, transported, and accessed in different jurisdictions.[25,26] Where multiple servers are located in different countries and where different activities in the incident were undertaken, it must be understood where each event occurred, as multiple courts may have jurisdiction for different aspects of the investigation.[5]

Even when the sought-after cloud-based evidence is resident in a single legal jurisdiction, data-distribution technologies may split the data across potentially thousands of storage devices the CSP has in that jurisdiction. An investigating officer would be required to seek and obtain the support of the CSP in obtaining the evidence and in demonstrating the integrity of the evidence.[6] Alternatively, the data of a specific user may be located across multiple legal jurisdictions, and if it is recovered, there is no guarantee that it will be in a format readable by humans.[17] Again, the support of the CSP will be of great value.

The location of data and backups on cloud-computing platforms may be difficult to determine, and the laws on storage and transmission of this data may contradict the obligations imposed by other jurisdictions.[25] Further complicating matters is that multijurisdiction and multitenancy models are the default settings for CSPs.[9] There may be instances where the location of the cloud event cannot be identified and determination of which court has jurisdiction cannot be made. There may also be instances where multiple jurisdictions may have the authority to hear a case, which raises the question of how the order of priority will be determined.[27]

To retain potentially volatile evidence on cloud servers, a legal consideration may involve speaking to the CSP to preserve the evidence, a process that is known as a "litigation hold." To identify where the evidence is located and to seek the legal authority of that court to obtain the held evidence, an investigator may have to request that the court serve a subpoena on the CSP.[18]

Different CSPs have different rules regarding data storage. Google provides the client with the option of all copies of their data residing in a single jurisdiction; however, if the client were not to specify this option, then their data could potentially reside across multiple servers in any of the listed countries where Google's data servers reside. Multiple countries result in multiple jurisdictions.[29]

As a CSP platform may be made up of many components from many suppliers, there is no guarantee that each component will be resident within the same jurisdiction. Inquiries may need to be made of the different suppliers for different sources of your evidence.

The investigator needs to understand where in the cloud infrastructure an alleged event (such as a data breach) takes place and in which country that server is located to identify jurisdiction. Even then the person or entity suspected of committing the event could potentially be located in a separate country and jurisdiction altogether.

When seeking evidence from a foreign legal jurisdiction and pursuing a court order to obtain the data, an investigator may need to identify whether the suspected offense they are investigating is an offense in the jurisdiction they are seeking evidence from. Because an action may be illegal in one country does not guarantee that it is illegal in another.[5] Should the alleged offense be a legal activity in the host jurisdiction, seeking redress or assistance through the court in that jurisdiction may have a lower chance of success.

There is agreement between academic research and industry that an investigator may find it impossible to identify the legal jurisdiction without obtaining the support of the CSP.[23] This is a major distinction when compared to investigating computer events in infrastructures owned and operated by the user, where the data center or servers containing the evidence reside in a known and geographically accessible location.

In summary, the identification of the jurisdiction where an alleged incident took place may be a complex matter requiring the assistance of the CSP. Collecting the evidence in an admissible manner from a foreign jurisdiction is a matter that must be planned, possibly with the assistance of extensive legal support prior to the active component of the investigation and evidence collection commencing. Understand that the cloud-computing environment is one that is very different for the investigator to navigate and having an understanding of the multijurisdictional environment in which you are operating will be of assistance to you.

Acquisition of Evidence

This section examines the legal and technical feasibility of obtaining evidence from a cloud-computing platform that may be resident in a foreign legal jurisdiction. The evidence being sought may be that of a complainant or a suspect and may be sought by a civilian or law enforcement examiner. Of particular relevance to this section is identifying the legality of such an action and an examination of what technical barriers may exist.

Conducting a forensic examination in the cloud creates problems that do not exist in traditional infrastructures. First, as the data may reside in foreign jurisdictions, legal advice needs to be sought so that any remote forensic analysis does not violate the laws of the foreign jurisdiction.[9] The ability to conduct remote forensic examination depends upon the identification of the host jurisdiction and their legislation, as data is subject to the laws of the country in which it resides.[28] Also of consideration is the protection of the data of other clients of the CSP that are not subject to the examination.[9]

Although the following reference is from 2009, it is still highly relevant to the multijurisdictional nature of cloud computing:

> Obtaining cloud-based evidence which is physically on a server in a foreign jurisdiction risks violating that country's privacy and criminal laws. So, regardless of where the subject of an investigation resides, investigators may now need to consult with their organisation's attorneys on whether they will legally be able to obtain data potentially not stored in their jurisdiction.[29]

The obtaining of forensic evidence from traditional storage devices is significantly different from obtaining it from a cloud platform. With cloud platforms, the underlying infrastructure is not available for full bit-by-bit imaging.

Acquiring the evidence requires an understanding of the legal requirements of the target jurisdiction. Legislation in the United States that a law enforcement officer may use to access data on a cloud platform includes the Electronic Communications Privacy Act of 1986 (ECPA), an ordinary search warrant, or the Foreign Intelligence Surveillance Act (FISA).[25] An ordinary search warrant can be issued under Rule 41 of the Federal Rules of Criminal Procedure (FRCP).[30]

As many cloud-computing data centers are located in the United States, when obtaining a search warrant from a CSP based in the United States a law enforcement officer must be aware of the Fourth Amendment to the US Constitution, which states that:

> The right of the people to be secure in their persons, houses, papers, and effects, against unreasonable searches and seizures, shall not be violated, and no warrants shall issue, but upon probable cause, supported by oath or affirmation, and particularly describing the place to be searched, and the persons or things to be seized. [31]

To assist in securing evidence that may be dynamic in nature and may be easily overwritten prior to the service of a court order, a request may be submitted to the CSP asking them to preserve the evidence until a court order may be obtained and served. In the United States, the instrument used to preserve data is an S2703(f) letter from title 18 of the *Code of Federal Regulations*. An S2703(d) order from title 18 of the *Code* is required for noncontent data that is more detailed than basic subscriber details. [32]

Obtaining cloud-based evidence from a jurisdiction such as the EU means that the investigator must navigate European privacy directives as well as host country legislation. [24] As an example, France has the Data Protection Act of 2004, which is administered by the Commission nationale de l'informatique et des libertés (CNIL), as well as the EU Data Protection Directive to protect data in their jurisdiction. This legislation places additional responsibilities on parties seeking to remove data from France to other countries, including potentially being required to seek separate notification and/or authorization from the CNIL prior to the data being removed from France should the data owner not have provided informed consent or the recipient country not have a level of data protection that is recognized by French authorities as being equivalent to their domestic legislation at the French or EU level. [33] Removing any data from the EU requires legal advice from your own resources and preferably the CSP.

Encryption in a cloud-based environment may also present an issue for investigators. It is a security provision recommended by CSPs. Encryption will particularly present hurdles when the data is sought from a party who is not the data owner, as the CSP may not hold the key to decrypt the data. [11] The key may be held by the owner or user of the data and not be accessible to the CSP. [17] Due to the increasing number of high-visibility data breaches being reported in the media, consumers are turning to encryption to protect their data in the event of a breach. CSP service level agreements often contain guarantees that data will be encrypted and that any person other than the data owner will be prevented from gaining access to the data. This means that an investigator may be able to legally access the data from the CSP but not be able to read it without the key being provided due to encryption.[17]

The cost of conducting an investigation may be extensive considering the number of jurisdictions involved, legal support needed, amount of bandwidth required to download evidence,[21] investigators' time, and amount of storage capacity required to be provided. The large volumes of data that may be accessed present challenges to the investigator.[19] The amount of data that may be obtained has the potential to overwhelm an investigator, with 1 GB of data equaling 894,000 pages of plain text and 1 TB equaling 916,000,000 pages of plain text. It is not realistic for an investigator to read and process these amounts of data.[34]

Prior to the commencement of a cloud forensic examination, the purpose of the examination must be clearly defined.[5] The priorities of law enforcement and a CSP may often differ. A CSP may prioritize the availability of a service to a client as being their top priority, whereas law enforcement may consider collecting evidence and prosecuting the offender as a higher priority.[5] From the customer's perspective, when an incident occurs, it may be a priority of the entity to recover their system by initiating a new virtualized instance. While this results in the entity recommencing operations, it however destroys the evidence that may not be recovered.

Gaining the cooperation of the CSP will advance an investigation in each instance as network-facing and load-balancing logs are controlled by the CSP and this evidence can assist in identifying relevant jurisdiction(s). A CSP may use proprietary data formats that are unique to them and subsequently require potentially extensive assistance to provide the evidence in a readable format.[6]

CSPs have concerns as to remote parties conducting digital forensic examinations of their servers. The chief security officer of a large US-based CSP stated:

> We do not allow clients to do remote forensics on our infrastructure. This is our proprietary network and we are protective of our clients. If people attempted remote forensics, then we would pick it up. We would even block an attempt to copy a VM or virtual server. The higher than usual bandwidth use would alert us, and upon investigation as to what was going on, we would cut our client off. We do not want our clients anywhere near the physical infrastructure and touching directory structures.[10]

Another CSP digital forensic examiner states:

> There is a difference between using our service and touching our infrastructure, and that is a line that we do not allow to be crossed. If they were, they would be getting into the substructures of the services they are using, such as service structures that could affect the structure of the service they are trying to forensically examine. It is contractually and physically prevented from forensic imaging the view. It is electronically prevented too. We are able to stop a customer from using our service if they are destabilizing the service we provide.[10]

(The identity of these individuals and their employers is confidential, as per the ethics consent agreement signed prior to the interviews for my doctoral research.)

A CSP does not provide the client with direct access to the underlying infrastructure, representing the platform to the client as a virtual instance. This subsequently reduces the access to what may be valuable evidence. Also, the Virtual Machine (VM) may itself be based on a VM from a CSP the client's CSP has leased a service from.[11] This is a process known as reselling, where the owner controls the architecture of the cloud and the reseller only has access to the virtual server provided by the infrastructure owner.

The CSA states that should an investigator consider conducting a remote forensic examination, consideration should be given to the fact that as cloud computing is a dynamic environment, it may be difficult for an investigator to replicate the original state of the data from the time of the alleged attack. The dynamic, distributed, and complex nature of the cloud system cannot be easily frozen, meaning that the documentation, qualifications, and processes used may not be recorded.[3]

When downloading evidence from the cloud, metadata may be lost that contains information—such as the time(s) and date(s) that files were created, modified, or accessed—that may have been used as evidence.[8] Access to evidence by the examiner may be restricted depending on whether the cloud is private or public. If it is private, then the investigator may have access to the physical infrastructure and be able to accurately conduct an analysis in a traditional environment.[5]

A wide range of endpoints may connect to a cloud platform, which exacerbates the challenge of data discovery. Synchronizing logs and time stamps has been an issue in network forensics and is made more challenging in a cloud environment. Different evidence from different jurisdictions, infrastructure, and remote clients, as well as log formats, makes the examination of evidence in a meaningful manner challenging.[9]

A public cloud is likely to cause more concerns for remote forensic investigators, as there is limited access to potential evidence because it is owned and operated by a separate independent organization with third parties potentially providing applications. The level of data an investigator has direct access to will differ depending on the product the client has.[35] IaaS provides more access to evidence and log data than PaaS, which in turn provides more access to log data than SaaS.[2,11] In a SaaS environment, the customer has no control over the underlying infrastructure, such as servers, network configuration, and the applications being used. If the CSP runs no logs, the client has limited opportunity to conduct a forensic examination. Subsequently, it may not be able to be determined what data has been compromised.[2]

IaaS provides more opportunity for remote forensic examination, as the customer can install and set up an image for forensic purposes. Data logs can be preserved. A snapshot of the virtual image can be taken that may include data from the system's memory in real time, without the need to shut down the system.[2,16] Log information can include logged users, open ports, running processes, and registry information. In the instance of a virtual IaaS facility, if no persistent storage synchronization exists, then should the attacker shut down the virtual environment all volatile data will be lost.[2]

It is anticipated that with the increased use of smart mobile devices and data sharing, the challenges for investigators in accessing and securing data for forensic examination will increase. Of note is the difficulty in acquiring forensically sound remote data, the large volumes of data that reside in the cloud, and the distributed and elastic nature of cloud storage, and proving the chain of custody and identifying the owner of data are some of the issues facing the forensic cloud examiner.[20]

Depending upon the product, more log evidence can be obtained from a CSP conducting a forensic analysis themselves than from a remote forensic analysis by a remote examiner. As the underlying infrastructure is not accessible to the data owner or investigator, potential evidence such as host access logs, virtualization platform logs, and registry evidence may not be available without the consent of the CSP.[3] Infrastructure logs are only accessible via the CSP.[16] Keyun Ruan and colleagues also observe that audit logs of shared resources in a public cloud may be shared among multiple tenants and be regularly overwritten. A customer has no access to the raw disk devices but views a virtualized instance. At the physical level, system audit logs of shared resources are shared among multiple tenants. The challenge for an investigator is to obtain the shared resource logs without breaching the confidentiality of other clients.[9]

The amount of data to be imaged creates a separate problem for remote investigators. The cost involved in imaging and then copying the target drive may be prohibitive for an investigation. IaaS uses very large volumes of data that may not be practicable or possible to image or download.[11]

> A typical cloud case could be 40,000 VM provided by 512 servers with 1,000 users. It may contain 128 TB storage across multiple storage technologies and 48 TB memory.[8]

Virtualization in the cloud means logs that would previously be stored on a server are kept in the virtual environment for the time of the session and may be deleted once the session is closed and thereby unavailable to an analyst.[5] When a virtual instance is closed, data that in a traditional system is written to the OS may be discarded. Obtaining and authenticating the metadata may be crucial to an investigation.[2] Isolating the portions on the physical drives where the user's data is stored may be complex, as the virtualized data may be spread across multiple devices.[11]

The proprietary nature of the platform may also create issues an investigator must address during the forensic examination process, as the unique technologies used may require extensive assistance from the CSP staff. Of further uncertainty is the skills and training of those staff members who take the forensic image for the investigator whose training and methodologies may not necessarily be consistent with those of the jurisdiction seeking the data.[11]

The multijurisdictional nature of cloud services means that although an examiner is seeking to deal with only one CSP, the data sought may be spread across different legal jurisdictions requiring multiple legal orders to obtain the forensic data. Further, different time zones would need synchronization.[11]

Despite the many issues identified in this section and the fact that forensic imaging in the cloud is in an immature state, the CSA believes that it does not mean that the evidence collected from a cloud platform cannot be seized in a forensically sound and accountable manner.[3] The CSPs interviewed for my doctoral thesis state that they can overcome many of these issues if you seek their cooperation at the commencement of your investigation.

Preservation of Evidence

The preservation of evidence obtained from cloud platforms where the examiner is in a location foreign to the server is the responsibility of the examiner.

These issues have been discussed in section the on preservation of evidence under "Forensic Investigations of Cloud-Computing Servers" and are equally relevant to remote forensic examinations.

The following section incorporates the issues identified throughout the remote examinations section and discusses the issues involved in presenting cloud-based evidence in a court of law. This section will expand on the four phases of the ISO evidence collection process and highlight the value of following an established and understood evidence collection methodology.

Presentation of Evidence

As the steps of the ISO standards are complied with, there may be a requirement to present some of the evidence received in a court of law. As each jurisdiction has their own legislation and legal precedents established by the courts, this section will provide a very generic view of the presentation of evidence in a court of law.

Evidence from the cloud is believed to be highly significant to criminal or civil litigation in the future.[2] Josiah Dykstra and Alan Sherman reinforce this statement by adding that evidence seized, collated, and presented must be done so in a manner that is not only admissible in a court of law, but is capable of surviving a potential legal challenge by another party.[16]

The court requires evidence to be authentic, reliably collected, complete, believable, and admissible.[8] Once the evidence has been acquired, preserved, filtered, and determined to contain evidentiary value, it must be presented to the court in a manner that complies with legislation and judicial rulings. Each jurisdiction has its own relevant legislation and judicial precedents and the acceptance of evidence will be determined on a jurisdiction-by-jurisdiction basis. Even though evidence has been obtained, there is no guarantee that it will meet the criteria of acceptance of a court. Failure to adhere to the rules of evidence may result in challenged evidence being eliminated from proceedings and a complainant's case being weakened. Alternatively, the evidence may carry a reduced level of weight. In summary, the production of evidence obtained from cloud-computing services may be difficult to present in court.[25]

In the first instance prior to the complaint being heard and the evidence introduced, Cristos Velasco San Martin states that the court needs to identify whether they have the authority to hear the matter. With cases involving cloud evidence, there may be instances where the location of the alleged offense cannot be identified and determination of which court has jurisdiction made.[27] Ruan and colleagues argue that as CSPs have data centers across the world in different jurisdictions, with the data being replicated in each of their centers to provide data backup,[9] this may require inquiries being made with the CSP. Consequently differing rules of evidence may apply in various court hearings, and these may require that further evidence be located.

Should an investigation determine a level of culpability of another party, the complainant may seek redress through the judicial system. This may be in a civil or criminal court. The basic process of obtaining evidence of any sort to present before a court is to collect, preserve, and filter, and then to present the evidence in court.[21] This process incorporates the standards introduced by the ISO and discussed throughout this section, and extends the boundaries to include filtering and presenting the evidence. This acknowledges that although evidence may be obtained and preserved as required by ISO standards, not all of the evidence may be required in a court hearing; the filtering process will eliminate evidence that has been lawfully acquired and preserved but that is not required after examination.

With limited established proceedings having been accepted by the court and differences existing between the collection of evidence in traditional and cloud environments, effort must be made to guide the court as to understanding the methods used to seize the data, the reasons why new methodologies have had to be created, and why the court may rely upon its credibility. The integrity of all the steps needs to be clearly explained and the credibility of the CSP needs to be established. This point is reinforced in the *United States Attorneys' Bulletin* of May 2011, which states that a coherent body of case law has yet to be established on the appropriate collection, management, and disclosure of electronically stored information (ESI) for presentation in the criminal courts. Procedures have, however, been developed for the civil courts, which have been codified into the Federal Rules of Civil Procedure.[36] Current research has failed to locate any significant updated research on this fact.

With the legal issues to be addressed by the investigator, the point has been raised in a US court that the failure of the prosecuting agency to seek and obtain potential evidence may weaken the case or cause it to be suppressed. In *United States v. Cross* in 2009, the court granted a motion to suppress evidence based on the failure of the prosecution to produce evidence of the metadata of the electronic evidence.[37] This is of particular relevance to cases involving cloud evidence, as the evidence collection process may take extensive time and involve the MLAT process and adherence to ISO best practices.

Due to the potential volume and complexity of the evidence, consideration must be given by the investigator to ensuring that the court is able to understand what may be very technical evidence provided by many different actors in the chain of custody. George Grispos, Tim Storer, and William Glisson explain that courts and juries are made up of representatives of society and may or may not include persons who have limited understanding of technology.[11] Dennis Reilly, Chris Wren, and Tom Berry explain further that information technology evidence is complex to those who may not have an established background in technology and who may struggle to understand the evidence presented.[8] The explanation of issues such as hypervisors, multitenancy of drives/resources, and differing platforms is difficult enough before introducing the separate subject of computer forensics. The challenge is to present evidence in a manner where the themes and the evidence of expert witnesses are understood.

As a part of the production of evidence, its relevance to the case must be established. The forensic evidence produced must also be validated as being of a high level of integrity and a true representation of the facts it represents.[5] Joseph Schwerha explains that should it be required, it is the responsibility of the person presenting the evidence to the court to prove to the court that the evidence was obtained in a legal manner in all jurisdictions using methodologies that show the integrity of the investigation, evidence collection, and storage. Further, should it have been obtained in breach of legislation in the target country, those involved may be subject to penalties under civil or criminal legislation.[23] Also, should evidence be obtained in a manner that is not to the satisfaction of the court to which it is presented, it may not be accepted at all by the judge and/or jury, who may determine that they do not have confidence in it.[5,16]

The manner in which the evidence is obtained must be disclosed and the methodology must be robust enough to ensure the integrity of the result. The procedures must be able to be repeated by an independent party and produce the same result.[5,11,15,38] Taylor and colleagues explain that if the manner in which the evidence is extracted, secured, and analyzed cannot be documented to be of the standard demanded by the court, then it is unlikely to be accepted as evidence.[5] Grispos, Storer, and Glisson state that the presiding judge has the ultimate responsibility of deciding whether evidence is accepted or not.[11] Specific care must be taken to ensure that the privacy of other clients of the CSP is not violated.[9] Having third-party suppliers involved in the supply of services to the cloud platform makes the presentation of evidence in court even more complicated. Evidence obtained from each third-party supplier must be treated as unique evidence requiring testimony from a representative of that entity.

Stewart believes that the constant demands on cloud-computing resources to store, move, delete, and access data, as well as changes by operating systems, cause changes to the cloud repositories. Application use also changes file metadata, and AV programs access and potentially alter data across the cloud ecosystem. Consequently this may affect the ability to present the required standard of data integrity that a court of law may require.[20]

The CSA argues that unless there is evidence of hacking or tampering, a document produced in the cloud should not be less admissible in evidence because it was produced and stored in the cloud than a document created and stored on traditional infrastructure.[39] Reilly, Wren, and Berry hold a different view, arguing that it is difficult, if not impossible, to maintain a chain of custody for data seized from the cloud and that the principles of the ACPO cannot be conformed to. They argue that ACPO guidelines are redundant and that this creates doubt as to the authenticity, integrity, and admissibility of evidence obtained.[8]

CLOUD BARRIERS TO A SUCCESSFUL INVESTIGATION

As cloud computing is very different from traditional forms of data storage, the preceding sections have shown the investigator that they will be operating within a challenging environment when dealing with cloud-computing evidence. Several barriers to an investigation have been introduced in the context of evidence identification, collection, acquisition, and presentation. This section expands on this list and introduces other barriers, which will need to be addressed either in the planning phase or throughout the investigation as events unfold. While this list is considerable it may not be conclusive, as you may identify other issues to be addressed or you may be fortunate and not be required to address many of them if the cloud-computing service is located entirely within your jurisdiction.

As you read this list, understand that many of these issues can be addressed by communicating with the CSP legal team. However, they can only provide assistance if you make the contact, explain the circumstances, and seek their support and advice early in the investigation. Note that the CSP lawyers interviewed requested that initial contact be made with them when you require assistance, and that some of the digital investigators for the CSP who were interviewed were previously law enforcement officers and therefore very aware of the requirements for evidence preservation, protecting the chain of evidence, and the like.[10]

- *Identification of the cloud-computing provider.* As we have identified, some cloud services are made up of components from different providers. This means that not all of the cloud service is under the control of one company. Using a public cloud SaaS product as an example, a cloud provider may provide the underlying physical infrastructure, Microsoft the operating system and office suite, Oracle the relational database, and so on. Each creates its own logs, which are most likely not available to other suppliers. For example, in the case presented Microsoft would not have access to the logs generated by the Oracle database and vice versa.

At first the investigator will not know the details of the underlying system architecture and agreements, so they will need to ask the CSP when making initial contact. The investigator may then need to identify who among these companies actually stores the requested data and logs. In reality, several requests seeking assistance may need to be forwarded to the different companies.

▪ *Obtaining the cooperation of the CSP.* While the most popular CSPs provide support to law enforcement and civilian investigators, smaller ones may not have the skills, capacity, or interest to provide any form of forensic support.

The EULA or Service Level Agreement (SLA) may provide an agreed level of support from the CSP to a client/investigator in the event of a cyber investigation. For example, they may be willing to provide some evidence without court orders, such as network capture, images of the database, or a copy of a web server.

▪ *Understand the structure of the CSP.* The way data is stored and preserved in CSPs seeks to maximize the storage capacity of the facility. Consequently the data stored moves in some instances by the microsecond across local and maybe different legal jurisdictions. Should you be required to explain this in court, you will need the assistance of the CSP (which cannot be guaranteed as you cannot compel them to give evidence in a court unless they are in your legal jurisdiction) or you will need to obtain an independent expert, such as a cloud architect, who can provide the court with an understanding as to how data is stored in cloud-computer architecture.

▪ *Understanding the CSP log formatting across all the differing components.* Event logs do not have a standard format and may be recorded using different time zones and formats. This was discussed in Chapter 11. It is the investigator's responsibility to make sense of the logs and identify what they are telling you, so they will need to be standardized using SIEM or similar software.

It may be of assistance when a cyber security event is occurring (or even in general day-to-day usage) if the CSP can provide a real-time feed into the client's SIEM and have real-time alerts provided to record potential issues. The CSP may provide clients access to their proprietary log management solution as a part of their service.

- *__The sheer volume of the data stored.__* Cloud-computing services excel in storing large volumes of data. The investigator will need to understand the boundaries of their investigation and exactly what they are looking for before securing evidence. Should they be allowed to download the evidence directly from the cloud, the demands on the corporate bandwidth may be excessive. This takes a significant amount of time and carries the cost of the digital investigator overseeing the downloads.

- *__Multijurisdiction evidence collection.__* As explained, cloud architecture crosses potentially many legal jurisdictions. The architecture also uses virtualization to expand capacity and services to clients. Virtual servers may be hosted from unknown jurisdictions and applications from different suppliers may run from these virtual servers. Consequently, the data sought may be spread across several jurisdictions, and the physical architecture of the CSP may also cross different legal jurisdictions. Virtual servers may be hosted from unknown locations and the applications hosted at other locations altogether.

- *__Ability to link a suspect to a CSP service or activity.__* Cloud computing provides many possible structures to clients, providing different levels of access to logs. In all cases some logs cannot be obtained without the express assistance of the CSP, as they are behind the CSP firewall and hypervisor and cannot be accessed except by CSP staff. The hypervisor is software or a device that operates the VM's operating systems.

  Unfortunately, some of these logs (such as authentication logs) may be critical to your investigation and immediate assistance from the CSP to ensure preservation may be required.

  As with a computer located on a desk, the investigator must find evidence to link a suspect to the cloud account under investigation and the crimes allegedly committed. Some evidence may be found on the personal device that was used to connect to the cloud account, such as web logs showing times of connections to the cloud server, File Transfer Protocol (FTP) logs showing data being removed from the cloud account to an external portable drive, and so on.

- *__Validating the cloud forensic image.__* As the infrastructure of a cloud instance is dynamic, obtaining a second image two minutes after the first will produce a different outcome even though there has been no user activity. This is because the system architecture is changing as data is being moved in the background by the CSP per their storage algorithms.

The inability to produce the same forensic outcome does not comply with ACPO principles, which state that images should be able to be replicated—which is the case with a static piece of evidence, such as a laptop computer. This does not mean that there is any question as to the legitimacy of the cloud image, just that you are dealing with a different environment, which is very different from a static device.

- *Where do you stand when there is a security incident in the cloud? Does the CSP prioritize other clients over you?* Should there be a security breach on the side of the CSP, where do you rate when ensuring the continuity of service and evidence collection when compared to other CSP clients? As an investigator you will seek all evidence promptly; however, when the party who is to provide the evidence to you is seeking to mitigate and eradicate their own breach, your requirements may be rated as low priorities if they are considered at all. Also, the CSP may direct their resources to looking after their major clients and not provide the initial assistance you require.

- *Access to logs is restricted, especially depending upon the CSP product being investigated.* The CSP maintains log records and these need to be obtained with a consent or court order. The larger cloud services, such as IaaS or PaaS, allow the client to maintain their own applications and OS, meaning some logs can be easily obtained.

  As discussed in Chapter 11, log evidence will likely be a critical part of your investigatory and prosecution strategies. Cloud-computing services are not an exception to this concept. With cloud services, the logs you will be seeking are stored with the logs generated by the numerous other clients the CSP has. This is a characteristic of multitenancy and resource pooling and obtaining the advantages of outsourcing of information technology requirements. The logs on a cloud server may also be on many servers in remote locations, as the many functions of the architecture of a cloud service are often remotely spread across data centers in different geographic locations. As an investigator you will not have direct access to logs outside of your client's level of service, and you will need the CSP to use their specialist applications to obtain the logs you require in a format that is understandable and usable.

  To the investigator, this means that your log evidence potentially will not always be in your legal jurisdiction, and depending upon the cloud architecture, may be in a foreign country. If you are fortunate, the cloud service will be entirely within your jurisdiction, meaning local court orders can be used without concern about having to deal with other jurisdictions.

If you are even more fortunate, your client may use a managed service where the log data generated by their CSP is imported into their local storage, where it can be easily accessed as required.

As logs are decentralized and different layers of the cloud platform create different logs in differing formats, logs are generated quickly and may be preserved for very short periods of time due to the massive level of logs being generated daily.

As discussed in Chapter 11, maintaining the authenticity of the cloud log files is a challenge the cyber investigator needs to understand and address in the planning phase of their investigation. In a cloud environment, many cloud services are made up of third-party providers of the infrastructure, and you may find no party has direct access to all the logs you require.

Examples of logs that may be generated include those from antimalware, (IDS) Intrusion Prevention System (IPS), vulnerability management, and remote access software, and those from web proxies, authentication servers, routers, and firewalls. Examples of OS logs include system events and audit records. Some application programs generate their own logs. Examples include client requests and server responses, account information, user information, and significant operational actions.[40]

- **What is the architecture of the CSP? Do they use resources from other CSP or third-party suppliers?** Cloud suppliers come in many shapes and sizes. As previously mentioned, CSP may use only their own infrastructure and suite of applications to make their cloud products, meaning they have visibility over the complete infrastructure of their cloud services. However, many cloud providers use third-party providers to provide aspects of their infrastructure, and the company selling the service will have limited visibility over the infrastructure and how it is operating.

  The relevance to the investigator is that when they are seeking cloud-based evidence, it needs to be determined whom and how many different parties to the CSP they need to contact to obtain evidence. Obtaining logs from multiple suppliers is a challenge in its own right but these need to be matched with those from the infrastructure provider as well.

- **Identifying where the offense actually occurred.** As there may be many legal jurisdictions involved, understand where the offense was actually committed. Because an action is an offense in your jurisdiction does not mean it is an offense in the foreign jurisdictions where the suspect is resident in the case of a cyber-attack. Hacking into a computer and removing all the data is not a criminal offense in every legal jurisdiction throughout the world.

- **Elasticity and forensic evidence.** One of the great benefits of cloud computing is the elasticity of the product obtained. That means you purchase and use the amount of storage and resources you require without having to purchase capacity you may not use. Moreover, elasticity works in both directions, with capacity being reduced should it not be required.

  Once capacity is returned to the CSP, it is made available to other customers and the space is overwritten. This space may contain the remnants of the evidence you require and cannot be recovered once lost. Consequently prompt action is required to notify the CSP and ask them to preserve all the evidence relating to the investigation, even if you are expanding the investigation boundaries wider than initially thought necessary.

- **Ability to obtain stored snapshots and backups for investigation and recovery.** CSPs generally store snapshots of their client's services as backup in the event they're needed for disaster recovery. These may be requested from the CSP directly. Remember, they are a snapshot of the client's cloud service at a specific point in time and may not record details of the offense you are investigating.

- **How to capture forensic evidence across multitenanted jurisdictions?** Along with being spread among different legal jurisdictions, the data stored may be spread across many physical data centers in different countries. Ask the CSP for support and obtain advice from a legal specialist.

- **Introduction of cloud-based evidence before the court.** Should the evidence be obtained from a CSP using remote forensics in a legal manner, the evidence still has to be presented before a court and accounted for, as any other evidence requires. The chain of custody must be addressed and the rules of evidence in each jurisdiction hearing the matter will consider whether there is a need for the testimony of the CSP as to the accuracy of the underlying infrastructure, and whether there is no concern as to the integrity of the data captured.

  Where there is the requirement to meet this hurdle, the CSP will be required to assist in the presentation of the evidence. While they may prefer to capture the evidence themselves and present it as evidence they have lawfully captured, this is one of many issues the investigator will need to address before the evidence-capture process commences.

- **Questions regarding cloud-based evidence.** As cloud-based evidence has rarely if ever been seriously challenged before a court, the investigator may not have judicial direction in determining what a court requires to verify the authenticity and credibility of the data obtained. Also, the questions of jurisdiction and the legality of local court orders being partially executed in foreign legal jurisdictions have not been settled, and therefore no judicial direction will be available to the cyber investigator on this issue, either. Consequently, the investigator will consider operating under established rules of evidence approved by a court in a given jurisdiction, as previously discussed.

- **Sufficient storage capacity.** Evidence from the cloud can be significant and require extensive storage capacity by the client.
- **Chain of custody.** The chain of custody may involve many parties: the CSP, their forensic technicians, and third-party suppliers. As an investigator you will be required to obtain statements from all parties required to prove the chain of custody of the evidence.
- **Imaging of evidence, including cloud servers.** As discussed throughout this chapter, seek legal advice and the cooperation of the CSP prior to imaging of evidence.
- **Obtain legal authority from multiple jurisdictions.** Is the fact the evidence is originating from multiple jurisdictions of any interest to a particular court?
- **Data integrity.** The capture of digital evidence is volatile and cannot be replicated by the opposing party at a later date. As with network forensics, this means that a special emphasis must be placed on the preservation of the data as it is captured and preserved.
- **Recovery of deleted data.** Depending upon the cloud product being used, there will be varying levels of access to deleted data, which may provide valuable evidence.
- **Suspect having continual remote access to the compromised device and the cloud server.** In our increasingly compromised world, the suspect may have the ability to remotely access the cloud server and delete evidence the forensic examiner or cyber investigator seeks to seize. To complicate matters further, the investigator may never know the suspect has remotely accessed the cloud evidence and deleted it.
- **Lack of ability to compel persons in overseas jurisdictions to support a prosecution.** An employee of a CSP may be a competent but noncompellable witness, meaning they cannot be forced to give evidence in a prosecution. This will reduce the ability to present cloud-based evidence, depending on the rulings of the court.
- **Obtaining a virtual image of a device or server may not capture necessary data, such as deleted data.** A VM image does not have access

to network logs, which are stored by the CSP. Depending upon the cloud product being used, there may be no access to authentication logs. Once data has been deleted in a VM, it may be difficult or impossible to recover.

▪ **Encrypted data.** Encryption of data is a standard safeguard in cyber security. Depending upon the cloud product being used in a cloud environment (such as IaaS), the data you are seeking may be encrypted but the encryption key may not be stored in the cloud environment and may not be available to CSP security. This is particularly relevant to a law enforcement officer who is investigating a suspect who has evidence stored in a cloud service.

If it is an offense in the identified foreign jurisdiction, identify whether the prosecution should be commenced in your jurisdiction or where the suspect resides. This is particularly the case in criminal matters.

SUGGESTED TIPS TO ASSIST YOUR CLOUD-BASED INVESTIGATION

As we have seen, investigating in the cloud can be a very challenging environment for the many reasons discussed throughout this chapter. This, however, does not mean that evidence is beyond the investigator or inquiries should not be pursued. It means that the investigator must understand and respect this challenging environment and that obtaining evidence from a cloud-computing environment is not business as usual.

The CSP provides a lawful product and does not like their services being misused by criminal entities. Many of the issues addressed in this chapter can be navigated by open communication with the CSP early in the investigation.

A few ideas to advance your investigation follow.

▪ **Establish cooperation with the CSP before the incident.** In a perfect world, gaining access to the required staff at a CSP would be as easy when responding to an incident as it was during the recruitment phase. However, this is not always the case. It is recommended that a data owner obtain the emergency contact details of the key people at their CSP in the event of an incident, and that this information be incorporated into their Incident Response (IR) plan.

▪ **Contact the CSP early in the investigation.** The issues discussed in this chapter are not new and CSP lawyers and digital investigators have the capability to greatly assist you. As has been mentioned regularly in this chapter, commence contact at the beginning of the investigation and seek their experienced advice. You will not be the first investigator navigating these issues, and should you ask, the CSP will be able to assist you in addressing many of these issues.

- *Work with lawyers who understand the cloud environment and contractual obligations with the CSP.* Prior to commencing evidence acquisition, ensure the legality of your actions after discussing them with your lawyers and the CSP lawyers. The consequences of getting this wrong can be extremely serious for the investigation team and the complainant.
- *Establish agreement of access to evidence, including logs, before incidents happen.* Obtaining access to logs generally needs to be done with the consent of the CSP; however, logs are often overwritten due to the large volume of space they take up over time. Consequently a data owner may make arrangements for their logs to be preserved as a part of their agreement or for them to be recorded to an external device under their control.
- *Identify relevant data sources pre-event.* Having an understanding of the data that may be obtained from a cloud-computing product allows the investigator to commence the evidence identification and seizure phase with the knowledge of the boundaries they are operating within. Earlier in this chapter, "What Is Cloud Computing?" described the three major configurations of cloud-based evidence and what can be obtained with and without the direct support of the CSP.
- *Define thresholds for investigation and calling in law enforcement from the start.* Investigation boundaries need to be established in the initial meeting with the complainant. However, as many experienced investigators will know, these boundaries may expand as a greater understanding of events unfolds and the scale of the offender's activity becomes known.

Calling police in to an investigation may occur at any time between the initial discovery of the event and the completion of the investigation, when a factual investigation report can be completed for referral. Not all matters will be referred to police, and whether the notification is made will depend on many matters, including the seriousness of the event.

When it appears that an event is very serious, an initial phone call to police cybercrime units may prove beneficial. The online report may follow. Examples of online reporting facilities include:

- *United States.* The Internet Crime Complaint Center (IC3), which can be located at https://www.ic3.gov/default.aspx

- *Singapore.* Singapore provides an eService for reporting online cybercrime, and this can be located at https://www.police.gov.sg/e-services/report/police-report
- *Hong Kong.* The Hong Kong police provide an online reporting facility for cybercrime at https://www.erc.police.gov.hk/cmiserc/CCC/PolicePublicPage?language=en
- *Australia.* The Australian Cybercrime Online Reporting Network (ACORN) portal, which can be located at www.acorn.gov.au
- *United Kingdom.* The Metropolitan Police provides an online reporting facility for fraud, including cybercrime, which can be located at https://www.met.police.uk/ro/report/fo/fraud

  Each of these systems provides value for complainants reporting cybercrime across international borders. The receiving law enforcement agency disseminates complaints throughout the country to the agency where the suspect is believed to be resident or refers it to the jurisdiction where the complaint will obtain a more thorough understanding of the crime being reported.
- *Understanding the attitude of the CSP toward remote forensic examinations.* There are many issues to be addressed when seeking to understand the attitude of the CSP toward remote forensic services being conducted on their servers. A few are:
  - When data is being removed, how can the CSP determine whether a client or law enforcement is copying the data for a legal reason? A hack into the cloud server via the client's machine looks the same to the CSP as a client seeking a copy of their data.
  - CSPs do not like untested forensic tools being used on their physical or virtual servers. The evidence in the registry is generally unavailable to the client, and should a digital examiner seek to breach the hypervisor and access this evidence, a security event will occur in the cloud service, which places other clients' data at risk.
  - CSPs are concerned that the forensic tools used may collect other client's data along with the clients' data you are seeking.
  - CSPs are concerned at the bandwidth demands involved in removing a client's data, especially an established corporate client who may have many terabytes of data being downloaded.
  - CSPs have stated that should a forensic examiner cause damage to their physical or virtual infrastructure while conducting an examination, they reserve the right to commence legal action against their client.

CLOUD-COMPUTING INVESTIGATION FRAMEWORK

As cloud computing is a significantly different platform for the investigator to operate within, the manner in which evidence is obtained may present legal and logistical challenges. Where the cloud servers are entirely within your local jurisdiction, many of the issues discussed will not be relevant; however, given the manner in which cloud servers are being built throughout the world there is a fair chance that at some stage in your career you will be seeking evidence from a cloud-computing server in a foreign international jurisdiction.

The following section presents a proposed methodology that may be used to legally obtain this form of evidence. It is a proposed methodology only, and the laws in your legal jurisdiction will affect the relevance of this proposal. As with many of the ideas presented throughout this book, use it as a basis for expanding your thinking about the legal and logistical issues you may encounter and modify as you require.

Throughout the methodology are references to law enforcement agencies using MLAT warrants as the circumstances dictate. Although civilian investigators do not have access to these warrants, they are able to access legal assistance using court orders in the target jurisdiction. In fact, civilian investigator may be able to progress their investigations more quickly than their law enforcement counterparts, as the MLAT process is known for being cumbersome and bureaucratic.

Proposed Investigative Framework

To assist in following the proposed framework, a flowchart is presented to provide a visual representation of the proposed investigative methodology. This section provides the proposed template only for your consideration and takes a generic view of locating and lawfully obtaining evidence from a public cloud facility. The order of events is a generic representation only and an investigator may find in their circumstances it is advantageous to alter the order of investigative steps. Also, the considerations may not be applicable in all instances, depending upon the multiple versions of cloud-computing products and structures that are available to clients as well as the laws in all jurisdictions involved.

The flowchart also attempts to incorporate the processes of criminal and civil investigators, which are identified in the explanations given for each step.

Figure 12.1 shows a framework that may be used in a cloud-computing environment.

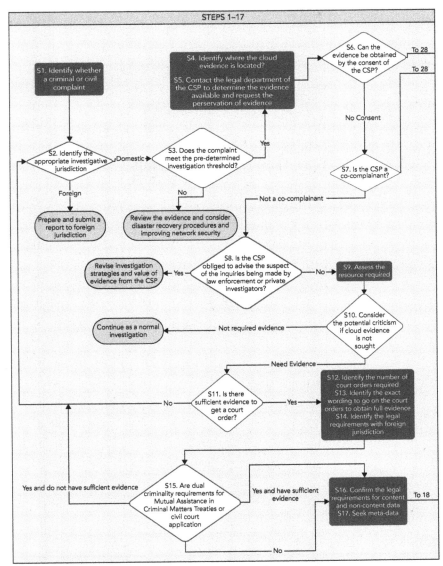

FIGURE 12.1 Cloud-computing investigation framework.
Source: Chart © Graeme Edwards

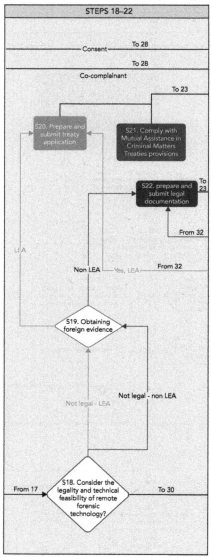

FIGURE 12.1 *(Continued)*

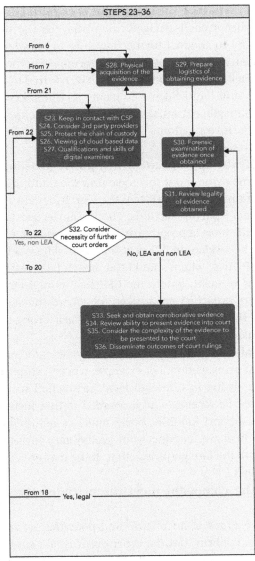

FIGURE 12.1 (Continued)

Step 1: Identify whether the complaint is criminal or civil.

As the cyber event is triaged, there may be the decision made by the victim entity to conduct further inquiries in an attempt to locate the offender. As soon as possible, attempt to determine whether the complaint is a criminal or civil matter. If the matter is to be referred to law enforcement, there must be sufficient evidence to justify a criminal complaint. If it is a civil matter, management must support the decision and supply adequate resources for the investigation.

Progress to step 2.

Step 2: Identify the appropriate investigative jurisdiction.

It is a theme throughout this topic that the multijurisdictional nature of cloud computing potentially brings the search for evidence into the realm of many different legal jurisdictions. This raises the question of which legal jurisdiction is the most appropriate in which to conduct an investigation, as evidence may be resident in different servers in different legal jurisdictions within the CSP. Also, where should the breach be investigated: where the complainant is resident, where the CSP has its registered offices, where the CSP servers breached are located, or where the suspect is resident? Depending on the circumstances, there may be a strong argument for any of these options.

Consider also the potential for multiple law enforcement agencies to conduct a joint investigation. For example, where a suspected offender can be identified as being in a foreign legal jurisdiction to the complainant, a complaint can be received and forwarded to that jurisdiction for investigation, with support inquiries being made as required by the referring police. In this instance, conduct your preliminary investigation and refer the complaint to the foreign jurisdiction. If the matter is not to be referred, progress to step 3.

Step 3: Does the complaint meet the predetermined investigation threshold?

If evidence exists of an offense and potential evidence resides on a cloud platform, confirm that the cyber event is of a sufficient nature and seriousness to continue the investigation. This level preferably needs to be determined pre-event in the IR plan or identified once facts about the event begin emerging.

The law enforcement investigator will assess whether the event is serious enough to conduct what may be an international investigation when compared to the other complaints they are processing, and whether the offense is serious enough to reach the legislated threshold of MLAT legislation.

The civilian investigator will continually monitor the costs of the investigation against the budget supplied. International legal costs may be very expensive and prove ultimately prohibitive to progressing the investigation past the initial defined budget.

If the investigation is to be progressed, then advance to step 4. If not, discuss other options with the complainant, such as commencing disaster recovery procedures and improving network security.

Step 4: Identify where the cloud evidence is located.

Assess whether the potential evidence to be obtained from a cloud server involves the location and seizure of evidence from a domestic or international jurisdiction. A complainant may be able to give advice as to whether their CSP data is stored in a specific region or international jurisdiction. If the complainant cannot identify this, communicating with the CSP's lawyers is recommend. If the evidence is located within the local jurisdiction, continue the investigation using traditional evidence collection methodologies and request evidence preservation. If the evidence is in an international or unknown jurisdiction, make inquiries with the CSP.

Progress to step 5.

Step 5: Contact the legal department of the CSP to determine what evidence is available and request that evidence be preserved.

Discuss what evidence is available and what may have been overwritten. Article 29 of the Budapest Convention holds that a law enforcement investigator may request that the CSP or central authority, in association with MLAT legislation, preserve a copy of the data sought pending the service of a legal instrument authorizing the release of such data. Despite a CSP mirroring their data for backup, not all data created in a data center may be replicated outside of that country due to local legislation, such as that in the EU. Consider whether the alleged suspect still has access to the cloud platform with the potential to commit further offenses or delete evidence. Also advise the complainant to update security settings and passwords to prevent a repetition of the attack.

The civilian investigator should also seek the support of the CSP legal team and identify which legal orders they are required to seek to obtain all the available evidence. Issues identified in the previous section may also be discussed with the CSP at this time.

Progress to step 6.

Step 6: Can the evidence be obtained by the consent of the CSP?

Assess from discussions what evidence can be obtained from the CSP with the consent of the data owner, complainant, or CSP, and the value this will have in the subsequent investigation, with consideration of the totality and integrity of the evidence. This step will largely depend on the nature of the complaint and the evidence that is being sought, such as where the cloud account of the complainant has been hacked. This step will also rely upon whether the evidence being sought is from the cloud server of the complainant or the suspect. If the former, then the CSP may be prepared to supply the evidence with the agreement of the complainant; however, if the evidence is from the suspect's cloud account, it is unlikely to be obtainable with consent. If the evidence can be obtained with the consent of the CSP, progress to step 28; otherwise proceed to step 7.

Step 7: Is the CSP a co-complainant?

Consider the nature of the offense and whether the CSP may also be a victim of the offense and interested in making a complaint. If the CSP becomes a co-complainant and is willing to provide the required evidence, progress to step 28; otherwise move to step 8.

Step 8: Is the CSP obliged to advise the suspect of the inquiries being made by law enforcement or private investigators?

Discuss with the CSP whether the service of a court order or law enforcement inquiries places a legal or contractual obligation upon them to notify the suspect party whose data is being obtained that a court order has been served on them. If so, reconsider options and whether they can continue with the investigation and seek such evidence after the suspect has been interviewed.

In some jurisdictions, such as in the United States, law enforcement can seek an order from the court prohibiting the CSP from advising their client that evidence is being sought against their cloud account

If the CSP will be advising the suspect, review the investigation timetable and the implications for it. If not, progress to step 9.

Step 9: Assess the resources required.

These resources may be in the form of financial, personnel, specialist IT, or legal support needed, and in a civilian investigation, will not be inexpensive. Do you have the storage capacity or forensic tools to deal with what may be a large volume of data that is written in a proprietary format?

Progress to step 10.

Step 10: Consider the potential criticism if cloud evidence is not sought.

Consider the potential to be criticized in court should you seek to conduct a prosecution and not seek the evidence from the CSP. If this evidence is not sought, does this render the investigation incomplete, and does it mean that you are providing the defense with an argument that the evidence showing their client's innocence has not been collected because of logistics, time, expense, complexity, or the lack of resources? Is evidence from the CSP required? Reconsider methodology (such as using screen capture of the evidence) that was to be used as an investigative tool. If the evidence from the CSP is not required, continue the investigation using traditional methodologies without the cloud-based evidence. If it is required, progress to step 11.

Step 11: Is there sufficient evidence to get a court order?

Is there sufficient evidence available to satisfy judicial authorities in all jurisdictions when seeking a court order for the evidence from the cloud platform that an offense has been committed and that evidence resides with the CSP? Failure to prove this point reduces the potential to obtain judicial orders from either jurisdiction. This applies equally to criminal and civil investigators. If sufficient evidence exists, progress to step 12. If not, refer back to step 2 and review the evidence held.

Step 12: Identify the number of court orders required.

Identify from discussions with the CSP whether multiple court orders need to be obtained for evidence held in different legal jurisdictions. The multijurisdictional nature of cloud storage, where the location of potential evidence is distributed throughout many different servers, and potentially in different legal jurisdictions, has been regularly discussed in other sections of the book. This is particularly relevant when the CSP is a reseller of cloud services.

Progress to step 13.

Step 13: Identify the exact wording to go on the court orders to obtain full evidence.

Discuss with the CSP the exact wording that they require to avoid confusion and ensure that you are obtaining the totality of evidence that you require. Issues have arisen in the past where court orders have been served on a CSP that do not make sense, that request evidence that does not exist, that apply to the wrong jurisdiction, that request only a portion of the available evidence, or that leave the CSP in the position of having to breach other legislation to comply.

Progress to step 14.

Step 14: Identify legal requirements with the foreign jurisdiction.

Discuss with the law enforcement agency or local lawyers in the target jurisdiction the legal process that must be undertaken and the level of evidence required to obtain data through a court order or a similar legal instrument. The laws of each country may vary markedly and what may be accessible in one country may not be accessible in another. Also, laws change and what may have been an acceptable legal application in a previous investigation may no longer be applicable.

Progress to step 15.

Step 15: Are dual criminality requirements for mutual legal assistance treaties or civil court applications met?

Establish whether the offense being investigated is also an offense in the jurisdiction in which the evidence is to be sought. In some countries dual criminality may be a necessity to obtain foreign cooperation in obtaining a court order and the seizure of evidence. If so, this may hinder the investigator's ability to obtain a court order to obtain evidence. Whether this is a condition of a treaty or civil application depends on the agreement in the legislation between both countries. If dual criminality requirements are met, progress to step 16. If not, refer to step 2 and reevaluate your evidence and options.

Step 16: Confirm the legal requirements for content and noncontent data.

Decide on what evidence you are seeking subject to the investigation you are undertaking, and the results of the advice provided by the CSP legal department and foreign-based legal advice. Generally, a subpoena may access noncontent data such as logs and a search warrant obtains both content and noncontent data.

Progress to step 17.

Step 17: Seek metadata.

When obtaining content data, seek the metadata that is behind the content rather than just a copy of the sought-after documentary evidence. This is valuable evidence and may significantly advance your investigation and help to identify the person behind the offense. An example of valuable metadata is the ability to identify who created a document, when it was created, and when it was last accessed.

Progress to step 18.

Step 18: Consider the legality and technical feasibility of remote forensic technology.

Despite technology being available to conduct a remote forensic examination of the target computer, this should only be of consideration when the issues of legality in all jurisdictions, cooperation of the CSP, and completeness of the sought-after evidence have been fully addressed. Failure to lawfully account for the collection of data can result in the evidence being excluded from court proceedings and the party doing the data capture in the remote jurisdiction may face legal proceedings in that jurisdiction. Also, being unable to prove lawful capture of data may make evidence inadmissible. If the decision is made not to use this technology, proceed to step 19; if technically and legally able to do so, undertake evidence capture and proceed to step 30.

Step 19: Obtaining foreign evidence.

Consider options to obtain evidence from the CSP. If using a traditional MLAT application, prepare the application and seek authority through designated channels to obtain a treaty request in the target jurisdiction.

If using civil lawyers in the target jurisdiction, the process of obtaining the evidence will be through the directions of your foreign lawyers, allowing for the different requirements of the different legal jurisdictions.

If a law enforcement agency, proceed to step 20. If a civilian investigator, proceed to step 22.

Again, steps 20 and 21 identify a proposed methodology for law enforcement investigators using MLAT legislation to obtain evidence from a CSP in a foreign legal jurisdiction. It is not applicable to civilian investigators.

Law Enforcement Investigator

Step 20: Prepare and submit treaty application.

MLAT requests must be prepared and forwarded to the law enforcement representatives in the target country through designated channels. The agency and their legal representatives will ensure the request complies with local legislation, including the rules of evidence.

If approval is given to forward the submission, progress to step 21.

Step 21: Comply with mutual legal assistance treaty applications.

MLAT legislation places requirements on law enforcement officers seeking evidence from foreign legal jurisdictions. It is outside of the boundaries of this book to examine such procedures, as each law enforcement agency will already have established procedures for obtaining such evidence through designated channels. In Australia, these channels operate through the Attorney-General's Department and in the United States through the office of the Department of Justice.

Progress to step 23.

If you are a civilian investigator, you will go to step 22 after step 19; as mentioned previously, steps 20 and 21 apply only to law enforcement investigators.

Civilian Investigator

Step 22: Prepare and submit legal documentation.

The civilian investigator will need to invest time with the lawyers in their jurisdiction as they prepare their international request for evidence. A partnership will need to be established with lawyers in the foreign jurisdiction.

Progress to step 23.

Law enforcement investigators will proceed from step 21 to 23; civilian investigators from step 22 to step 23.

Step 23: Keep in contact with CSP.

The requesting officer must keep in regular contact with the CSP and advise them of the progress of the treaty application, as an application can take a significant period of time depending on the workloads of the legal representatives in all related jurisdictions as well as the quality of the treaty application. Failure to keep in contact with the CSP may result in the stored evidence being considered as no longer required and disposed of. Speak to the CSP regularly and confirm how often they need to be kept informed of the progress of the legal proceedings.

Note that MLAT applications from outside the United States may take a very long time to pass through the layers of bureaucracy. It is not unusual for MLAT requests to take up to two years from the time of preparation to obtaining the evidence from the CSP. Many CSPs are not aware of the layers of bureaucracy involved and may need to be advised that the delay between the request for evidence preservation and the court order authorizing its release is not the investigator's fault.

Progress to step 24.

Step 24: Consider potential for third-party providers.

Should the third-party providers of the CSP's infrastructure component have evidence that cannot be obtained from the CSP, a separate court order via a treaty application seeking the data may be considered.

Progress to step 25.

Step 25: Protect the chain of custody.

Plan and prepare for preservation of the chain of custody with signed, legally admissible witness statements.

Progress to step 26.

Step 26: Viewing of cloud-based data.

Discussions may be undertaken between technical representatives of the requesting law enforcement agency and the CSP as to the manner in which the target data may be viewed, establishing confidence in the integrity of the evidence. This is of particular relevance if the CSP acquires the data using proprietary forensics or if the data is stored in a manner where it cannot be viewed with traditional applications.

Progress to step 27.

Step 27: Qualifications and skills of digital investigators.

Evidence of the qualifications and skills of the digital investigator are required to be presented to the court as evidence of the accuracy and completeness of the evidence. This statement would be sought at the time that the evidence was extracted from the CSP's servers. A forensic examiner may be requested by the court to state their qualifications and experience in the field of the seizure of digital evidence.

Progress to step 28.

The following section progresses the evidence collection process by examining the investigative template using the legislation proposed in this thesis from the initial application to the courts to seize a suspect's online account to the receipt of evidence from the CSP.

Seizure of Evidence

Step 28: Physical acquisition of the evidence.

The physical relocation of the evidence must be planned; this can be through an investigating officer going to the target country to collect it from the CSP or law enforcement agency that obtained the data. Alternatively, it may be forwarded through a secure registered courier or electronic transfer where feasible. Always consider the preservation of the chain of custody when making this decision.

Progress to step 29.

Step 29: Prepare logistics of obtaining evidence.

Plan for the receipt of the evidence, as cloud data can be considerable in size and require significant amounts of storage. This consideration can be addressed in discussions with the CSP, who can advise you as to the amount of data that the court order can produce and how much storage capacity you will need.

Progress to step 30.

Step 30: Forensic examination of evidence once obtained.

Upon receipt of the evidence, traditional forensic techniques can be applied depending on the format in which the evidence is obtained.

Proceed to step 31.

Step 31: Legality of possession of evidence.

Consideration needs to be made of the nature of the evidence being sought. Should you obtain a virtual image of the material in the cloud account you have successfully sought, you may discover during your examination of it illegal material, such as stolen IP, fraudulent identities, stolen credit card numbers, or CEM. Should you discover this material, seek immediate legal advice and contact your local police for direction.

Progress to step 32.

Step 32: Consider the necessity of further court orders or evidence capture.

Upon review of the evidence, consider whether further court orders are required from foreign jurisdictions. The potential exists for further court orders to be executed, indicating that the initial application may open new avenues of investigation.

Should there be a requirement to obtain further evidence from an international jurisdiction, the law enforcement investigator will return to step 20. The civilian investigator will return to step 22. If further orders are not required, progress to step 33.

Step 33: Seek and obtain corroborative evidence.

Evidence corroborating that obtained from the CSP must be sought where available to increase the integrity of the evidence obtained. This may be obtained from open source material, evidence from the suspect's electronic devices, inquiries made in the investigating jurisdictions (such as telecommunication/banking records), and so on.

Progress to step 34.

Step 34: Review ability to present evidence into court.

Should the evidence not be able to be supported by way of a witness statement and no legal instrument exist to compel a member of the CSP to produce the evidence, then the evidence may be accepted by the court within its discretion. Alternatively, it may not be acceptable or it may have a reduced standard of value. Review how the inability to obtain all the relevant witness statements affects the strength of your case.

Progress to step 35.

Step 35: Consider the complexity of the evidence to be presented to the court.

Should the cloud-based evidence be required to be introduced in a court of law as evidence, consideration should be given as to its complexity and the ability of a judge and jury to understand it. To assist in this, consider the use of an independent expert.

Progress to step 36.

Step 36: Disseminate outcomes of court rulings.

Outcomes of court hearings where the cloud-based evidence has been challenged and a determination of the evidence provided by the court needs to be disseminated through legal channels, so the decision can be factored into future investigations and an understanding of the direction the courts are taking with cloud-based evidence gained.

This chapter has provided a template to be considered and modified by civilian and law enforcement investigators. It is not intended to be a definitive guide, but provides a basis that can be modified to meet the unique circumstances of your investigation and the legal boundaries within which you operate. As a final point to be repeated, you will likely be operating in multiple legal jurisdictions so always consider the legality of the target legal jurisdiction and seek professional legal advice.

CYBERCRIME CASE STUDY

John (not his real name) worked in a technical position in a successful company. He was highly respected and produced high-quality work in conjunction with his two employees. However, unknown to management, John had a crush on one of his female staff that was not reciprocated.

The business had a downturn in the market and decided to let several staff go, one of whom was the female whom John was infatuated with. The day he was told she was leaving the company he was furious and aggressively fought against management for her to keep her job. While the severance package was generous with training support, John refused to allow her to leave the company without a fight.

In a sign of very visible solidarity, John resigned his position and made sure all of the staff knew the reason why. After a meeting where he was given the opportunity to reconsider his decision over the coming days, John insisted that he would leave at the same time as his employee.

After his resignation was reluctantly accepted, he returned to his desk and worked on his computer for several minutes before storming from the office.

Fellow workers were suspicious of his actions and decided to check his activities. As his computer was not logged off they were able to check his email, where they discovered he had forwarded the entirety of the company's IP, conservatively valued at $15 million, to his personal cloud-computing account.

A complaint was immediately made to police and a preservation request was made to the CSP through the authority of an MLAT and with the cooperation of the CSP. The request sought a copy of the suspect's cloud account, including metadata.

The immediate concern of the complainant and police was what the suspect had done with the data since he'd left the office. As it was sent to a cloud account, he could have moved it to multiple locations as well as downloading copies to his home computer and external storage devices. Another cause of concern was that competitors were trying to obtain the IP of the company, including through an offer to buy the company, and if John had released the IP to them the complainant was effectively facing bankruptcy within six months.

As the data was in the suspect's personal cloud, the complainant and police had no access to it to prevent further offenses while the initial phase of the investigation was continuing.

A search warrant was executed on John's residential address that evening, as links could be made between the data theft and his home. John was very surprised at police raiding his home and stated that he believed at worst he would be liable for an Employment Court hearing and not a criminal investigation for the theft of $15 million of property. He made a full confession, and despite having the law explained to him he refused to believe that he had done anything wrong (which is very common when employees take corporate data when they move to new employment).

Although he had signed a document at the commencement of his employment stating that he had no ownership or rights to the IP he'd helped to develop, he felt that as he worked on the IP, he had a right to a copy of it when he left the company. He also liked to keep a collection of his best work, which included large volumes of the company IP, for his resume.

An examination of his personal computer devices showed that he had not downloaded the IP from the cloud service. An examination of the cloud service showed that he had not moved the IP to any other account. An examination of his computer at home identified that he had already taken several copies of the company IP over the preceding year as well as personnel, salary, board, and management files.

In this instance, the usual offender motivations were not applicable and the reasons for the crime were seen as irrational. However, the motivators were very important to him and motivated him to commit a very serious criminal offense.

Although he had admitted the offense, as the evidence was spread through international jurisdictions via the cloud, he still had access to the IP and could still cause damage to the company. Once he worked out how much trouble he was in, he decided to assist police in their investigations and agreed to sign the ownership of the cloud account over to the police service, where passwords and account recovery options were changed.

The computers were seized with evidence wiped clean of all copies of the IP once court proceedings were completed.

NOTES

1. International Organization for Standardization (ISO) and the International Electrotechnical Commission (IEC), *Information Technology—Cloud Computing—Overview and Vocabulary*, ISO/IEC 17788:2014.
2. Dominik Birk and Christoph Wegner, "Technical Challenges of Forensic Investigations in Cloud Computing Environments" in *Proceedings of the 2011 Sixth IEEE International Workshop on Systematic Approaches to Digital Forensic Engineering* (Washington, DC: IEEE Computer Society, 2011).
3. Cloud Security Alliance, "Mapping the Forensic Standard ISO/IEC 27037 to Cloud Computing," June 2013.
4. Peter Mell and Timothy Grance, *The NIST Definition of Cloud Computing*, Special Publication 800-145, September 2011, National Institute of Standards and Technology, United States Department of Commerce.
5. Mark Taylor, John Haggerty, David Gresty, and David Lamb, "Forensic Investigation of Cloud Computing Systems," *Network Security* 2011, no. 3 (2011): 4–10, https://www.sciencedirect.com/science/article/pii/S1353485811700241.
6. Christopher Hooper, Ben Martini, and Kim-Kwang Raymond Choo, "Cloud Computing and Its Implications for Cybercrime Investigations in Australia," *Computer Law and Security Review* 29 (2013): 152–163, https://doi.org/10.1016/j.clsr.2013.01.006.
7. Ellen Messmer, "Gartner on Cloud Security: 'Our Nightmare Scenario Is Here Now,'" *Computerworld*, October 22, 2009.
8. Dennis Reilly, Chris Wren, and Tom Berry, "Cloud Computing: Pros and Cons for Computer Forensic Examination," *International Journal of Multimedia and Image Processing* 1, no. 1 (2011): 26–34, https://pdfs

.semanticscholar.org/366e/05c9bb441247afee11f97f125c9a5ce0fc2a
.pdf.

9. Keyun Ruan, Joe McCarthy, Tahar, Kechadi, and Mark Crosbie, "Cloud
Forensics: An Overview," 2011, Centre for Cybercrime Investigation,
University College Dublin, https://www.researchgate.net/publication/
229021339_Cloud_forensics_An_overview.

10. Graeme Edwards, "Investigating Cybercrime in a Cloud-Computing
Environment" (doctoral thesis, Queensland University of Technology,
2016).

11. George Grispos, Tim Storer, and William Bradley Glisson, "Calm Before
the Storm: The Challenges of Cloud Computing in Digital Forensics,"
International Journal of Digital Crime and Forensics 4 (2012), http://doi.org/
10.4018/jdcf.2012040103.

12. Neha Thethi and Anthony Keane, "Digital Forensics Investigations in
the Cloud," in *Proceedings of the 2014 IEEE Advance Computing Conference*
(Gurgaon, India, February 21–22, 2014), https://ieeexplore.ieee.org/
document/6779543.

13. Regional Computer Forensics Laboratory, *Annual Report 2012*, Federal
Bureau of Investigation, United States Department of Justice.

14. Regional Computer Forensics Laboratory, *Annual Report 2013*, Federal
Bureau of Investigation, United States Department of Justice.

15. International Organization for Standardization (ISO) and the Inter-
national Electrotechnical Commission (IEC), *Information Technology—
Security Techniques: Guidelines for Identification, Collection, Acquisition, and
Preservation of Digital Evidence*, ISO/IEC 27037:2012.

16. Josiah Dykstra and Alan Sherman, "Acquiring Forensic Evidence from
IaaS Cloud Computing: Exploring and Evaluating Tools, Trust, and
Techniques" (paper, Digital Forensic Research Conference, Washington
DC, August 6–8, 2012).

17. John Cauthen, "Executing Search Warrants in the Cloud," *FBI Law
Enforcement Bulletin*, October 7, 2014, https://leb.fbi.gov/articles/
featured-articles/executing-search-warrants-in-the-cloud.

18. Allison Stanton and Andrew Victor, "What We See in the Clouds: A
Practical Overview of Litigating Against and on Behalf of Organizations
Using Cloud Computing," *United States Attorneys' Bulletin* 59, no. 3
(2011): 34–43.

19. Mark L. Krotoski and Jason Passwaters, "Using Log Evidence Analysis to
Show Internet and Computer Activity in Criminal Cases," *United States
Attorneys' Bulletin* 59, no. 6 (2011): 1–15.

20. Dennis Stewart, "Challenges with Cloud Forensics, Masters of Cybercrime and Security," Utica College, 2014.

21. Scott Zimmerman and Dominick Glavach, *Cyber Forensics in the Cloud, IAnewsletter* 14, no. 1 (2011): 4–7.

22. Bernd Grobauer and Thomas Schreck, "Towards Incident Handling in the Cloud: Challenges and Approaches," in *Proceedings of the 2nd ACM Cloud Computing Security Workshop* (Chicago, IL, 2010).

23. Joseph Schwerha, "Law Enforcement Challenges in Transborder Acquisition of Electronic Evidence from 'Cloud Computing Providers,'" January 2010, Council of Europe.

24. Winston Maxwell and Christopher Wolf, "A Global Reality: Governmental access to Data in the Cloud," (white paper, July 2012, HI Data Protection).

25. Ivana Deyrup et al., Cloud Computing and National Security Law, 2010, Lawfare.

26. Stephen Mason and Esther George, "Digital Evidence and Cloud Computing," *Computer Law and Security Review* 27, no. 5 (2011): 524–528. https://doi.org.10.1016/j.clsr.2011.07.005.

27. Cristos Velasco San Martin, "Jurisdictional Aspects of Cloud Computing," Council of Europe.

28. Connie Carnabuci and Heather Tropman, "The Cloud and US Cross-Border Risks," Austlii.

29. Todd Shipley, "Collection of Evidence from the Internet: Part 2," *Forensic Magazine*, 2009.

30. Josiah Dykstra, "Seizing Electronic Evidence from Cloud Computing Platforms," ResearchGate.

31. United States Constitution 1788, accessed April 3, 2014, https://www.wdl.org/en/item/2708.

32. United States Code 1874, accessed April 2, 2014, http://uscode.house.gov/detailed_guide.xhtml.

33. Loi Informatique et Liberties 1978 Chapter XII (France), accessed December 22, 2018, https://www.cnil.fr/sites/default/files/typo/document/Act78-17VA.pdf.

34. John Haried, "Flying Cars and Web Glasses: How the Digital Revolution Is Changing Law Enforcement," *United States Attorneys' Bulletin* 59, no. 3 (2011): 2–15, https://www.justice.gov/sites/default/files/usao/legacy/2011/07/08/usab5903.pdf.

35. NIST Cloud Computing Forensic Science Working Group, *NIST Cloud Computing Forensic Science Challenges*, Draft NISTIR 8006, June 2014,

National Institute of Standards and Technology, United States Department of Commerce.

36. Andrew Goldsmith, "Trends or Lack Thereof in Criminal eDiscovery: A Pragmatic Survey of Recent Case Law," *United States Attorneys' Bulletin* 59, no. 3 (2011): 2–15, https://www.justice.gov/sites/default/files/usao/legacy/2011/07/08/usab5903.pdf.

37. United States v. Cross, WL 3233267 (E.D.N.Y. Oct. 2009).

38. Christopher Marsico, "Computer Evidence v. Daubert: The Coming Conflict," Perdue University.

39. Cloud Security Alliance, "Defined Categories of Service 2011."

40. Karen Kent and Murugiah Souppaya, *Guide to Computer Security Log Management*, Special Publication 800-92, September 2006, National Institute of Standards and Technology, United States Department of Commerce.

41. Janet Williams, *ACPO Good Practice Guide for Digital Evidence*, March 2012, Association of Chief Police Officers.

CHAPTER THIRTEEN

Identifying, Seizing, and Preserving Evidence from Internet of Things Devices

A S TECHNOLOGY HAS developed, its role in our lives has become more intrusive. With the new generation of technology being introduced into our homes, workplaces, community areas, and other spaces, it is fast reaching the stage where there is little the connected person can do that is not recorded on a digital device somewhere. While a separate discussion can be held on the privacy and security relevance of technology monitoring and creating DNA personality profiles on individuals, this chapter places a focus on how the investigator can use this technology to progress their investigation. This new generation of connected devices is called the "Internet of Things" and is becoming well established in society and our lives.

WHAT IS THE INTERNET OF THINGS?

The Internet of Things (IoT) refers to the billions of devices that are connected to the Internet. Although we are familiar with computers and phones being connected, now we have dryers, refrigerators, thermostats, and car components that are connected, as well as smart homes and buildings. While many IoT devices may not initially be seen as being relevant to the cybercrime investigator, with a bit of lateral thinking they can become highly relevant and provide previously unattainable evidence.

Examples of IoT devices that may be relevant to the investigator (excluding traditional devices such as computers) include sensors in buildings, swipe-card access devices, light sensors; Bluetooth-enabled motor vehicle peripherals, remote security cameras, and more. Each of these and many more may be relevant to understanding how a security breach occurred and to placing a particular person at a particular location at the specific point in time that the alleged offense occurred. The scope of the IoT devices that may be used to assist the investigator is limited only by their understanding of what digital devices are, or may have been, at a crime scene.

The idea with IoT devices is to understand what the device is doing and what data it is capturing. The home assistant will capture a lot of data that may provide evidence to the criminal investigator as to who was at the crime scene at the time of a homicide. The smart building may provide evidence to the cybercrime investigator as to who was behind the keyboard of a compromised computer at 2:00 p.m. when corporate Intellectual Property (IP) was copied.

This chapter seeks to expand the cybercrime investigator's thinking so that the IoT environment is incorporated into the investigation plan, especially when a suspect is an internal employee of a business or a person who had physical access (approved or not) to the cybercrime scene.

WHAT IS THE RELEVANCE TO YOUR INVESTIGATION?

Digital evidence is everywhere, including in wearable technology such as Internet-connected watches. Everything that captures data tells a portion of a story: even if it is a seemingly unrelated piece of data, it may provide assistance in the future.

Computers record what they observe in log files, and while they may tell an investigator that IP was taken by a person in an office using a specific device, knowing who was at the keyboard of that device may be difficult to work out, especially if it is a shared device with a shared password. However, evidence from the IoT may provide a few clues as to who was near the device at the time the IP was taken. As a very simple example: while five people may have had access to the suspect device used to copy IP onto a USB, devices within a smart room may identify that three of these people were not near the device at the time in question, leaving two suspects.

Devices such as Bluetooth and mobile wireless routers are continually searching for devices to connect to, and they leave a unique trace of their presence. An examination of a router may find the (Media Access Control) MAC address of the suspect's phone, placing them at the crime scene at the time of the suspected offense.

With IoT, the location of your cybercrime scene potentially expands to include many varied locations. Hospitals have seen the potential for IoT products to assist in the efficient delivery of health-care services, with items such as drug-delivery pumps being connected to an intranet.[1] Health care is an area of potential cybercrime, as implanted devices such as pacemakers and insulin pumps are connected online. The US Food and Drug Administration has identified the potential for a cybercriminal to unlawfully access an implanted medical device, such as a pacemaker, and modify the commands sent to the device.[2] As of the time of the writing of this book, there have been no actual attacks against this technology recorded, but this cannot be guaranteed into the future.

Distributed Denial of Service (DDoS) attacks can be launched using IoT devices that are not secure. The Mirai botnet used IoT devices.[3] With many IoT devices having weak or no security, the semiskilled attacker can locate these nonsecure devices online, build their own IoT botnet, and launch very powerful DDoS attacks against their targets.

IoT evidence will also be very valuable to the investigator who is investigating crimes that are not cybercrimes, as IoT expands into all aspects of our lives. The homicide detective at the domestic homicide scene who wishes to know what happened may use IoT evidence from the smart house to obtain logs from the doors, lights, smart watch (recording the time of death), sensors, home assistant, air conditioning (adjusting to doors opened), refrigerator (opening), shower (suspect showering after the homicide), and more. A smart phone with the wireless connection left on will leave evidence of a Media Access Control (MAC) address as the phone attempts to connect to the router. The logs of the suspect's motor vehicle can be used to track their movements, including placing them at the scene at the time of the homicide. The potential for using IoT to investigate traditional forms of criminal offenses is limited only by the imagination of the investigator.

As the cybercrime investigator, expanding your thinking to include IoT places you one step ahead of the criminal internal to the victim entity. Often they will be so focused on committing the crime and obtaining their data that they will be unaware that their devices are leaving digital fingerprints behind or recording that they are at a location that in the future they intend to deny being anywhere near at the time in question. They will also be largely unaware of the many IoT devices within the workplace, which will be recording evidence of their activities and locations.

WHERE IS YOUR INTERNET OF THINGS DIGITAL EVIDENCE LOCATED?

As with cloud evidence, the investigator should understand where an IoT device stores its evidence. Unlike the cloud, physical devices can be accessed, triaged, and examined in the traditional manner. If the logs of the IoT device are not stored in the device, inquiries may be made of the system administrator or device manufacturer to locate them. Reading the device's End User Licence Agreement (EULA) may also provide some direction.

In summary, IoT evidence may be stored in the device, on an internal storage drive, or on a remote server operated by the IoT device manufacturer.

LAWFUL SEIZURE OF INTERNET OF THINGS EVIDENCE

As with all evidence, seizure must be lawful. A complainant will be able to provide authority in most instances, but be aware of the value of IoT-connected devices when petitioning a court for a search warrant or civil court order. If it is likely to provide evidence and examination can be justified to the court official, explain its relevance and seek authority to seize and examine the device.

The key point of this chapter is to look broadly when seeking evidence in a digital investigation. As society becomes more connected digital fingerprints are being left in numerous locations, providing evidence toward identifying a suspect. As many IoT devices have little or no built-in security they can become a very valuable attack vector for the cybercriminal, leading to network intrusions through unexpected devices—such as smoke detectors, webcams, refrigerators, and televisions—which are connected to a network that is unpatched and not secure.

As the lack of security provides opportunity to the cyber- or internal criminal, so it also provides opportunity to the investigator, as the breadcrumbs of evidence these devices will leave in and around the criminal scene will provide the opportunity to uniquely identify a person and place them at the crime scene at the time of the activity under investigation.

NOTES

1. Steve Mansfield-Devine, "Securing the Internet of Things," *Computer Fraud & Security* 2016, no. 4 (2016): 15–20.

2. United States Food and Drug Administration, "Cybersecurity Vulnerabilities Identified in St. Jude Medical's Implantable Cardiac Devices and Merlin@home Transmitter: FDA Safety Communication," January 2017.

3. Josh Fruhlinger, "The Mirai Botnet Explained: How Teen Scammers and CCTV Cameras Almost Brought Down the Internet," March 2018, CSO Online.

CHAPTER FOURTEEN

Open Source Evidence

OPEN SOURCE EVIDENCE is that which may be captured online from services such as social media, government and corporate databases, and news sites. There are numerous categories of open source material available to assist an investigation and specialist investigators exist who do nothing but seek open source material for their clients. In essence, the Internet is their workspace.

THE VALUE OF OPEN SOURCE EVIDENCE

The value of open source material is that it is freely available so that obtaining it rarely requires a search warrant. The most commonly searched open source sites are social media sites, such as Facebook, where many a criminal with an open profile has been caught bragging about their crimes or leaving behind evidence of their associates. While some criminals are very protective of their social media profile, others are very careless, and the evidence they leave open to investigators has been used in court by the prosecution.

Open source material is particularly valuable as it can be captured by one of the many device-based recording devices, such as Microsoft's Expression Encoder. If the website or social media site is open to public view, the European

231

Convention on Cybercrime allows signatory countries to view the page subject to the laws of your jurisdiction.[1] Expression Encoder records the page as seen by a web user and allows it to be stored in an easy-to-view format.

To produce the most accurate and complete version of a recording as possible, download and display an atomic clock, which may be adjusted for time accuracy at the commencement of the recording and viewed throughout the evidence capture. This allows a viewer to see a complete capture of the evidence and the time it was captured, providing proof that no manipulation of the evidence (such as content being edited out of the recording) has taken place.

There are numerous forms of open source evidence that may be available to an investigator and there are many excellent books and courses covering this material. Open source toolkits are produced by many organizations and individuals, including Toddington International (www.toddington.com), IntelTechniques (https://inteltechniques.com), Qwarie (https://www.qwarie.com), and OSINT Framework (http://osintframework.com).

Should you decide to capture open source material, there is a specific skill set required to do so without compromising your investigation. Technically skilled cybercriminals conduct counterintelligence on their websites to see who has been visiting and what they have been looking at. For example, using their web analytic tools they may find an Internet Protocol (IP) address they wish to find out more about and determine that it can be traced to a law enforcement agency, private investigator, or similar investigatory entity. This will alert them that they are under investigation and may lead them to destroy the evidence you are seeking or launch a counterattack against you.

Open source investigations require their own skill sets and it is recommended that you seek specialist advice before progressing in this area. Several examples of the skills you will require include:

- Using a specialist laptop device that can have the Operating System (OS) reinstalled without concern
- Using a Virtual Private Network (VPN) for connection before commencing your investigation
- Using a virtual system
- Using a connection that has no link to your organization
- Having a high level of security on your device and ensuring that the OS and all applications have recently been patched

As referenced in previous chapters: understand the laws in the relevant jurisdictions to understand the legality of undertaking open source investigations.

This chapter will introduce examples of the forms of open source material available to an investigator and discuss their benefits.

▩ EXAMPLES OF OPEN SOURCE EVIDENCE

There are numerous online locations to locate evidence, which is freely accessible. Some examples follow.

- **Blogs.** A blog is a website where author(s) discuss issues of interest to them and their readers. Depending on the mood and interest of the author(s), it may address a specific subject, such as politics, or cover a wide range of topics.

  There are several hundred million blogs in existence, with more emerging daily. Of value to the investigator is the potential to link a person to a user name, which may be used across different sites. It is also helpful to understand the dynamics of a specific topic of relevance to an investigation.

- **Dark web.** The dark web is a portion of the Internet where traditional search engine tools (such as Google) do not operate due to restrictions imposed on them. Although there are legitimate reasons for using the dark web, it is commonly understood to be a place where criminals communicate and host markets selling many different forms of illegal goods and services, such as stolen credit cards, stolen identities, Intellectual Property (IP), and more. Specific tools and applications are needed to enter the dark web.

  The investigator who believes evidence for their investigation resides on the dark web should practice extreme caution before proceeding, as the criminal community conduct robust countersurveillance in this environment and show suspicion toward persons they suspect of being investigators, law enforcement officers, and others who may pose a risk to them. If you are not confident in this environment, unsure about the legality of going onto the dark web from your jurisdiction, or have concerns about your security (personal or digital), refer this area of inquiry to specialist investigators who have knowledge and experience in this field.

  The dark web will be discussed in more detail in Chapter 15.

- **Domain lookup tools.** Domain lookup tools provide details about the registered owner of an Internet domain. While the details regarding the owner of a domain may be blocked or false, they are a very useful place to commence inquiries, as many registrations do contain correct information.

  Domain lookup tools also provide information on where a web page or email server is located. Examples of tools include CentralOps (https://centralops.net), Whois Lookup (https://www.whois.com.au/whois/index.html), and the reverse Internet Protocol domain check at ViewDNS (http://viewdns.info/reverseip/).

- **Email tracing.** The header information included on an email may provide the Internet Protocol address of the sender. This is not always the case, as some web hosting services do not preserve the sender's IP address. Once the Internet Protocol address has been located, further inquiries can be obtained from the domain search tools listed above.

- **Email services.** Email services provide the investigator valuable support in understanding the metadata contents of and other information about a suspect's email. A service such as an email header analyzer (mxtoolbox.com or whatismyip.com) allows the investigator to upload an email under investigation and have the program put the metadata into a readable format.

  DidTheyReadIt (didtheyreadit.com) and ReadNotify (readnotify.com) allow an investigator to send an email and identify whether it was read and when.

- **Image search.** In social engineering crimes in particular, the criminal sends their target an image, often purporting to be him- or herself, as a part of the relationship-building process. These images are usually obtained from open source sites such as Facebook and Google Images. To identify where the image originated from, search tools such as Google Images (images.google.com) and TinEye (tineye.com) allow the image to be uploaded, where it will be analyzed and a list provided of where else online these images are located.

- **Internet archive.** As web pages disappear or are modified, how a web page looked several months previously may be very different from how it looks today. The investigator may need to know how a specific site looked several months ago at the time of an alleged criminal activity involving the website.

  Sites such as Internet Archive (https://archive.org) contain (as the name suggests) an archive of web pages dating back several decades. There may not be a complete archive of each page and link associated with the site, but such sites may provide the investigator with some assistance and direction.

- **Internet Protocol address tracing.** Tracking an Internet Protocol address may require a court order from an Internet Service Provider (ISP) to identify the account that the address is attached to. Some open source tools will provide an approximate location as to where the address is located, however these are approximate only. Use these tools as a guide only and not as support evidence in legal documents such as search warrant applications, with more definitive emphasis being placed on inquiries with the ISP.

- **Maps.** Open source maps can be used to input GPS data obtained from devices or embedded in photos. They are generally accurate; however, care must be taken to corroborate the data against other evidence before acting upon it. As an example: should you be applying for a court order, the data from maps may be beneficial but care should be taken before presenting it as definitive evidence before a court. Use this data as helpful but not necessarily definitive evidence.

- **Network tools.** There are many network tools—such as netstat and ping—that can be used to locate evidence.
- **Open Source Intelligence toolkits.** As mentioned in the introduction to this chapter, organizations such as Qwarie (https://www.qwarie .com), Toddington International (www.toddington.com), IntelTechniques (https://inteltechniques.com), and OSINT Framework (http:// osintframework.com) provide a large number of open source intelligence (OSINT) materials that you may use to advance your investigation. There are many more sites containing a wide range of open source material and the investigator may find many avenues of inquiry from these resources.
- **People finder.** There are many useful open source tools available to make background inquiries about persons of interest in an investigation. Before going down this path, check local legislation for laws about collecting and storing Personally Identifiable Information (PII).

   Examples of popular people-finder sites are Pipl, PeopleSmart, and Spokeo. Some of these sites focus on US records but it is certainly worth a look.
- **Phone number search.** Locating the name of the person linked to a phone number often requires a court order, but there are many online sites providing this information through reverse phone checks. This is particularly useful when attempting to identify whether a phone call that was received is linked to a fraud site.
- **Search engines.** There are numerous search engines online, with Google being the obvious example. Do not restrict your searches to Google only; try out the many other search engines available, such as DuckDuckGo, Yahoo, Bing, and others.

   The search returns you receive from each search engines may differ, especially if a person has tried to bury their history in Google search returns but has left their history exposed in other search engine returns.
- **Social media.** The most common social media platforms are Facebook and Twitter. There are numerous other platforms being used and different countries have their favorites. Social media platforms include:
   - Facebook
   - Flickr
   - Instagram

- LinkedIn
- Myspace
- Periscope
- Tagged
- Tumblr
- Twitter

- **Translation tools.** These tools translate languages into one usable by the reader. While often not 100 percent accurate and allowing for differences in grammar, they are very useful for gaining an understanding of the contents of a communication. Use such a tool as a guide, and if you need a definitive translation of a communication, consider using a professional translation service or consulting graduate student or lecturer at a university fluent in the language in question.
- *Website copy.* Occasionally there will be a need to obtain a copy of a website for evidence or to advance a line of inquiry. A web copy facility takes a copy of the whole website, including the code that operates the site.

When considering using these tools, understand the laws of your jurisdiction as well as the one where the website is hosted to ensure there is lawful authority for such data capture.

There are numerous open source tools available for the investigator. Some of the categories have been mentioned in this chapter but understanding and operating open source material is a full course in its own right. Having a person on your investigation team as an open source specialist may be an invaluable investigation resource.

Once you have accumulated your evidence from the numerous sources listed so far, there comes a time when interviews must be conducted to take the investigation to the next level. Interviews may be conducted as evidence is collected, and this is a good idea, as the person providing key evidence may leave the company tomorrow and be unable to be located.

▩ NOTE

1. Cybercrime Convention Committee, *Transborder Access to Data (Article 32)*, T-CY Guidance Note #3, December 2014, Council of Europe.

CHAPTER FIFTEEN

The Dark Web

T HE DARK web is that portion of the Internet where search engines such as Google, Yahoo, and Bing do not index the content of the websites. Dark web sites specifically block these legitimate companies from indexing their pages to increase the privacy of the activities that take place on them.

The US Naval Research Laboratory created the concept of the dark web for the legitimate purpose of helping their people to communicate over the Internet using an increased form of security.[1] It is also highly beneficial for persons who are in countries hostile to human rights to be able to communicate over the Internet using a secure communications channel that prevents the host government from spying on their communications.[2]

To access the dark web a user needs to use a specific browser, such as Tor, whose name is derived from The Onion Router, the original project name. The Tor browser is available at www.torproject.com. There are other options available but the Tor browser is the one most commonly used.

Your pathway onto the dark web is made up of specific locations that are in different legal jurisdictions, meaning tracing the activity of Internet Protocol (IP) addresses via traditional investigative strategies is not feasible due to the time required to locate this form of evidence. Also, Tor network nodes do not keep log records beyond a session.

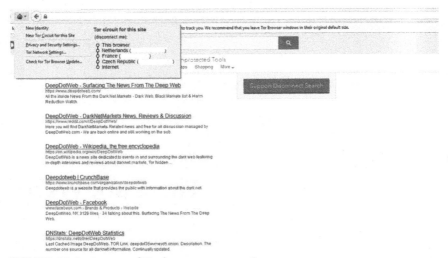

FIGURE 15.1 Image of Tor browser connections.
Source: Screenshot captured by Graeme Edwards.

Figure 15.1 shows a Tor browser with the pathway being used shown in the top-left corner. The IP addresses have been removed, as it is unknown whether these addresses are still part of the Tor network.

It is worth repeating at this time previous warnings about the dark web. Before considering operating in this environment, understand the skills required to operate in what is sometimes a very hostile environment and where professional criminals like to conduct counterintelligence inquiries about people visiting their vendor store or loitering at a criminal market. Also check the legality of visiting the dark web and its markets in your jurisdiction, as some countries strictly prohibit their citizens being on the dark web or having applications such as the Tor browser on devices.

If you have any doubts about your ability to secure your computer and navigate the dark web safely and legally, reconsider the necessity for your investigating there. Where legal, obtain the services of specialist investigators, many of whom were previously law enforcement investigators with specialist training in this environment.

CRIME AND THE DARK WEB

The criminal community has identified the dark web as being of specific benefit to them, as this secure method of communicating while hiding their identity meant that they, too, could communicate covertly with less chance of law enforcement interference. An initial criminal market called Silk Road was created, allowing cybercriminals to buy and sell goods and services in a market forum where buyers could check the credibility of the vendor and their products/services before placing an order. Many new markets have appeared since Silk Road was closed by US law enforcement, some in existence only for short periods of time and others operating for years. An advantage of the criminal markets cited by many purchasers is that they take away the necessity of meeting sellers face-to-face, which and increases anonymity.

There are numerous criminal goods and services available on dark web markets, including the following:

- Drugs
- Weapons
- Child Exploitation Material (CEM)
- Credit cards
- Identities
- Intellectual Property (IP)
- Bank accounts
- Compromised user names and passwords
- Hacking services
- Cybercrime escrow accounts
- How-to books
- Corporate databases
- Compromised social media accounts
- Cybercrime package kits
- Tobacco
- Forgery services
- Alcohol
- Zero-day vulnerabilities

An example of an advertisement for counterfeit currency is shown in Figure 15.2. All identifiers have been removed, even though the Middle Earth marketplace no longer exists. Note that in the bottom-right corner is an atomic time clock. This is used to record activity and time should the web image be used as evidence.

Although the markets supply the criminal community, unusual requests for assistance sometimes appear, as shown in Figure 15.3.

Markets are based on the model of an online auction site, where vendors advertise their goods and services and buyers assess the product and vendor. A purchaser will review the feedback of the vendor from previous customers and assess the quality of goods/services provided. They may also go to the

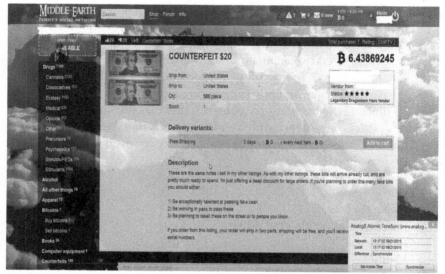

FIGURE 15.2 Image of counterfeit currency for sale.
Source: Screenshot captured by Graeme Edwards.

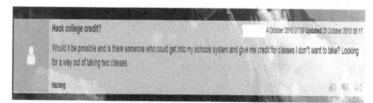

FIGURE 15.3 Image of hacking service.
Source: Screenshot captured by Graeme Edwards.

bulletin boards on the site and ask a question of the community as to the reputation of a vendor they are interested in or who is selling a particular item or service they are trying to find.

Figure 15.4 shows an example of a vendor's user profile with the review rating and comments from purchasers. All identifying particulars have been removed.

The investigator may find that the dark markets are where their client's data ends up after a cyber breach. It may also be the place your attacker learned their craft from more experienced cybercriminals.

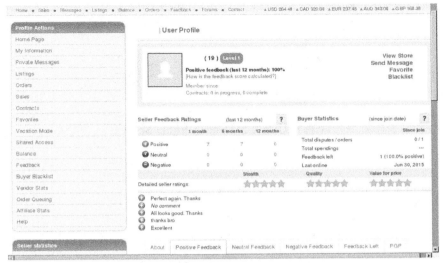

FIGURE 15.4 Image of a vendor's user profile with review ratings and comments from purchasers.
Source: Open Source.

On the markets, the people trading are generally members of the criminal community. They are there for their own motives and understand the risks involved in being identified. Many are very serious about trading and take their cyber security very seriously, including, as previously mentioned, taking measures such as attempting to identify who has been looking at vendor stores, not interacting with vendors, and not meeting purchasers. People in these categories are viewed as police, private investigators, or journalists. Despite the need for caution, the criminal markets are a legitimate place for the investigator to go to locate evidence and/or upgrade their own knowledge of emerging criminal methodologies.

International law enforcement agencies have closed many markets, but more continue to be established to replace those shut down. An example of a site taken down by law enforcement is shown as Figure 15.5.

Should you require more knowledge about the dark web and markets there are surface websites devoted to understanding what is happening on the markets. These sites provide basic information on what markets exist and provide a lot of information for those wishing to learn more.

THIS HIDDEN SITE HAS BEEN SEIZED

FIGURE 15.5 Image of a criminal market being shut down by law enforcement. Source: Screenshot captured by Graeme Edwards.

Chapter 16 will provide some ideas about interviewing witnesses and suspects. It provides many lists that may serve as templates and may also help in obtaining further information, which is the point of an interview!

 NOTES

1. "Tor: Inception," Tor Project, www.torproject.com.
2. Ibid.

CHAPTER SIXTEEN

Interviewing Witnesses and Suspects

NTERVIEWING IS an art, and the more interviews you do the more you improve. There is no fast way to become an expert interviewer, as it is a skill that requires many years of continual practice. When interviewing, accept that your 100th interview will be infinitely better than your first and that your 200th will be significantly better than your 100th. This is an art that you are always learning, as each subject is different and has varying motivations, and human personalities are dynamic, so an interviewing strategy that is an outstanding success in one instance may be a dramatic failure in the next.

There are many factors involved in being a skilled interviewer, with different models being used by law enforcement and private investigators. This book does not seek to teach the art of the interview, but to provide content that may be used with your chosen strategy as you see relevant in the circumstances facing you.

The interview is a search for facts to deepen your understanding of the person's knowledge of and relevance to the matter being investigated. Their relevance may be very clear from the time you first approach them to take part in the interview, or you may be interviewing them to be thorough and to ensure that all potential avenues of inquiry are covered. In both circumstances your initial thoughts may prove correct or alternatively, as you listen to them, your opinion may undergo a radical shift. The witness you felt had key evidence may not have any at all, and the witness you were only speaking to as a matter of being thorough in your investigative methodology may disclose information that brings them right into the center of the investigation as a crucial witness or a suspect. The key in both instances is to treat each interview as a unique event, to actively remove any bias you have in what you expect to hear, and to be prepared for the interview to be very different from what you expected.

One piece of advice this chapter can provide is to listen and allow the person being interviewed to do the talking. This applies equally to suspect and to witness interviews. An interviewing trap many fall into is asking a question, then focusing on the next question to be asked instead of actively listening and digesting the words that the interviewee is saying. In this scenario valuable information will be missed and the point of the interview, which is to gain all the knowledge the subject has to offer, defeated. This is where having a colleague as your interview partner will help, as they may be able to identify evidence that you as the main interviewer may miss.

Silence is also a powerful interview strategy. Suspects in particular may provide a rehearsed answer to a question that they expected and anticipate that a new question be asked immediately after they have stopped speaking, allowing them to lead the interview away from an area they feel uncomfortable with. By staying silent, the interviewer is projecting the impression that they see the answer provided as being only partly complete and that they are waiting for the suspect to provide more information. Depending upon the personality of the suspect and their experience in being interviewed, many will inadvertently start speaking again, saying things they had previously rehearsed not saying. Many lawyers in court are experts at using this strategy when cross-examining witnesses.

In contrast to using silence as an interview strategy, many interviewers feel they need to be constantly talking over the other party as a sign of controlling the interview, or that they need to immediately challenge the interviewee when something is said that is different from what the interviewer expects or wants to hear. As a very rough rule of thumb, try to have the witness/suspect speak about 90 percent of the time compared to your 10 percent.

As a general guide, if you are conducting an interview and it resembles something from your favorite cop show on television, the chances are you are doing it wrong, as many of the police interviews on television are necessarily dramatized for story development and entertainment, and not portrayed with the rigorous accountability you will need to demonstrate in court up to two years later. That joke or put-down that seemed highly effective during the suspect interview looks very ugly when it is played before a judge and jury while you are sitting in the witness box waiting for the defense lawyer to spend the next several hours questioning you regarding your comedic skills and attitude toward their client. This may lead to a line of questioning along the lines of, if you lack professionalism in the interview, what else about your investigation lacks professionalism? Juries also do not seem to like the use of sarcasm by interviewers.

SUSPECT INTERVIEWS

Should you be in a position where you are considering interviewing a suspect, think whether you are the right person to conduct the interview or if there is someone on your team who would be more appropriate. The most senior person is not always the best interviewer. Also consider whether a member of your team has a rapport with the suspect, as this may prove to be a tactical advantage or benefit the interview. It is not uncommon for a suspect to build resentment toward the lead investigator who has been designated the interviewer, but have a rapport with the person designated to do another job, such as collecting the exhibits. This may be a matter of personal chemistry and ego should not play any part in an interview.

As an example, early in my police career I arrested a young male for stealing a car, a charge that he denied in the interview despite being caught driving it at 2:00 a.m., not being able to give the name of the owner, and having plenty of prior convictions for stealing cars. He was not prepared to make any admissions about driving a stolen car, but my partner, a female officer who along with her husband raced cars at a local raceway, took over the interview and spoke the language of motor racing to him, and he could not confess to stealing the car and several others quickly enough. As the arresting officer and lead interviewer I was happy to pass over control of the interview to her, as results were being obtained and I did not care which of us obtained the confession as admissible evidence. Although he was going to be arrested for stealing the car all along, the admission during the interview meant that he pleaded guilty to the initial charge and several others as soon as he faced the court.

As a civilian investigator involved in an investigation likely to be referred to police, consider whether the best policy is to not interview the suspect and leave it to police, as was mentioned previously. Often a suspect will provide only one interview and that may be best left to police. Regardless of whether you or a colleague interview the suspect, remember they are to be provided safeguards to protect themselves in an interview in which they are considered to have committed a civil or criminal offense. These rights vary according to jurisdictions, however several of the most common ones are:

- The right to speak to a lawyer and/or support person and have them present during the interview
- The right to silence and/or to not incriminate themselves
- The right to speak to a union representative and have them present during an interview in a civil investigation
- The right to fully understand what the interview is about and what they are being accused of
- The right to decline to be interviewed unless compelled by local legislation
- The right for the interview to be electronically recorded and to be provided a copy of the recording (check local laws on electronically recording interviews)
- The right to terminate the interview part of the way through if desired
- The right to the interview not being oppressive
- The right to a translator if the suspect cannot communicate in the language spoken by the interviewer
- The possible right to have the home country's embassy/consulate alerted should the suspect be a national of a foreign country (this requirement may exist in the instance of a law enforcement investigator)

Failure to provide any or all of the safeguards a jurisdiction demands means that the interview and all the evidence from it may be excluded when the matter goes before the court or that its value may be diminished. This in turn will damage your reputation among your colleagues and the court, especially should you lose the case and your company is liable for costs.

 WITNESS INTERVIEWS

The witness interview is different from that of the suspect; however, many of the same courtesies apply. In most cases the witness is there voluntarily and is keen to help. You will find some rare instances where the witness is more evasive than a suspect and extracting information from them is nearly impossible. This will be because of reasons important to them, such as might be the case if you are interviewing a manager whose employee has committed a large-scale fraud against the company. While the manager is not suspected of being involved, they are scared for their career, being blamed for being negligent, and losing their job.

For example, I interviewed a middle manager of a large organization whose member of their staff had allegedly fraudulently obtained in excess of $15 million. The manager was highly evasive and obstructive in the witness interview, despite being told on many occasions that they were not a suspect and were only viewed as a witness providing background on the suspect and their duties.

This manager was not trying to be disruptive, but their interview goal was to extricate themselves from the investigation, as they were concerned that the interview would provide evidence of their negligence as a manager, which would then be used by their supervisors for dismissal. This would have meant losing their job and home and having to remove children from their private school, so in their mind avoiding dismissal was a higher priority than the investigation.

Alternatively, witnesses may try to be very helpful to an investigation, and this is to be appreciated. However, sometimes evidence may be inadvertently embellished by the witness. This is not a measure of their dishonesty, but an unconscious attempt to provide as much information to the investigation as possible. Their evidence must be restricted to the events within their knowledge and not hearsay, which includes telling of events they have heard of from other parties (not the suspect). Information the suspect has told them themselves may be acceptable evidence, but stories they've heard in the lunchroom will most likely not be.

Finally, think about the order in which you interview people. One strategy is to build as much understanding as possible about events from witnesses before you approach a suspect. Your circumstances may dictate the order of interviews due to witness availability, suspects being nearby, or a lack of knowledge about events and the need to build a deep understanding of events and the environment.

PREPARING FOR AN INTERVIEW

Regardless of whether an interview is of a suspect or witness, preparing for an interview saves time and embarrassment later. Having a well-prepared interview room with experienced interviewers greeting the subject projects a professional image.

Whether you are interviewing a witness or suspect, the success of an interview is in the planning. Creating an environment that allows the person being interviewed to provide the information during a more engaging process is preferable to the traditional police interview where the questions are asked by the police officer and answered by the interviewee in the order of interest to the police officer. What is important to the police officer conducting the interview may be very different from information the interviewee wants to give in the first place.

When interviewing staff members of the organization that is the victim of the cyber event, understand the business and the role of the person being interviewed before the interview begins. This not only saves time, it shows the interviewee that you are briefed on your topic and do not need to waste valuable interview time on unnecessary basics. Even so, asking some very basic questions of the interviewee allows them to work their way into the interview with some simple answers unrelated to the mechanics of the event. Some examples include:

- How long has the business been in existence?
- How long have you been with the organization?
- What is your role?

Along with the legislated safeguards a particular jurisdiction provides, there are other matters that a skilled interviewer will attend to. Examples include:

- **Plan for the safety of yourself, other persons present, and the interviewee.**
- Plan the interview for a mutually acceptable time should circumstances allow.
- Have the interview in a quiet place where there is no background noise or chance to be interrupted by people walking into an office. Background noise could come from the lunchroom next door or a noisy air conditioner in the room itself. Alternatively, depending on the circumstances you may need to electronically record a preliminary interview with a witness at the side of a road with traffic driving past—which although not desirable, may be necessary due to the unique circumstances of the case.
- Build a rapport with the person to be interviewed. Learn their background and interests to encourage a friendly conversation before the interview begins in order to break down barriers and settle nerves.
- Be careful what you tell a witness about a case. Do not make any negative offhand comments about the suspect, as this will likely be repeated to other witnesses or may even be recorded by a witness who wants their own electronic copy of the interview.

- Check to ensure that the witness/suspect will not need to leave the interview for some reason, such as picking up children from school in a half hour.
- Provide water, tea, coffee, or some kind of beverage.
- Ensure that they understand the language you're speaking, and if they do not, arrange for an interpreter. Also avoid jargon and acronyms, as this will likely confuse not only your witness, but also the jury who watches/listens to your interview several years later after a suspect has been charged.
- Check on their physical and mental well-being and whether they need to take any prescribed medication or if there are any other issues you need to be aware of.
- Ensure there is sufficient airflow in the room, as a closed interview room with poor airflow detracts from the interview for all parties.
- Electronically record the interview in accordance with the laws of your jurisdiction.
- Provide them a copy of their statement.
- At the conclusion of the interview, tell them what happens next and assess their well-being. Thank them for their time. Ensure they can get home safely.
- Mobile devices should be turned off or set on silent, as they can interrupt the flow of the interview.
- Consider the value of having a second person at the interview as a corroborator to support you. This may be for personal safety, exhibit management, or to have another person observe the mannerisms of the interviewee and to provide a line of questioning you may have not thought of but which the corroborator may identify through the interviewee's answers.
- If the witness is a vulnerable person or likely to be seen as being at a significant disadvantage with respect to the interviewer, plan for a support person to be present to ensure that their evidence is obtained fairly while showing respect for their needs and any impairments, which may include physical/mental health disabilities.

A valuable consideration pre-interview is planning to control your evidence. A second person in the interview may be tasked with ensuring that the suspect has no physical access to evidence they may destroy or things that can be used as weapons. Copies of important documents may be of benefit for showing to the suspect, and asking them to sign and date these copies provides a level of authenticity.

THE INTERVIEW PROCESS

This section provides a general introduction to the interview and its structure. As has been stated in other sections, your local laws and regulations will dictate how your interview is conducted and the standards required by your courts. Use the following sections as a guideline only and incorporate them into your interview plan as your laws and circumstances allow.

Introduction to the Witness Interview

When the safeguards have been provided and you are ready to begin the interview, start with the basics to establish who the interviewee is and their relevance to the investigation. Being able to answer questions they are comfortable with also allows them to build up their confidence. This is just as relevant in both witness and suspect interviews.

The questions you ask during the interview will be determined by events; however, the list of questions that follow may be used for either a witness or a suspect interview. Use open-ended questions (questions starting with "explain," "who," "what," "when," "where," "why," and "how"), which preclude yes or no answers. Also keep questions brief, as there are few things more difficult for the person being interviewed than a question that lasts several minutes and includes several subquestions.

Examples include:

- Where do you work?
- What are your duties?
- Who is your manager?
- How many staff do you have reporting to you?
- How long have you been in your current position?
- When did you join the company?
- What would a routine day consist of with respect to your duties?

These questions are very general in nature and allow the subject to ease their way into the interview by being able to give detailed answers to questions that they are familiar and comfortable with. As the interviewee's confidence builds, more evidence-related questions can be asked.

Body of Interview

Allowing the interviewee to talk about what is important to them is a valuable way of opening the main body of the interview process. The witness/suspect may have valuable information they wish to disclose and are looking for the first opportunity in the interview to disclose it.

Note what they are saying and the manner in which they are saying it. This technique may also allow evidence to be disclosed that you had not even thought of. The experienced interviewer will note that a witness may provide details on many of the points being raised, whereas the suspect may provide great detail on unrelated matters but noticeably minimal information on the specifics of the offense being investigated.

Once you have established the relevance of the person to the matter under investigation you may move into more relevant questions. Again, ensure that the questions being asked are open ended and designed to solicit detailed answers. Should you identify inconsistencies between what the subject is saying and what you know, do not jump in and contradict them, as this breaks their flow and their confidence.

The type of offense being investigated will dictate the direction of the interview from now on. Interviewing the senior executive will be different from interviewing the line manager of a suspect, as their knowledge of events is likely to be very different.

The following list covers a wide range of interview questions that may be covered in an interview; where possible, it would be helpful to know some of this information prior to the interview. This is not always possible; however, pre-interview preparation is often as important as the interview itself. The list is very general in nature, as it is not practical to provide a schedule of interview questions covering each of the many types of cybercrimes.

Witness's Knowledge of Devices Related to the Investigation

- What devices do you use?
- Who owns the device? (This question pertains to interviews conducted at a suspect's home or when a Bring Your Own Device (BYOD is involved.)
- What duties do you carry out on these devices?
- Who else has access to these devices? (Is the device in a person's office or in a shared space?)
- How do you gain access to the device? Do you use an individual or a shared password to gain access?

- Who is(are) the person(s) in charge of providing access to these devices?
- Who is(are) the persons(s) who can modify access privileges as required? (Here you are looking to see if access privileges to data have been unlawfully upgraded by a hacker.)
- How long has the subject device been on the network?
- What is the password to the device? (This is particularly important for the digital investigator and can include encryption keys for the device and network traffic.)
- What security applications and protocols are on the device and network?
- What are the Media Access Control (MAC) and subnet Internet Protocol (IP) addresses? (This is a question for technical staff.)
- Who owns the device the security breach relates to, the complainant business or a witness/suspect? If a BYOD device, what is the agreement with management relating to access to the device for examination?
- Who has remote access to the device or network? What security is attached to the remote access?
- Who creates the backup storage?
- Who has access to backup storage? (Access is established for potential background evidence, especially when evidence on the device has been destroyed by the attacker.)
- Who has a list of the authorized applications on the device? (Identify any unauthorized programs and how they got there. Identify what they do.)
- What is normal user behavior on the device? Examples include amount of traffic and users.
- What cloud-computing access is involved in the network? (Identify whether data is routinely stored in the cloud.)
- What external storage devices are associated with the subject device? Examples include USB devices, mobile phones, and portable hard drives.
- What examples are there of shadow IT (Information Technology)? (This includes applications and services installed by a user without the approval or knowledge of the system administrator.)
- What is your account identifier and email address? Do you have any other user names associated with the device/network?
- What cleaner programs (such as CCleaner or BleachBit) are used on the computer? When were they installed and by whom?
- If an internal employee committed a suspected offense, how can it be determined that it was a deliberate action of dishonesty and not a person exceeding their authority?

Witness's Knowledge of Suspect

- Who do you think may be behind the cybercrime being investigated?
- Describe any unusual events that have occurred recently, especially involving technology.
- How did you become aware of the cyber incident that occurred?
- How do you know this person? (This question is relevant for an internal investigation.)
- How long have you known this person? (This question is relevant for an internal investigation.)
- What are their daily duties? (This question is relevant for an internal investigation.)
- What does a typical day look like for this person? (This question is relevant for an internal investigation.)
- Who is their manager? (This question is relevant for an internal investigation.)
- What is their attitude toward the workplace and management like? (This question is relevant for an internal investigation.)
- Describe any instances of negative or suspicious behavior from this person. (This question is relevant for an internal investigation.)
- Describe your knowledge of their skills with respect to technology. (This question is relevant for an internal investigation.)

Witness's Knowledge of the Event under Investigation

- What is your understanding of the event under investigation?
- How was it discovered?
- What is your involvement in this investigation?
- What evidence is there that a offense was committed?
- When did the incident occur?
- When was the incident initially discovered?
- Who discovered the incident?
- Who has been responsible for the investigation?
- What are the estimated damages from the incident? (This question is for senior managers and may include financial, reputation, and opportunity cost losses.)
- Who gave the order to secure the evidence? (Relevant when a person has been directed to secure evidence)
- Who identified what evidence was to be secured?
- Where is the evidence collected to date stored and who has had access to it?
- What actions have been taken to identify, collect, preserve, or analyze the data and devices involved?

- Explain in your own words the relevance of the evidence that has been secured.
- What is your relationship to the evidence? (This question is relevant if the witness has access to a shared device.)

Note that the questions are all open ended, meaning that the interviewee cannot answer with a yes or no. Also note that the questions are all very short and direct.

 ## CLOSING THE INTERVIEW

Once you are satisfied that you have obtained all the evidence you can from the interviewee, it is time to close the interview. At this time, it is helpful to repeat your understanding of the information obtained from the interviewee in your own words, which allows the interviewee to correct you on your understanding and possibly add any new material they have suddenly remembered.

Closing the interview can involve several questions to prove that the interview process has been fair to the witness/suspect and to protect your integrity before the court. Examples of such questioning may include:

- Did you take part in this interview of your own free will?
- Do you have any further information you think may be relevant to this matter that I have not asked of you?
- Do you have any complaints about the manner in which you have been treated?
- Was any threat, promise, or inducement given today to persuade you to undertake this interview?

Always thank the interviewee for their time and keep them informed of developments where practical.

 ## REVIEW OF THE INTERVIEW

Once an interview is completed, the temptation is to move on to the next line of inquiry and to build on what benefit you've gained from the interview. Experienced interviewers understand that there may have been important evidence or indicators they missed during the interview, and they will review the recording to see if there is anything of value they've missed. Some examples of indictors are identifying that a person was uncomfortable with a line of questioning, gave very specific answers to some questions but was vague in answering others, changed references to themselves from the first to the third person, moved about in their chair when uncomfortable, or moved their eyes nervously when discussing certain points. While these may seem obvious after the fact, when conducting the interview the interviewer may be concentrating on the evidence and miss some vital nonverbal indicators of discomfort or nerves.

Sometimes as an investigation develops there may be a need to reinterview a witness. This is not a sign that the original interview was not conducted well but instead that new information develops through any investigation and new lines of questioning evolve, meaning questions never originally considered become relevant.

Depending on your local laws, record a new statement and reference the original. For example, the introductory sentence of the new statement may read:

> This statement is an addendum to the statement I provided on October 2, 2018.

PREPARATION OF BRIEF FOR REFERRAL TO POLICE

Whether or not it is the initial goal of the client/complainant to have their complaint referred to police for a follow-up investigation, there will be instances when the facts uncovered during the investigation require a referral to police. When preparing the investigation for referral, remember your covering report will be read by police who have no knowledge of the matter and need to identify within the first two paragraphs the most important information about your referral. If you require that police go searching through your report for details about what the complaint is about, who the complainant/suspect is, what evidence you have, and why it is a criminal matter, the chances are very high that police will lose interest in your referral very quickly. They do not have the time to go searching for the facts, which should be highlighted by the person making the referral.

When a cybercrime is very serious, you may contact your police cybercrime experts for advice and they may (depending on resource available) be prepared to take your complaint at once.

When referring your cybercrime complaint to police, presenting a sharp, accurate case will be greatly appreciated by the detective the case is to be assigned to. This may lead to your complaint having priority over other referrals where less attention to detail has been provided

Where possible have the following information available and prepared:

- Internet or written submission
- Executive summary
- Clearly identify the alleged crimes
- Modus Operandi of alleged offenses
- Investigation schedule of inquiries undertaken
- Affidavits of key witnesses
- Evidence schedule (facts versus the particulars of potential offenses)
- Draft summary of facts
- Draft search warrant application
- Schedule of further inquiries to be undertaken by police
- Digital copy of brief available for police
- Key word schedule used in computer examination of suspect and/or complainant devices
- Passwords for evidence submitted
- Supporting documents, including consent to examination forms
- Points of contact
- Timeline of events in chronological order

Once the human and digital evidence has been collected, the next process is to review the evidence; this is covered in Chapter 17.

CHAPTER SEVENTEEN

Review of Evidence

O NCE THE scene examination has been completed, exhibits examined and safely stored, interviews conducted, and open source inquiries completed, there comes a time to review all the evidence gained in the investigation and to attempt to gain a clear picture of the event and what evidence you have. This picture may develop very quickly or be very complex. You may find that avenues of inquiry that originally looked very promising end up leading to dead ends and that other lines of inquiry that were being undertaken primarily as a matter of being thorough lead to the smoking-gun evidence.

During the initial phase of your investigation you have been building the foundation. As mentioned previously, although it is always a great outcome when you find evidence linking the offender to the crime while still at the scene, this is often not the case. It is through the review of the evidence that the picture becomes clearer and you gain a greater understanding of what has occurred.

Avoid having a preconception of events and suspects as you review the evidence. This may not always be easy, as the evidence may initially seem quite conclusive. If you wish in your mind for the evidence to point to a specific person or Modus Operandi (MO), your thinking will subconsciously make the evidence point to your theory, even if it is hopelessly wrong. If you do not challenge the evidence and your theories, you can be sure that the defendant's lawyer will walk you through the exercise in minute detail should you appear in court and be required to defend your investigation. Follow the evidence with an open mind and see where it leads you!

During the investigation, you will have obtained a lot of material from potentially many sources. Some will carry more weight than others and some evidence will be determined to have no value. In some jurisdictions there will be a requirement to return seized exhibits once you have examined them and identified them to be of no value. In these circumstances keeping a copy of the exhibit may be beneficial, as the evidence determined to be of no value today may develop into a crucial exhibit several weeks later in the investigation.

In large investigations there is a benefit to creating a spreadsheet that is a who's who of the many people you have encountered and that includes their different roles in the investigation and evidence related to them. Creating a chronological timeline of events will also allow a wide variety of complex evidence to be presented in a manner that any person reviewing the investigation can use to get a quick grasp of events.

In summary, when reviewing your investigation and the evidence, here are 12 quick tips to assist your review:

1. Review all interviews to ensure that you have a strong understanding of the nature of the complaint and what has allegedly happened. Obtain an addendum (second statement) if required. This is not a sign of weakness in your initial interview, as reviewing the case in its totality will provide a greater understanding of events, the witnesses' roles, and potentially new lines of questioning of witnesses. Having addendum statements is a sign you are being thorough in your investigation and you are chasing down every lead.

2. Review the digital evidence, including the reports provided by the technicians. If you cannot understand the technical evidence there is an excellent chance the jury will not, either. This is the opportunity for you to walk through the technical evidence, with your experts so that you can understand exactly what they are saying in their report. Take lots of notes if you need to, as these will be helpful in understing the evidence.

   One useful way of gaining an understanding of technical evidence is having an opportunity to use the forensic tools the examiner used, under their supervision and on a separate device. This will be done on a copy of the initial image to ensure that no damage is done to the integrity of the evidence. People who learn by doing an activity will find this helpful.

For example, the forensic examiner may be able to guide you in following the recorded evidence as the attacker moved through the network and gained access to valuable corporate data.

Ideally your technician will provide their report in clear language and avoid technical terms where possible. As you review the evidence, you do not need to be an expert on what the expert is saying, but you must be able to accurately describe the evidence in court if the defense lawyer asks you.

3. Witness statements are to be completed and signed during the initial phase of your investigation, as people may leave the company or even the country and it may be impossible to locate them later. This also completes a line of inquiry. Many times statements will have been recorded using digital recordings at the scene and then translated into formal interview statements back in the office. These statements will then need to be reviewed and endorsed by the witness.

The temptation may be to record the statement and focus on more promising lines of inquiry, such as suspect identification, with the intention of meeting the witness to review the statement at a later date. You will find your investigation is clearer when you have the written statement recorded and signed by the witness, as it means they have formally adopted a version of events as the investigation continues. It is one less thing you have to plan to complete and provides a solid foundation to your investigation.

4. Human Resource (HR) documents are particularly useful when there is an internal security breach. Secure them early and identify which member of staff can introduce them as evidence and explain the contents.

Your investigation into an internal data breach may depend on the HR documentation, as it details acceptable use of computers, policies regarding the use of Bring Your Own Devices (BYOD), and ownership of Intellectual Property (IP) created during the term of employment. When dealing with a suspected internal data breach, speaking to HR officers and obtaining the personnel file with these documents will determine early in your investigation the potential legality of a suspect's actions.

When reviewing evidence gained from examination of the scene, HR documents may determine whether your investigation should continue or is complete. For example, if there is no document detailing ownership of IP created during the suspect's term of employment, seek legal advice as to whether there was any offense committed when the suspect copied it.

5. Continue to ensure the chain of custody of the exhibits when conducting the review. Prepare a schedule explaining all movements of and security for the exhibits, as this is very useful should the exhibits officer be cross-examined in court regarding the exhibit chain of custody. Your legal team will also greatly appreciate this document to help them clarify exhibit custody.

   As the investigating officer, when reviewing the chain of evidence you may find there is evidence you did not know was seized or evidence whose relevance you did not understand at the time. For example, a notebook seized from a suspect's desk may contain numerous notes covering their daily duties but also contain their passwords or details of other staff members' passwords that they have accumulated.

6. Keep the client informed of the investigation progress. There is no need to explain every theory, as these may change regularly, but the client will be very interested in the investigation progress, cost, and potential to identify a suspect, especially if there is suspicion of an internal offender.

   As you review the evidence, suspects may change, new theories develop, legal issues be encountered, and the relevance of evidence change. The complainant has placed a lot of trust in the investigation team, and as you review the evidence and the case in general, they will be wondering about what is happening and the progression of the evidence, and will appreciate regular communication from you, even if it is only a five-minute courtesy phone call.

7. When making a recommendation to the client or making a decision to prosecute, ensure every claim in the recommendation is supported by admissible evidence.

   Compare the evidence against the elements of the offenses being investigated. If there are elements of the potential charges that cannot be proved, then further inquiries will be required or the investigation will have to terminate. Clearly identify which witnesses are presenting or supporting the evidence that substantiates the elements of the alleged offense.

   Your evidence review will project the professionalism of your investigation and knowledge of events. Understand the laws you are considering and link the evidence to the ingredients of the offense. If you cannot support the claim, be prepared to say so.

8. Question whether the evidence supports the allegation. This is not always the case, as you may find the person referring the complaint made it based

on an honest misunderstanding of circumstances. They may be relieved to find your investigation found no evidence of an internal fraudster or security breach.

As an investigator, there will be times that you are required to tell the complainant/client things they do not want to hear, such as agreeing with them that there was a data breach and that a certain employee is a strong suspect, but that there is no standard of evidence to prove it. Reviewing the evidence and investigation will direct you toward the offender, but there will be times in your career when you know who the offender is but will not be able to meet the required standards of evidence to prove it in a court of law. In these circumstances avoid the temptation to interpret the evidence to meet your assumptions or client's expectations, as this will cause major problems for you as an investigator and for the complainant when challenged in court.

9. Create an events timeline in a chronological order for clarity of vision to assist the review. As you review your evidence, you will find many instances of activity around certain dates and times and it becomes very difficult to follow what is happening. The chronological timeline places every event in the correct order so that you can understand what has happened.

   As you review the chronological timeline, add a column in your spreadsheet that shows where a piece of evidence came from. For example:

   10/25/2018 10:43am   Unauthorized access to Jake Smith's desktop computer ABD 1234E Sourced from statement of Jacobs (digital examiner)

10. Be prepared to have an independent party review the case to obtain a fresh view of the investigation, evidence obtained, and conclusions reached.

   Despite your best efforts, you may have decided on a motive, suspect, and methodology. Having an independent person review the evidence may confirm this or challenge your perceptions. The review of another person may also identify evidence or theories you had not been aware of, as that person brings their professional experience and knowledge into your investigation.

   No person in the field of investigations knows everything, and a fresh perspective may also locate weaknesses in your investigation that you were unaware of.

11. Challenge yourself and the evidence obtained to ensure that you have a robust conclusion.

    As you review your investigation, also think about it from the perspective of what a defense lawyer may ask when they do their review of your case. They will be very critical and may seek to raise suspicions about other persons you have eliminated from your suspects list.

12. All investigators' statements should be comprehensive and completed before moving on to the next investigation. This includes preservation of notes made during the investigation, as they may be required as evidence in their own right.

    An investigation concluded today might be resurrected next year when unexpected new evidence becomes available. For example, new technology may be able to locate evidence on a digital device that could not be accessed previously. Having everything completed and preserved means the investigation can be easily picked up and continued without wondering what needs to be completed that was not initially done.

When reviewing the evidence in technological investigations, avoid placing total focus on digital evidence at the expense of understanding the personalities and motivations of the attackers involved. This is particularly so when you identify a potential suspect, such as an internal employee or business competitor. Think about their motivations and what benefit they would obtain from the actions in question, and what evidence you can obtain from examining their offline activities.

Looking at a suspect's behavior post-offense is a very good way of corroborating the evidence you have gained throughout your investigation. For example, do they appear to have a more luxurious lifestyle post-offense, or have they suddenly paid off outstanding debts they were previously unable to? Alternatively, has the internal employee obtained a new job at a competitor in excess of their known skills?

Following this theme, the scene examination of a suspect's home often shows signs of lifestyle far in excess of the suspect's income. This evidence may also be able to be located on their mobile phone or social media account, where there may be photos of extravagant homes, meals at expensive restaurants, or major shopping trips at high-quality retailers. Use this open source material to your advantage. Tax returns and bank statements located at the suspect's address provide strong evidence of their lawful income and may be very relevant evidence when compared to the suspect's expenditures. Also, look at store receipts located at the suspect's address, which will provide information as to spending activities.

These are common investigation techniques of the fraud examiner. Locating receipts or photos of high-value purchases will provide dates of expenditure, which in turn can be linked to the time of the alleged offense.

Depending upon the circumstances and your legal authority, evidence of large expenditures can be traced back through bank accounts to find out where this money came from. At this time, bringing in an accountant with specialist skills in financial investigations and/or a fraud examiner will provide the cyber-crime investigator valuable support.

Once you have reviewed the investigation and evidence, there comes the time when you decide whether to commence a prosecution. Should this occur, Chapter 18 will provide some ideas for presenting your evidence, digital and otherwise, to the court. You will find there are times when despite the extensive nature of your investigations you are unable to locate a suspect. This may be because the evidence you need such as log files do not exist, the attacker has used technology such as proxy servers, anonymizers or compromised devices or alternatively they cannot be located in a foreign jurisdiction. Preparing a detailed report on your investigation and findings provides the complainant information to understand the extent of the attack and damage, providing them information to understand the attack and how to remediate the compromise of the systems and data.

CHAPTER EIGHTEEN

Producing Evidence for Court

A FTER REVIEWING the investigation and evidence, a person may be identified who can be prosecuted for the event. This may be in a tribunal (such as an employment court), or be a civil—or even a criminal—prosecution. With rare exceptions, the party bringing the matter before the court has the burden of proving the case against the other party.

This is where the professionalism and thoroughness of your investigation will be examined critically. The defense lawyer will see their job as challenging your conclusion that their client has committed the alleged offense, but they may also extend their challenge by questioning your team about the scene examination, evidence collection, protection of the chain of custody, and qualifications of your investigation team for the work they undertook. While your review of the investigation focused on questioning the evidence, the defense lawyer's job is to represent their client to the best of their abilities and this involves focusing strongly on your investigation, evidence, and conclusions.

Consequently, in your pre-court evaluation be prepared to not only explain why the accused person committed the offense, but also why the person next to them did not. For example, if a computer device is shared by five people who use a shared user name and password, why is this suspect before the court as the defendant and not the other four? As part of your court preparation, be able to explain with evidence why these people are not also in the courtroom as defendants.

A defense lawyer may introduce alternative theories as to who the offender is, and in your preparation anticipate these theories and think about whether they have any validity. Build your case around not only producing the evidence of why the defendant has been placed before the court, but why other people who could have been involved are not defendants as well.

A common circumstance is where an employee steals Intellectual Property (IP) to take to their new employer because the understanding when they are offered the new job is that they will get it only if they bring the IP with them. The laws of conspiracy to commit an offense require that at least two persons be involved: in this instance, the person stealing the IP and the new employer who offers the person a job as long as they bring the IP with them. You may have strong evidence to prosecute the employee, but no more than a strong suspicion about the person who is suspected of receiving the IP. Their explanation may be to agree that the employee brought the IP with them but that they had no knowledge it was owned by their competitor as the defendant stated that they were the owner of it.

The defense lawyer may introduce this theory to you in cross-examination in court in an attempt to mitigate the involvement of their client, so be prepared to admit that although this is a possibility, you do not have the evidence to progress this theory. Admitting there is insufficient evidence to prosecute a suspected coconspirator will show that you are objective in your decision making. Your prosecution will then rely on a charge based on the stealing of the IP and not a charge of conspiracy.

Your evidence will be technical and nontechnical. The piece of paper found on a suspect's desk on the day of the scene examination that was considered to be of limited value may end up being the most critical piece of evidence in the whole case. Even though you are investigating a technical matter, do not discount the value of a piece of paper you locate at the scene.

All evidence tells a story and your job is to make sure it is told as clearly and concisely as possible. The defense lawyer's job may involve confusing the jury with technical details to the point that no one can understand what the evidence means, and this has proven to be a successful strategy in its own right. That is their job and your job is to negate this legitimate legal strategy before it can be used against your case.

As with all evidence, a primary consideration is to consider its admissibility in the court in which you are seeking to have your matter heard. The legal representative on your team will be playing a major role here, so seek their advice early and regularly. The greatest piece of evidence you have is of no value if it is inadmissible.

DIGITAL EVIDENCE AND ITS ADMISSIBILITY

In a civil matter, a civil lawyer may potentially be added to the investigation team to assist in obtaining court orders, restraining the suspect from using the data unlawfully obtained, obtaining computer evidence, or freezing bank accounts and assets of the suspect. This may then lead to further court action or even be a prelude to a criminal complaint being made to police. As each jurisdiction is different, obtaining the legal advice of an experienced lawyer may be time and money well spent before planning any such action.

Your digital evidence will be as relevant to the court hearing as any other evidence. However, digital evidence needs care in its presentation to ensure its relevance is understood.

All matters of evidence will be decided by your local jurisdiction(s) and rules of evidence are decided with local legislation and judicial rulings. Examples of considerations when placing evidence before the court with very brief non-legal descriptions are as follows:

1. *Relevant.* Evidence that goes toward proving or disproving an element of the charges before the court.
2. *Authentic.* This rule is to show that the evidence placed before the court is what it purports to be. For example, that a document presented as evidence is authentic and not a fraudulently created document to prove or disprove an element of the charge. A witness who gives credible evidence, accepted by the court, that they created the specific document can prove authentication of the document.
3. *Not hearsay or admissible hearsay.* Evidence where the witness provides evidence of that which is within their direct knowledge. For example, hearing a rumor in the office lunchroom that a specific person admitted to committing a crime would not be admissible evidence in most jurisdictions because the witness has no direct knowledge of the alleged confession.
4. *Best evidence.* In a perfect world, original copies of documents and images are presented to the court. With digital evidence, the original may be a digital copy which is generated and presented as evidence. A court will generally accept this unless there are legal or other reasons why not to.

5. *Not unduly prejudicial.* The evidence presented does not create an unfair prejudice against the accused, such as presenting evidence of similar convictions in the past. Also, because you located material on their computer showing that the suspect is of bad character does not mean it can be introduced to the court as evidence unless it is relevant to the prosecution. For example, finding evidence on the suspect's computer that they have been have been misbehaving on social media is unlikely to be admissible evidence when you are investigating them for stealing corporate data from their employer.

 ## PREPARING FOR COURT

Technology can be extremely complex, and although the evidence presented may be very relevant, the party presenting it needs to ensure its value is highlighted and not lost in the complexity of the underlying technology, as can be the case with cloud-based evidence. Consequently, investing time in developing a technology plan for the court is time well spent, especially when the defendant's lawyer is using a strategy of making the technology sound as complex as possible to the jury.

If your technological evidence is highly complex, having an independent expert as a witness who knows little about the case but a lot about the technology helps to present the court with an understanding of the crucial technology in the case without any hint of bias toward the party who asked them to give testimony. This person is an expert witness to the court and not to the party who brought them to court to testify. If you are introducing a person as an expert in their field, they will not be accepted by the court as an expert until they have established their qualifications and expertise and the other side's lawyers have had the opportunity to challenge them if they choose. In most jurisdictions a person is only an expert in court when the judge agrees they are.

A problem juries have had is following the volume of evidence in complex cases. Evidence moves quickly across witnesses, and it is human nature to take time to understand the complex evidence and its meaning in the context of the case. If a piece of evidence is highly complex but provides limited value, review with your lawyers whether it should be presented, as its value may be overwhelmed by its complexity.

Providing a monitor and/or device (tablet) for the jurors to have access to the digital evidence as it is presented allows them to hear the testimony at the same time that they are seeing it operate. They may also review exhibits from the device as they require. This assists those who learn by doing as well as those who learn by listening.

When reviewing the range of offending by the defendant, should there be a long period of offending consider whether there is any benefit in prosecuting every instance of offending over several years and confusing the court. An alternative strategy is to identify the main period of offending and to prosecute based on this time frame. The potential sentence for using technology to fraudulently obtain $15 million is not much different from using technology to fraudulently obtain $16 million, especially when there is no possibility of reparation. So if the main period of offending involves the $15 million and your evidence is very strong, but the evidence is weaker and confusing for the remaining $1 million, a common strategy is to stick to your strengths.

When choosing your experts, determine their qualifications and experience. While not every digital investigator needs to be an expert, they must be able to show their qualifications and experience in using the technology used to capture and assess digital evidence to the standard required by the court. In effect, the court wants to see competency in their actions and the credibility of the results and interpretations.

Assisting your lawyers in understanding your investigation is an often overlooked ingredient of an investigation. Lawyers are often overrun with matters and sometimes have limited time to get an understanding of the nuances of the case they are to prosecute. It is in your interests to prepare a complete summary of matters and the evidence to ensure they have the knowledge to represent your case in a court/tribunal. A well-crafted executive summary is worth the time taken to prepare it. Include a schedule of the main evidence and why it is relevant. Preparing a chain of custody schedule will also be greatly appreciated. If you cannot convince your lawyers of your evidence and case in a clear and precise manner, you will struggle to convince a jury.

Working with your lawyers is an investment. You may have a legal representative on your team and this may not be the same person who presents the case in court. Be prepared to accept the advice of your lawyers even when you do not like it, as they are the ones who have to present your case in court and have learned the hard-won lessons from the courtroom and the requirements of the judiciary. If they want a line of inquiry investigated further, this must be treated as a priority.

From the time of initially commencing your investigation, understand that everything you do may be questioned in court where you will be required to justify your actions. This applies to your investigation methodologies as well as evidence management. We have discussed taking notes of decisions made and circumstances known at a particular time, and this is where they will prove valuable. A decision made may be later proven wrong; however, when you are working at a scene or speaking with a suspect, you do not have the luxury of waiting for all the information you require, and that decision may have been reasonable at the time. You work with what you know and use your experience. It is a rare occurrence when you conduct a post-investigation review and do not think that you would have made different decisions at key times if you had information that became available later at the time decisions were made.

When you make a claim before the court, ensure that your evidence is strong enough to prove it. As mentioned, having an independent party, such as a lawyer, review your case and evidence will be beneficial, as it provides an opportunity for the beliefs you have developed during the investigation to be challenged. Unfortunately, despite the best efforts of the investigation team, they may become so convinced of their theories involving evidence and a suspect that alternative theories for the facts uncovered may be missed. Having your evidence challenged before you begin a prosecution and correcting any shortcomings is preferable to the shortcomings being identified and highlighted by the defendant's lawyers in the courtroom. Standards of proof to win a case may vary between criminal and civil law. Understand the thresholds for conviction required in the court in which you are seeking to prosecute.

With the development of technology, the seizure, examination, and storage of the device and image may be a factor in the court determining its admissibility. When choosing the method of seizing digital evidence, understand that the court wishes to see methodologies it can place reliance upon. The courts have ruled upon matters involving technology and digital evidence over many years and your jurisdictions will have plenty of legal precedents providing guidance.

If your methodologies seem very complex, plan the explanation carefully. Courts have been interpreting complex evidence for generations. Once, fingerprint evidence was new and challenging; now it has been accepted without question for decades. Since then, courts have successfully understood many new forms of evidence, including computers, mobile devices, and DNA. In each case the explanations of this evidence and its accuracy would have been carefully planned prior to its introduction.

New technology is evolving faster than the courts can be introduced to them. For example, cloud-computing technology is no longer new to the marketplace and the Internet of Things (IoT) is already rapidly evolving, meaning evidence is being placed before the court that judicial officers may not be familiar with and that may not have a clear precedent to rely upon when they consider its integrity and authenticity. There may be instances in the future when important evidence comes from a new form of digital device and the opposing party puts the technology and its accuracy on trial rather than focus on the evidence it produces and its implication for their client. This evidence often does not get challenged because the parties involved do not understand the technology themselves and do not know the questions to ask.

As a part of your preparation for court, prepare your witnesses. Many people who are witnesses have never been in a courtroom before and their understanding of court is what they have seen on TV. It is common for witnesses to be nervous about attending court, as they are stepping into the unknown against skilled lawyers who see the courtroom as their second home and know the rules of the court intimately.

A positive strategy is to take key or nervous witnesses to show them an empty courtroom before they are to give evidence. Show them where they are to sit, where the lawyers will be situated, and teach them court protocol, such as how to respectfully address the judge and present themselves in the best positive light. In effect, take the mystery out of the courtroom. Allow them to review their statement to refresh their memory (where local laws allow), as the court hearing may take place several years after the alleged offense when their statement was taken. Also introduce them to your lawyers, who will appreciate the opportunity to review the evidence with their witness and clarify any matters.

Explain courtroom procedures, such as the role of the court registrar (or similar official, depending on your jurisdiction), who provides the oath or affirmation and what their role is. In a high-profile matter, there may be media present and they have their own role, which is to record events in the courtroom. Explain that there may be members of the community present who have no involvement in the case but are interested because of the media reports.Teaching your witnesses some of the tricks of giving evidence is a valuable strategy you can apply in preparing for court. Some good advice includes sticking to what you know; not providing opinion evidence unless you are an expert witness and the court allows such evidence; and being aware of the tactic of silence, where the witness provides their answer and the defense lawyer stays silent, waiting for further information the witness had no intention of giving. The silence prompts the witness subconsciously that more information is required, and they may say something they later regret.

Other tips are to stay professional, to not make derogatory comments about the defendant, to not make smart/sarcastic comments, and to attend court dressed professionally and respectfully. The witness should not use foul language unless it is a direct quote directly relevant to the evidence and testimony, such as "When challenged as to stealing the intellectual property, the defendant said *******." The judge and jury will assess the character of the person providing evidence as rigorously as the evidence itself, and showing professionalism and respect to the court is a foundation of being a quality and credible witness.

A further tip to give your witnesses is that they are allowed to say they do not know the answer to a question or that they cannot remember when they are giving evidence. Making up answers from fragments of memory is not quality evidence and they may be questioned as to why these memories were not included in their original statement but only recalled several years later. If something is remembered that was not included in the original statement, an addendum statement should be recorded and supplied to the defense lawyer before the hearing.

Defense lawyers are skilled practitioners at reading witnesses and identifying strategies to reduce the impact of their evidence. This is their job and they are there to represent their client to the best of their ability.

In summary, your investigation may provide very strong evidence to identify the offender, their methodologies, and their motivations for committing a cybercrime. However, unless you are able to prove the facts when required to, your conclusions will remain unproven.

CHAPTER NINETEEN

Conclusion

A
S THE world becomes more connected and technology expands into every aspect of our lives, targets become easier to locate and attack for cybercriminals. With the development of technology, it is often said you can reach out and touch the world from your home. However, the inverse of this is that the cybercriminal can now reach into your home and/or business from their location anywhere in the world. The cybercriminal has realized that it is easier and safer to commit a cybercrime against a person or company on the other side of the world than it is to commit a crime against their neighbor.

The threshold for becoming a cybercriminal is very low, and there is no turf war between cybercriminals demanding that no other person intrudes on their turf, which is not the case with all crime types. The Internet is open season on everyone by anyone. The emerging cybercriminal needs to have only a very limited skill set, as there are volumes of training resources available online provided by more experienced cybercriminals sharing their trade, as well as automated tools doing the hard work of breaking into home devices and corporate networks. The rewards are unfortunately great, and the damage done to the innocent victims is often horrific and life changing.

Due to the many technical issues discussed throughout this book, from the cybercrime investigator's perspective locating the offender and holding them to account for their actions may be a very difficult and complex operation requiring a significant investment in time and resources, regardless of whether a law enforcement or civilian investigator is tasked to work the case. Most of the luck and advantage is with the cybercriminal; however, the investigator will find many leave breadcrumbs that reveal their true identity. These breadcrumbs originate from the cybercrime scene and many a cybercriminal has been surprised to find the knock on their front door is from law enforcement seeking their arrest, especially when they believed they were 100 percent anonymous online.

Despite the perception, not all cybercriminals are located in international jurisdictions, hiding behind many layers of technology. Many are within our organizations, or have links to them, such as being a business competitor. These people are accessible within your jurisdiction and may be held accountable. This is where your scene examination and evidence management is so important, as your investigation methodologies will be examined in depth in the courtroom.

As technology develops, more evidence becomes available to criminal and civil investigators. Locating evidence is restricted only by the imagination of the investigator, as our increasingly interconnected world collects more and more data on our activities. The Internet of Things (IoT) can make the cybercriminal's job easier, but it can also be used to your advantage as you investigate offenses where you suspect the criminal physically has been at the crime scene.

As an investigator, your job has become more complex; however, there is significantly more evidence available to progress your investigations if you know where to look for it and what devices do and the evidence they may contain. Incorporating this evidence into your investigation is a skill you will refine throughout your career, with positive results achieved, honest mistakes made, lessons learned, and a higher-skilled investigator emerging.

The digital evidence you obtain may be very volatile, and the skills you learn and practice will be crucial in many investigations. As a digital/cyber investigator, you will be of value to many forms of investigations, not only those involving cyber or internal fraud. Wherever an offense takes place, in today's society there is a very strong expectation that digital evidence will be involved in the investigation. For example, a homicide scene at a home with many connected devices may reveal a lot to investigators about the actions leading to the deceased's death and who is culpable.

As you investigate the many forms of cybercrime, you will have your wins and you will have investigations where you cannot identify a suspect. On some occasions, your investigation will work perfectly using the methodology you have developed through your experience, and on other occasions you will use the same methodology and find you do not get off first base. This is the nature of conducting any form of investigation and the law enforcement officer who has been working cases will understand the frustration of doing everything right and not solving the case as they wish.

Each investigation is an opportunity to learn and develop your skills and share lessons learned.

Glossary

THIS GLOSSARY provides a general understanding of technical terms located throughout this book. It is to provide a working understanding only and does not provide a detailed analysis of the terms listed.

APT: advanced persistent threat   A compromise of a device or network, usually by a highly skilled attacker, group, or nation state. Once the attack is successful and the attackers are within the device/network, they navigate to the data they are looking to extract. Many APT attackers stay within a device/network for months, collecting new data as it is created.

ARP: Address Resolution Protocol   The ARP is used within a network to relate an internal IP address to a media access control (MAC) address. A MAC address uniquely identifies a device on a network. The MAC address can be located on the NIC, which is the physical device allowing communication between one device and others. A device also has an internal IP address, which is known as the subnet address. The ARP table correlates the MAC and IP addresses and sits within the router that the device is connected to.

authentication server   A computer server that determines whether a person or application is who it represents itself to be when trying to access a computer network.

AV: antivirus   AV software detects and eliminates computer viruses.

botnet   A collection of compromised computer devices used to commit a distributed denial of service (DDoS) attack. A botnet may be made up of hundreds of thousands of compromised devices. Compromised devices can include desktop computers, laptops, and any of a multitude of IoT devices.

BYOD: bring your own device   A device belonging to an employee on which the employee has been authorized to perform company work, and which has access to the corporate network and data.

CEM: child exploitation material   Pornographic images of children.

CERT: computer emergency response team　CERT teams have different roles in each country; however generally provide education and training, information sharing (indicators of compromise, cyber security briefings), linkage between Government and industry, international collaboration and direct incident response support to government as well as critical infrastructure. Some CERT teams provide paid services to industry clients.

CSP: cloud service provider　A business that provides cloud-computing services to customers. Examples include Amazon Web Services and Microsoft Azure.

DHCP: Dynamic Host Configuration Protocol　DHCP is the method by which a server dynamically assigns IP addresses to computers on its network; it takes the place of a system administrator assigning addresses manually.

DMZ: demilitarized zone　A layer of security facing the Internet that provides a first line of defense to a local area network against cyber-attacks.

DNS: domain name server　A DNS is the location your computer sends a request to when attempting to locate the address of a computer on the Internet you have not previously visited. Your computer asks the DNS server the address and is sent the location. Your computer then directs its request to the site you wish to visit. In most cases your DNS is also your Internet service provider.

DDoS: distributed denial of service　A DDoS is a multitude of computers that attack a device with the intention of damaging the capacity of the target device to function and be accessible to other computers.

DoS: denial of service　A DoS is a computer attack from a device with intention of damaging the capacity of the target device to function and be accessible to other computers.

Faraday bag　A bag designed to stop external communication channels from reaching the devices inside. A Faraday bag may be used to store a cell phone in order to prevent a suspect from remotely logging into the device and deleting your evidence.

FTP: File Transfer Protocol　A protocol for transferring files from one platform to another, for example, from a laptop computer to a USB drive.

GDPR: General Data Protection Regulation　GDPR is European Union legislation covering security and response in a breach of personally identifiable information of citizens of the European Union.

hash　A hash algorithm makes a mathematical compilation of data and produces a specified output. The value returned is a unique number, so if you change a single character in the data being subject to the hash process, you will get a different result. For example, the hash value for the word "cyber-crime" is 507C9BFA28900497DE242262C755ECDE. However, if we add another character to the word—for example, change it to "cybercrime!"—the hash value becomes FF5D162B91779BD2897F277972E1A2CC, using one of the hash protocols available.

A hash value is used to validate the authenticity of the evidence you have secured to ensure that it has integrity and has not been manipulated, as if even one character is changed in the source data, the output changes.

hypervisor   The hypervisor is software or a device that operates a virtual machine's operating systems.

IaaS: infrastructure as a service   A form of cloud computing where the CSP provides the basic infrastructure and the client provides the operating system and applications. An example of IaaS is Amazon EC2.

IDS: intrusion detection system   Monitors a device or network for activity that may harm it and reports it for review and possible action.

IoT: Internet of Things   The collective term for the multitude of devices connected to the Internet.

IP: intellectual property   Data that has been created by an entity that is unique to it and has value.

IP: Internet protocol [address]   A unique identifier for an ISP account. The ISP assigns an IP address to their client for a fixed or dynamic period of time. When you trace an IP address, you are generally tracing it to the account at the ISP.

IPS: intrusion prevention system   Monitors a network for activity that may harm it and has the capacity to respond automatically to threats.

IR: incident response   Action involved in responding to a cyber event.

ISP: Internet service provider   Provides a client access to the Internet. May also act as the DNS server.

IT: information technology   A very general descriptor for the many forms of technology in our society.

LEA: law enforcement agency   The police or an associated agency involved in investigating breaches of the law.

MAC: media access control [address]   A unique identifier for a device attempting to access network resources. The MAC address is resident on the physical network interface card (NIC) within a device. The device may have one unique MAC address for Ethernet access and a separate one for wireless access.

MLAT: mutual legal assistance treaty   An international treaty where law enforcement agencies provide assistance to each other upon request from fellow treaty members.

NIC: network interface card   An NIC is a physical board within a computer that facilitates access to a network. A device may have separate NICs for Ethernet and wireless connections.

NIST: National Institute of Standards and Technology   The NIST is an agency of the United States Department of Commerce.

OS: operating system   An operating system is a computer program that allows a physical computer device to operate and interface with the multitude of applications attached to it. Common operating systems include Microsoft Windows 10 and Apple Mojave.

PaaS: platform as a service   A form of cloud computing where the CSP provides the basic infrastructure and tools required for application development. An example of PaaS is Google's App Engine.

PII: personally identifying information   Specific identifying data about a unique individual, such as full name, address, Social Security number, and date of birth.

port   A location within a computer where data travels to and from. Ports are specific to the application using them; for example, port 80 is used for web traffic and port 25 is for email traffic.

proxy server   A computer server whose function is to receive requests from network devices seeking resources from other networked devices. Examples include web and email servers.

RAID: Redundant Array of Independent Disks [system]   Data is stored across a series of drives in the system to increase redundancy and performance quality.

RAM: random access memory   Stores data and code as it is being used so that the device will not have to direct every instruction to the operating system and specific applications within the device.

SaaS: software as a service   A form of cloud computing where the CSP provides the basic infrastructure as well as the operating system and applications chosen by the user. The user has little to no control over a SaaS system, as they have contracted with the CSP to provide and manage the services. An example of SaaS is Microsoft's Office 365.

SANS Institute   The SANS Institute provides high-quality education and training to security professionals across a wide range of IT disciplines.

shadow IT   Applications and online services installed on a device/network without the authority of the system's security administrators. Examples include cloud-computing services that users operate to assist them when working outside of the office when they do not have VPN access.

SIEM: security information and event management   SIEM software provides security information and event management for real-time analysis of potential threats to a network. It is an integrated system that gathers data from multiple sources and provides alerts about potential security violations.

subnet   A subnet is the division in an IP address providing two or more distinct networks within that IP address. It is used in domestic and corporate environments with subnetworks communicating with each other through routers on that internal network. For example, there may be separate subnets for the human resources, finance, and research departments.

vulnerability management software   The process of identifying and correcting vulnerabilities within an operating system or application.

zero-day exploit   A new piece of computer malware not known to security vendors, operating systems, and applications.

Index